HUMAN RIGHTS ENCOUNTER LEGAL PLURALISM

This collection of essays interrogates how human rights law and practice acquire meaning in relation to legal pluralism, ie, the co-existence of more than one regulatory order in a same social field. As a social phenomenon, legal pluralism exists in all societies. As a legal construction, it is characteristic of particular regions, such as post-colonial contexts. Drawing on experiences from Latin America, Sub-Saharan Africa and Europe, the contributions in this volume analyse how different configurations of legal pluralism interplay with the legal and the social life of human rights. At the same time, they enquire into how human rights law and practice influence interactions that are subject to regulation by more than one normative regime. Aware of numerous misunderstandings and of the mutual suspicion that tends to exist between human rights scholars and anthropologists, the volume includes contributions from experts in both disciplines and intends to build bridges between normative and empirical theory.

Recent titles in this series

Human Rights Encounter Legal Pluralism

Normative and Empirical Approaches

Edited by
Giselle Corradi, Eva Brems and Mark Goodale

Oñati International Series in Law and Society

A SERIES PUBLISHED FOR THE OÑATI INSTITUTE
FOR THE SOCIOLOGY OF LAW

·HART·
OXFORD · LONDON · NEW YORK · NEW DELHI · SYDNEY

HART PUBLISHING
Bloomsbury Publishing Plc
Kemp House, Chawley Park, Cumnor Hill, Oxford, OX2 9PH, UK

HART PUBLISHING, the Hart/Stag logo, BLOOMSBURY and the Diana logo are
trademarks of Bloomsbury Publishing Plc
First published in Great Britain 2017

First published in hardback, 2017
Paperback edition, 2019

A catalogue record for this book is available from the British Library.

Library of Congress Cataloging-in-Publication Data

Names: Brems, Eva, editor. | Corradi, Giselle, editor. | Goodale, Mark, editor.

Title: Human rights encounter legal pluralism / edited by Eva Brems,
Giselle Corradi, and Mark Goodale.

Description: Oxford [UK] ; Portland, Oregon : Hart Publishing, 2017. | Series: Oñati international
series in law and society | Includes bibliographical references and index.

Identifiers: LCCN 2016057791 (print) | LCCN 2016058888 (ebook) | ISBN 9781849467612
(hardback) | ISBN 9781849467711 (Epub)

Subjects: LCSH: Human rights. | Human rights and international law. | Legal polycentricity.

Classification: LCC K3240 .H85665 2017 (print) | LCC K3240 (ebook) | DDC 342.08/5—dc23

LC record available at https://lccn.loc.gov/2016057791

ISBN: HB: 978-1-84946-761-2
PB: 978-1-50993-223-8
ePDF: 978-1-84946-772-8
ePub: 978-1-84946-771-1

Typeset by Compuscript Ltd, Shannon

Acknowledgements

We would like to express our gratitude to Emily Braggins and the staff at Hart Publishing for their kind assistance during the production of this book. We are also very grateful to the staff at the International Institute for the Sociology of Law in Oñati. Their support in the organization of the workshop 'How Does legal Pluralism Interplay with the Promotion of Human Rights?', which took place on 2 and 3 May 2013, is very much appreciated. In particular, we wish to thank Malen Gordoa for her invaluable help before and during the meeting. The exchanges and reflections that took place during that encounter led to the publication of this volume. We would like to thank the participants in the workshop, most of whom are the authors of this collection, for their insightful contributions during the discussions and for their commitment to this project and scholarly debate. Finally, we acknowledge with gratitude a grant from the Research Foundation Flanders (FWO) for the research project 'Reconciling Human Rights and Customary Justice', and of the Belgian Federal Public Planning Service Science Policy (BELSPO) for the research project 'The Global Challenge of Human Rights Integration: Toward a Users' Perspective'.

Contents

Contributors

Eva Brems is Professor of Human Rights Law and Co-founder of the Human Rights Centre of Ghent University.

Catherine Buerger is a PhD candidate at the Department of Anthropology of the University of Connecticut.

Giselle Corradi is a postdoctoral researcher at the Human Rights Centre of Ghent University.

Ellen Desmet is Research Coordinator at the Human Rights Centre of Ghent University and a postdoctoral researcher at the Law and Development Research Group of Antwerp University.

Mark Goodale is Professor of Cultural and Social Anthropology at the University of Lausanne.

Felipe Gómez Isa is Professor of Public International Law and Researcher at the Pedro Arrupe Institute of Human Rights of the University of Deusto.

Anne Hellum is Professor and Director of the Institute of Women's Law at the Department of Public and International Law of Oslo University.

Kari Henquinet is Director of the Peace Corps Master's International Programs and Senior Lecturer at the Department of Social Sciences of the Michigan Technological University.

Andre Hoekema is Emeritus Professor of Sociology of Law at the Law Faculty of the University of Amsterdam.

Rosalie Katsande is Senior Lecturer at the Southern and Eastern African Regional Centre for Women's Law of the University of Zimbabwe.

Kim Lecoyer is a PhD candidate at the Human Rights Centre of Ghent University.

Olivier Struelens is a researcher at the Centre of History and Anthropology of Law of the Free University of Brussels.

Barbara Truffin is Professor of Law and Anthropology and Member of the Centre of History and Anthropology of Law of the Free University of Brussels.

1

Introduction

Human Rights and Legal Pluralism: Four Research Agendas

GISELLE CORRADI[1]

OVER THE PAST two decades, scholarly endeavours to understand social and cultural diversity in relation to human rights have shifted from concerns over universalism and relativism towards the analysis of how human rights operate in different contexts, and with which effects. A number of reasons explain this. In the first place, one could say that the sharpest edges of the so-called 'universality debate' have been polished. On the one hand, human rights scholars have advanced critical approaches to universality (An-Na'im 1995; Bell et al 2001; Brems 2001; Donnelly 2007, 1984). Rather than a priori given, the universal legitimacy of human rights may be constructed a posteriori. Since human rights standards are flexible and evolve, they can become responsive to diverse realities. For example, existing rights may acquire novel interpretations and new rights may be endorsed (Brems 2001). On the other hand, anthropologists have dismissed reified conceptions of culture that portray it as static, consensual and self-contained (Cowen et al 2001; Merry 1998, 2003; Preis 1996; Wilson 1997). Both material and immaterial aspects of culture, such as practices, habits, symbols and systems of meaning, have been shown to be reproduced, modified, acquired and rejected within histories of contact and exchange, embedded in relationships of unequal power.[2] Current anthropological understandings of culture recognise its structuring and agentic dimensions, while underscoring its changing, contested and porous character. This dynamic view of culture and human rights has recast the 'universality debate'.

[1] I wish to thank Eva Brems and Mark Goodale for their valuable comments on previous versions of this introduction.
[2] See eg Comaroff and Comaroff (1991), Garcia Canclini (1990), Rosaldo (1989).

Although it is possible that tension exists between aspects of cultural traditions and certain standards, or even the entire idea of (human) rights, this perspective allows us to focus on diachronic processes of co-constitution and change (Merry 1997, 2003, 2010). In addition, a number of scholars have reflected on how areas of tension could be resolved. They propose intercultural dialogues as means to redefine culture and human rights, and consider how epistemological bias and power differentials across and within social groups interplay with these undertakings (An-Na'im 1995; Eberhard 2002; Santos De Sousa 2002).

But next to these theoretical advancements, an empirical reality has prompted scholars to reorient their lines of enquiry. By the late 1990s, it was clear that human rights had become a global language for the articulation of a wide range of social struggles the world over. This inspired a wave of studies of the 'social life' of human rights (Cowan et al 2001; Englund 2006; Goodale 2009; Goodale and Merry 2007; Merry 2006a; Speed 2007; Wilson 1997; Wilson and Mitchell 2003). By inspecting the ways in which human rights become platforms for action, these detailed, often ethnographic, accounts of how human rights are mobilised in specific situations demonstrate that a broad spectrum of actors linked through trans-local networks are involved in the sociocultural production of human rights (Goodale 2007). From this viewpoint, UN monitoring bodies and human rights courts produce human rights discourses and practices as much as peasant intellectuals and the team members of development projects debating human rights in rural villages. These studies show that the meanings attached to human rights vary and do not necessarily correspond with the letter of the law. For example, Goldstein has identified discourses on the human right to security in Bolivia that are violent and at odds with international law (Goldstein 2007). In other words, which sources inform these multi-vocal and multi-sited human rights discourses and practices, and which role human rights law plays therein, are matters of empirical investigation. In this context, the extent to which this pluralising human rights landscape enables or constrains processes of emancipation remains a central question.[3]

In this volume, we interrogate how human rights law and practice acquire meaning in contexts of legal pluralism, and influence interactions that are subject to regulation by more than one normative regime.[4] Legal pluralism refers to the coexistence of more than one legal order in a particular field of social relations (Griffiths 1986; Merry 1988; Von Benda-Beckmann

---

[3] For example, Englund documents how a narrow approach to human rights in terms of freedom impedes the struggle against poverty and injustice in Malawi (Englund 2006). In the area of gender, see Henquinet in this volume.

[4] Theoretically, this interrogation rests on what Eckert et al have called 'the two sides of the sociality of law', ie law's formative impact of the social, and its very constitution in the social (Eckert et al 2012: 1).

2002; Woodman 1998).[5] The concept denotes a plurality of laws and/or mechanisms for processing disputes stemming from different sources of legitimation, such as the state, religion or custom, which operate within a same sociopolitical, temporal and geographical space.[6] In the Global South, legal pluralism is often officially endorsed by state policies, and is mainly, although not exclusively, linked to customary and religious legal orders operating alongside the legal institutions inherited from former colonial powers (Merry 1988).[7] In the Global North, it is mostly unofficial and relates to the coexistence of state and non-state forms of ordering, increasingly prevalent due to migration and intensified transnational relations (Hellum et al 2011; Von Benda-Beckmann et al 2005). As a result, legal pluralism constitutes an important element of the contexts in which human rights operate. Moreover, a legal pluralist perspective on the polycentric production and implementation of human rights law sheds light on how different users of human rights law relate to its many layers.[8]

As in the case of human rights, legal pluralism also has a 'legal' and a 'social' face, or what we would call normative and empirical dimensions. At the normative level, legal pluralism constitutes a policy field embodied in legislation and case law stipulating how the coexistence of different legal orders should function. These policy frameworks may deal with the status of different legal orders or elements thereof, and their interfaces. For example, they may mandate, make optional or prohibit that customary, religious or state laws are applied in certain domains. They may also regulate the judicial competence of different authorities and the possibility to appeal from one jurisdiction to another (Connolly 2005; Forsyth 2007; Morse and Woodman 1987). When policies take a 'positive' stance towards legal pluralism, ie non-state legal orders are not criminalised or ignored, they may dictate that state courts apply non-state laws, that non-state disputing forums are integrated into the state court hierarchy, or that non-state laws and disputing mechanisms are applicable but remain autonomous from the state judiciary. The latter may entail or not that the decisions of these forums can be enforced by recourse to state mechanisms of coercion.

Empirically, or as a social phenomenon, legal pluralism denotes the de facto ways in which a multiplicity of legal orders operate and articulate with

---

[5] We are not concerned with making a contribution to theoretical debates about which social phenomena should be labelled 'law' (see eg Tamanaha 1993, 2000). Our interest lies in understanding the variety of norms and disputing institutions that characterise the contexts in which human rights operate. Therefore, throughout the volume, the terms 'law' or 'legal' and 'norm' or 'normative' are used interchangeably.

[6] There may be no equivalence between these two realms. For example, in many countries of sub-Saharan Africa, state courts may handle cases according to customary law, and chiefs may combine custom and state law when processing disputes.

[7] For example, see Weilenmann (2009) on 'project law' produced by development agencies.

[8] See, for example, the contributions of Brems and Desmet in this volume.

each other in a given space. This may be more or less influenced by policies on legal pluralism. Classical empirical studies of legal pluralism reveal the co-constitutive dynamics among coexisting forms of ordering (Galanter 1981; Merry 1988; Moore 1973; Von Benda-Beckmann 1981). In her influential article, 'Law and Social Change: The Semi-Autonomous Social Field as an Appropriate Subject of Study', Moore introduced the notion that social fields have rule-making capacities and the means to induce or coerce compliance, while they are also part of a larger social matrix that invades and affects their operation (Moore 1973). In other words, the regulation of social fields results from intended and unintended intersections amongst normative orders. The concept 'inter-legality' mirrors this idea from an actor perspective (Santos De Sousa, 2002). Since the life of most people takes place at the crossroads of multiple regulatory regimes, 'a mixture and interpenetration of elements from different legal orders arises both in our minds and in our actions. Consequently, social practice is a constant bridging between legal orders' (Santos 2002: 437). However, in some cases, different legal orders sanction forms of subjectivity that are difficult to reconcile. Merry employs the term 'double consciousness' regarding situations in which people move in between normative frameworks that produce disparate understandings of the self (Merry 2006a: 179–217).[9] Processes of exposure to and mobilisation of multiple registers of law affect the legal consciousness of individuals in unpredictable ways.[10] In turn, this may lead to the emergency of new 'hybrid' legal institutions, entrench 'old ways' or produce changes in existing legal orders (Eckert et al 2012; Merry 2010). Studies of legal pluralism as a social phenomenon seek to capture these dynamics.

In this collection of essays, we explore how the legal and social dimensions of legal pluralism interplay with the legal and social life of human rights. Consequently, the relationship between human rights and legal pluralism is investigated at four levels of analysis: normative legal pluralism and human rights law, human rights law and empirical legal pluralism, empirical legal pluralism and human rights practice, and human rights practice and normative legal pluralism. By distinguishing these sub-fields, we hope to contribute to the development of a fertile ground for enriched exchange across disciplinary boundaries. Misunderstandings, particularly between legal and social science scholars, may easily stem from implicit differences in the use of the concepts 'human rights' and 'legal pluralism'. For example, social scientists may question the usefulness of debating whether legal pluralism

---

[9] For example, being a rights-bearing subject that is assertive in denouncing gender violence is incompatible with being 'a good wife' who accepts this violence as a natural, regrettable fact of life (Merry 2006: 186).

[10] Legal consciousness refers to the ways in which people use and understand the law, which is closely connected to their experiences with it (Merry 1990: 5).

is 'good' or 'bad', since it is a fact. This may preclude a discussion on how different policies on legal pluralism affect human rights. Furthermore, this fourfold framework allows us to situate existing knowledge and the insights that emerge from the contributions in this volume within more specific, and sometimes quite disparate, research agendas. At the same time, we acknowledge the need to understand the connections between empirical and normative theory, and build bridges between the multiple scholarly projects that are conducted under the umbrella of 'human rights and legal pluralism'. The present volume reflects our commitment to generating such encounters.

1. NORMATIVE LEGAL PLURALISM AND HUMAN RIGHTS LAW

Studying the relationship between policies on legal pluralism and human rights law entails two sets of questions. On the one hand, how should states respond to legal pluralism according to human rights law? Does human rights law recognise a right to 'one's own law'? Are there particular policies on legal pluralism that are prohibited, permitted or mandatory according to international standards? And on the other hand, how should states respond to legal pluralism in order to protect human rights? Which specific legislation and case law enable or constrain this protection? Reflections on the second set of questions have sometimes crystallised in the adoption of international standards, and international standards or their interpretation may be subject to criticism and debate, so both levels of enquiry are connected. As demonstrated by Brems in chapter 2, human rights law is not that coherent when it comes to legal pluralism. And although it contains some guidance on the treatment of legal pluralism, it also presents many gaps (ICHRP 2009; Quane 2013).

At present, the status of 'the right to legal pluralism' in human rights law is ambivalent. While there is no universal right to 'one's own law', in some cases legal pluralism is mandatory, in others it is permissible, and yet in others it is prohibited (Brems in this volume; Megret 2012; Quane 2013). In the second chapter of this volume, Brems demonstrates that when looking at human rights law from an integrated perspective, this state of affairs is problematic. It means that states may find themselves in a double bind. One branch of human rights law, ie the regime governing the rights of indigenous peoples, makes the recognition of legal pluralism mandatory, whereas another branch of human rights law, ie the case law of the European Court of Human Rights, forbids it as a violation of human rights. Since both duties may apply to the same state simultaneously, this inconsistency is untenable.

In this context, a fundamental question is why adopting a policy of endorsement of legal pluralism would be desirable or undesirable from the perspective of human rights. This interrogation is part of more general debates about how states should respond to legal diversity as an aspect

of cultural diversity, and promote social cohesion in multicultural societies (Megret 2012). In this regard, two issues are of concern. First, that the
imposition of a unitary system of law may not be neutral, but reflect the
particular viewpoint of hegemonic groups to the exclusion of those that are
marginalised. And second, that granting official status to legal orders associated with marginalised groups could entrench power inequalities within
those groups, resulting in the exclusion of minorities within the minority.
In other words, the adoption of policies that endorse legal pluralism may
advance the collective rights of minorities, but may also entail the risk of
violating the individual rights of their members. Some scholars have suggested that we look beyond this frame of reasoning, and consider instead
whether the recognition of multiple legal orders may be beneficial for society at large (Ardito 1997; Megret 2012). In other words, in multicultural
settings, the endorsement of legal pluralism not only concerns minorities,
but raises questions on how to capitalise on diversity and strengthen democracy in general (ibid).

The conclusions of Gómez Isa and Corradi in chapters 4 and 6 resonate with this view. These chapters show how the interpretation of human
rights may be enriched by the inclusion of voices that have been largely
excluded from the definition of these standards. Gómez Isa illustrates how
indigenous relationships with a territory have become the platform for a
renewed interpretation of the right to property under the Inter-American
system for the protection of human rights. In recognition of indigenous legal
orders, the Inter-American Court of Human Rights extended the scope of
this right to protect not only individual, but also collective property. Considering the socioeconomic realities of Latin America, it is not unthinkable
that this broader interpretation of the right to property may not only benefit
indigenous peoples, but also other groups with collective claims to land.[11]
Similarly, Corradi's analysis of how the right to a fair trial may be interpreted cross-culturally suggests that areas of tension between indigenous
procedural norms and mainstream interpretations of this right may open
windows of opportunity for exchange and collaboration between state and
indigenous authorities, which may strengthen both indigenous and state
legal orders.

At the same time, the human rights implications of policies that endorse
legal pluralism depend on the concrete substance of these policies. For
example, how is the enjoyment of human rights affected by different normative orders and disputing forums being declared mandatory or optional

---

[11] For the moment, the case law of the Inter-American Court relies on culture and identity
as the basis for this recognition, eg *Sawhoyamaxa Indigenous Community v Paraguay* (2006),
Kichwa Indigenous People of Sarayaku v Ecuador (2012), *Kuna Indigenous People of Madun-
gandí and the Emberá Indigenous People of Bayano and their Members v Panama* (2014).
However, there is no reason to assume that culture and identity should be the only grounds to
protect collective property.

for different persons in different fields? Human rights law does not contain ultimate answers to these questions. According to the UN Human Rights Committee, when states recognise the judicial functions of customary or religious courts they need to ensure that these courts cannot hand down binding judgments unless the proceedings are limited to minor civil and criminal matters, meet the basic requirements of fair trial, ensure equal treatment, are validated by the state in the light of human rights and can be challenged in a state court.[12] But apart from these guidelines, states can decide according to their discretion. This is not wholly surprising. After all, the human rights effects of particular policies on legal pluralism are difficult to evaluate in the abstract. This means that these questions remain contested and their answers highly contingent upon empirical realities (ICHRP 2009: 92). Sieder and McNeish note the importance of looking at the legacies of different colonial and postcolonial histories, and how these shaped current constellations of power and governance (Sieder and McNeish 2013: 4–7). In regions such as Latin America, where indigenous forms of justice were either criminalised or ignored by the postcolonial state, the recent adoption of policies that give official status to indigenous law is celebrated as the result of a long struggle for emancipation. By contrast, in most of sub-Saharan Africa, colonial and postcolonial policies on legal pluralism sought to co-opt customary law institutions as instruments of domination. Therefore, the official status of customary legal orders may not convey progressive connotations, and is often met with suspicion (ibid). Bearing this in mind, a crucial issue is the extent to which policies endorsing legal pluralism foresee mechanisms of downwards accountability that keep the power of legal institutions in check (Nyamu-Musembi 2000; ICHRP 2009).

In this respect, human rights law does demand that states ensure that international standards apply to official non-state legal orders.[13] This is the case in several postcolonial countries, where customary legal orders are recognised by the state, except for when they breach human rights. For example, in the famous case *Bhe v Magistrate Khayelitsha*, the South African Constitutional Court ruled that the customary law rule of male primogeniture could not be endorsed because it was incompatible with the rights to equality and dignity enshrined in the Bill of Rights.[14] In contrast, in Sierra Leone and Lesotho, customary laws are officially applicable but exempted from the constitutional prohibition of discrimination on the basis of gender. This results in the legalisation of discrimination against women who fall under the jurisdiction of customary law (Odinkalu 2006: 155; Nyamu-Musembi 2000). In addition, human rights soft law recommends that states

---

[12] Human Rights Committee, General Comment on the Right to Equality before the Courts and Tribunals and to a Fair Trial, UN Doc CCPR/C/GC/32 (2007).
[13] See Quane (2013) for an extensive discussion of this duty.
[14] *Bhe and Others v Khayelitsha Magistrate and Others* (CCT 49/03) [2004].

take positive measures so that non-state legal orders comply with human rights[15]—for example, by reinterpreting non-state laws in line with international standards, providing human rights training to authorities in non-state courts, and adopting a participatory and inclusive process of law reform (Quane 2013). A key concern here is whether these policies see non-state and human rights law as inherently incompatible or as reconcilable (Perry 2011). As discussed above, to a large extent this depends on how human rights and culture are conceptualised. However, in the final analysis, the potential of policies on legal pluralism to advance or constrain the enjoyment of human rights hinges on the actual influence of these policies on the ground. This brings us to the study of empirical realities and legal pluralism as a social phenomenon.

2. HUMAN RIGHTS LAW AND EMPIRICAL LEGAL PLURALISM

The connection between human rights law and legal pluralism as a social phenomenon may be examined from the following two points of view. First, which actors and normative frameworks regulate in practice the social fields in which international standards are applicable? How can international human rights law come to grips with realities of plural regulation and multidimensional power? And second, to which extent are the norms and practices sustained by plural forms of ordering aligned with standards of human rights? This last question may involve assessments of the appropriate interpretation of these standards in the light of legal and cultural diversity.

The first question revolves around the issue of where power resides, and hence, the ability to violate or realise human rights. International human rights law is primarily concerned with the behaviour of states. By observing how social fields are regulated in practice, empirical studies of legal pluralism may question the assumption that the state is the most influential agent (Provost and Sheppard 2013: 2, 3). The limits of the state-centred architecture of international human rights law have already been exposed from other angles. Studies have shown that state sovereignty is increasingly fragmented and linked to complex interfaces between global, national and local scales of governance (Eilenberg 2014; Peluso and Lund 2011). In this context, scholars have examined whether and how international human rights law could impose direct obligations upon transnational non-state actors, such as corporations and international organisations (Clapham 2013; Vandenhole 2015; Noortmann et al 2015).[16] Although most international human rights

[15] See Quane (2013: fns 102 and 103) for numerous examples of such recommendations by UN human rights treaty bodies and independent experts established within the UN Charter-based system.

[16] For the moment, only norms of customary international law concerned with crimes that entail massive violations of human rights apply directly to non-state actors (eg genocide, war

law mechanisms continue to focus on states' behaviour, initiatives such as the UN Global Compact constitute a step in this direction.

Empirical studies of legal pluralism may further inform ongoing reflections on the reach and limits of the Westphalian architecture of international human rights law. On the one hand, these studies show that state institutions may be absent, share or compete with other regulatory sources in different arenas.[17] This may concern an entire geographical space, as it is often the case in conflict, postconflict and some developing regions, but it may also apply to specific domains of social interaction in all societies. By uncovering 'the state of the state' and explaining the reasons behind particular configurations of plural regulation, these studies may provide elements to appraise the ability and willingness of states to protect individuals and entities under their jurisdiction for human rights violations committed by non-state actors. On the other hand, these studies bring to our attention non-state actors with governance capacities at the intra-state level, such as chiefs, indigenous and religious leaders, that have rarely been considered in these discussions.[18] These studies increase our understanding of the sources and nature of these actors' power. As demonstrated by Hellum and Katsande in chapter 7 and by Henquinet in chapter 8, in the context of neoliberal policies and the downsizing or retreat of the state from certain public domains, the influence of customary and religious authorities may derive from or be strengthened by alliances with transnational actors, such as private businesses and transnational aid organisations. In addition, these chapters uncover the spaces in which different forms of power are exercised, enabling or constraining the implementation of human rights. Hellum and Katsande discuss how women's options to challenge discriminatory customary laws opened and closed in a changing political terrain in Zimbabwe. They indicate that the 'hidden power' exercised by traditional institutions and the 'invisible power' embedded in social and religious structures that upheld patriarchal perceptions and practices dominated over the 'visible power' of state laws granting equal inheritance rights to men and women. Although Henquinet's chapter does not refer explicitly to these different dimensions of power, her study

crimes, crimes against humanity, slavery and complicity with state-sponsored abuses). Under the existing soft law, ie the Guiding Principles on Business and Human Rights endorsed by the Human Rights Council by resolution 17/4 of 16 June 2011, businesses' legal liability for human rights violations arises at the national level.

[17] See, for example, the 2011 special issue of the *Journal of Legal Pluralism* on 'Legal Pluralism and International Development Interventions', *Journal of Legal Pluralism*, vol 43, issue 63.

[18] Under international human rights law, state obligations in respect of these actors' behaviour differ depending on whether these actors are considered state agents or not. In the former case, such as when state policies on legal pluralism grant jurisdictional powers to non-state disputing forums, human rights violations committed by these forums are directly attributable to the state, which has the duty to take measures in order to ensure that its agents respect, protect and fulfil human rights. In the latter case, state obligations are limited to taking ex ante and ex post measures to protect individuals for human rights violations committed by third parties.

of transnational women's rights interventions in Niger also exemplifies how the hidden and invisible power of religious networks moulded the scope of these interventions, preventing the incorporation of certain international standards into national legislation. All these insights point to the need to continue to think critically about the way in which human rights law understands power and devices mechanisms to contain it.

Regarding the second entry point to research in this sub-field, ie the extent to which these configurations of plural regulation uphold or violate human rights, two sub-questions may be distinguished. Firstly, whether the substantive, procedural and structural elements of different legal orders abide by human rights law. For example, to what extent are existing normative orders attuned with these standards? Are the decisions made within different disputing institutions aligned with human rights? The same applies to the procedures and structural aspects of different disputing forums. A considerable amount of research entitled 'human rights and legal pluralism' concerns precisely these questions (eg Danish Institute for Human Rights 2013; Farran 2006; Fluet et al 2006; Oppermann 2006; Wojkowska 2006). As discussed before, these assessments are not straightforward but depend on how human rights and non-state norms are interpreted.

Chapters 3–6 in this book suggest that disputes occurring at the intersection of legal orders represent potential spaces of intercultural dialogue that may result in the reinterpretation of international standards. The contributions by Desmet and Gómez Isa in chapters 3 and 4 analyse how these standards acquired new meaning informed by indigenous legal orders. They show, however, that the overlap is never complete. Even in cases of 'alliance' between human rights and indigenous norms, such as in the area of rights to territory, these encounters may also reflect tension. In chapters 5 and 6, Hoekema and Corradi deal with how indigenous legal orders call for flexibility in the interpretation of certain standards. In chapter 5, Hoekema provides examples regarding the right not to be subjected to cruel and inhuman forms of treatment.[19] Amongst others, he describes how the Constitutional Court of Colombia came to the decision that corporal punishments applied by indigenous justice did not violate this right because the indigenous community that applied them saw them as a form of cleansing. In chapter 6, Corradi explores how different modes of processing disputes (eg mediation v adjudication) underpinned by different forms of social organisation (eg simplex v multiplex societies) influence how certain elements of the right to a fair trial may be interpreted. As these chapters show, cultural essentialism always looms in this line of enquiry. One way to mitigate it is by questioning the effects of declaring particular interpretations of norms and practices compatible with human rights.

---

[19] On the cross-cultural examination of corporal punishments, see also An-Na'im (1995).

A second sub-question in this area is how the articulation between different disputing institutions affects the enjoyment of human rights. For example, standards of fair trial such as *ne bis in idem* would be breached if the same person or entity was punished twice for the same offence, eg first by state courts and then by non-state courts or vice versa. Alternatively, the treatment of a case by multiple disputing forums at the same level may lead to contradictory outcomes, non-implementation of decisions, impunity and lack of accountability. Although existing studies remark that this aspect of the relationship between legal pluralism and human rights is highly relevant (ICHRP 2009: 32; UN Women 2011), so far this issue has remained under-researched.

3. EMPIRICAL LEGAL PLURALISM AND THE PRACTICE OF HUMAN RIGHTS

In the previous section, the analysis of legal pluralism as social phenomenon served as the basis for the evaluation of how human rights law should address these realities. By contrast, in this sub-section questions centre around understanding how human rights norms articulate with other norms in the production of legal subjectivities and social change. What is the role of human rights in processes of normative transformation? How are experiences and representations of grievance, entitlement and duty influenced by ideas of human rights? To what extent are these ideas informed by multiple normative repertoires? Which factors influence this and what are their consequences?

These questions have been dealt with at length by Merry in her ethnography of the transnational production of violence against women as a violation of human rights (Merry 2006a,b). She has traced human rights approaches to gender violence from the sites in which legal documents and policies are formulated to those in which they are supposed to have effects. This revealed the key role played by intermediaries, such as community leaders, non-governmental organisations, and social movement activists, in generating variation in the meaning of human rights. As she explains, the logic that underpins transnational human rights does not always resonate with local ways of thinking and interpreting the world. Therefore, these intermediaries, who are acquainted with both systems of knowledge, translate 'up' and 'down'. In order to attract international attention and funding, they articulate local grievances in the language of human rights. At the same time, they reframe human rights in terms that make them 'speak' to local concerns. Merry calls this process of downwards translation 'vernacularisation'.[20] Against this backdrop, Eckert et al have argued that it is necessary

---

[20] She distinguishes between two sub-types: 'replication' and 'hybridisation'. In the former, the transnational idea remains the same but it is framed in a language that is locally familiar.

to look beyond the role of professional translators (Eckert et al 2012: 10). Subjects of law also make meaning of human rights norms and thus extend the chain of translation. Moreover, their concerns are not uniform. Therefore, Eckert et al suggest processes of normative transformation should be studied through the notion of 'iteration' (ibid). Iterations entail interactions in which norms are interpreted. These processes do not involve the meeting and mixing of normative orders but rather subsuming certain concerns under varying interpretations of specific norms. This goes hand in hand with contestations over the meaning of norms and the validity of different interpretations thereof, which may be fuelled by knowledge of different normative orders. As a result, iterations need to be understood in terms of social struggles (ibid).

In chapter 8, Henquinet provides good illustrations of the reach and limits of normative transformations facilitated by human rights development projects in which the meaning of human rights was informed by religious normative orders. She shows how the scope and success of the women's rights interventions of CARE and UNICEF in Niger were heavily influenced by religious norms used to interpret women's rights. These prevailed over 'global' interpretations of those rights due to the power of religious networks. Religious norms supported the improvement of women's position in public spheres, such as politics and education, but rejected ideas of gender equality in private relations, such as those addressed by sexual and reproductive rights.

Chapter 7 by Hellum and Katsande and chapter 10 by Lecoyer suggest that knowledge of various normative orders constitutes a crucial factor allowing disadvantaged groups to contest the meaning of norms and redefine them in ways that respond to their experiences and stakes. Drawing on the case of inheritance rights in Zimbabwe, Hellum and Katsande elucidate how legal literacy and advice rooted in a plural conception of law enabled women to challenge patriarchal norms and discourses on inheritance operating at different levels. Lecoyer makes the same point when she argues that strategies seeking to improve Belgian Muslim women's equal access to divorce need to engage with all the normative frameworks at play, ie human rights, state law and religious normative discourses.

At the same time, the adoption of a rights-defined subjectivity depends on individuals' experiences with mobilising law (Merry 2006a). In chapter 11, Truffin and Struelens show that state policies that ignore normative diversity may undermine young people's rights consciousness, and their enjoyment of the right to family life. Their examination of the experiences of Belgian families with Congolese roots resorting to state law for the resolution

---

In the latter, the transnational idea merges with local ideas and gets a more interactive form. An extreme form of hybridisation is 'subversion' in which the name of the transnational idea (human rights) is kept but applied to what are fundamentally local ideas.

of family conflicts points to a plurality of family models (ie egalitarian and hierarchical) operating both within these families and within state law. They argue that in this context of 'inter-normativity', the protection of the right to family life and the provision of adequate support for young people requires that state policies deconstruct these contradictions in order to understand how they fuel family conflicts in the first place.

Finally, chapter 9 by Buerger demonstrates that strategic resort to customary norms within a human rights campaign conducted in Ghana increased the chances of achieving the campaign's goal, while at the same time undermining the acceptability of using the human rights label. Her chapter illustrates how different actors contest and police the boundaries of social action that can be carried out in the name of human rights.

4. HUMAN RIGHTS PRACTICE AND NORMATIVE LEGAL PLURALISM

To what extent are policies on legal pluralism influenced by human rights ideas? How do these policies in turn affect people's experiences with human rights? The interface between the practice of human rights and policies on legal pluralism is a relatively recent area of study. Nevertheless, a growing body of knowledge is concerned with these questions, particularly in the Global South. In several developing regions, neoliberal policies seeking to make the state more efficient have relied on decentralisation and the delegation of governance tasks to local actors, such as customary authorities (Buur and Kyed 2006; Zips and Weilenmann 2011). This has often led to reforms in the legal frameworks dealing with customary law institutions. At the same time, in recent years, legal development interventions supported by transnational aid organisations have been criticised for their exclusive focus on the state (Derman et al 2013; Harper 2011; Tamanaha 2012). Recognising that most development regions are characterised by legal pluralism, these organisations increasingly engage with non-state legal orders (eg DfID 2004; Danida 2010). These agencies' adoption of human-rights-based approaches to development has resulted in interventions to promote human rights at the level of non-state law. In this context, studies have examined how existing policies on legal pluralism interplay with these initiatives. They show that normative frameworks for legal pluralism tend to define which non-state actors and layers of law are included or excluded from these interventions (Brems et al 2015; Corradi 2014).

In chapter 8, Henquinet shows that policies on legal pluralism that grant official status to discriminatory religious laws may obstruct initiatives to debate and redefine these laws at more grassroots levels. In chapter 7, Hellum and Katsande indicate that even when gender equality clauses are in place and apply to non-state law, individuals may be unable to mobilise them effectively. They identify lack of knowledge and social pressure as

14   *Giselle Corradi*

powerful constraints for women, limiting the effectiveness of these policies on the ground. In chapter 5, Hoekema reflects on the positive aspects of non-implementing these clauses. He argues that representations of indigenous justice as inherently at odds with human rights has often led to policies that restrict its jurisdiction.[21] He is particularly critical of policies that demand the compliance of non-state legal orders with international standards without requiring the adoption of an intercultural approach to the interpretation of these standards. According to him, such policies render human rights into an arrogant discourse that justifies the oppression of the legal institutions and practices of marginalised groups. Drawing on examples from Peru, he shows that in practice, local actors may decide to put these policies aside. He concludes that the way in which state and indigenous authorities articulate with each other in practice counterbalances the ethnocentric bias of these policies, and opens spaces for bottom-up approaches to the cross-cultural understanding of human rights.

In chapters 10 and 11, Lecoyer and Truffin and Struelens demonstrate that these debates are also relevant in the Global North. In chapter 10, Lecoyer reflects on how popular sentiments that reject legal pluralism 'at home' in the name of human rights lead to a narrow focus on state law as the only means to promote Belgian Muslim women's rights. This diverts policy-makers' attention from other non-legal strategies that may be more appropriate in supporting these women and which require engagement with religious normative discourses. Similarly, chapter 11 by Truffin and Struelens suggests that state policies that ignore or essentialise the role of cultural diversity within different layers of law fuel conflicts within families, and undermine social cohesion.

5. THE CONTRIBUTIONS IN THIS BOOK

The insights emerging from most of the chapters in this book may be situated within one or more of the sub-fields sketched out above. Nevertheless, the contributions in part 1 can be said to advance arguments that are mainly of a normative nature, whereas part 2 is primarily concerned with empirical findings.

Part 1 opens with a chapter by Brems, in which she analyses the inconsistent treatment of legal pluralism by human rights law as a whole. Brems remarks that one layer of human rights law, ie the regime governing the rights of indigenous peoples, mandates state recognition of legal pluralism, whereas another layer, ie the case law of the European Court of Human Rights, forbids it as a violation of human rights. After examining several

[21] See also the recent decision of the Constitutional Court of Ecuador in the *La Cocha* case, which excludes murder from the jurisdiction of indigenous justice. Sentence 113-14-SEP-CC, 30 July 2014.

arguments that may be advanced in order to justify this contradiction, Brems concludes that the latter cannot be explained in a coherent manner and shows the negative consequences that follow from it. According to Brems, both the privileged treatment of indigenous peoples and the ban on legal pluralism endorsed by the European Court of Human Rights are problematic. The former may be seen as an instance of unjustified discrimination against other groups that may have similar grounds to claim the recognition of their legal institutions. The latter ignores the potential of policies that recognise legal pluralism to foster the protection of human rights, eg by regulating the operation of non-state legal orders. Drawing on the case of legal pluralism, Brems demonstrates that the pluralist nature of human rights law may lead to incongruities that undermine the coherent protection of human rights as a whole. She concludes that in order to counter this, it is necessary to look at human rights law from an integrated perspective, and identify gaps, areas of divergence and alignment, as well as cross-cutting and isolated dynamics.

In chapter 3, Desmet deals with the relationship between international human rights law and legal pluralism at two levels. First, she reflects on the analytical purchase of the concept 'legal pluralism' when applied to ever-smaller bodies of law, such as international human rights law itself. She proposes a distinction between 'legal pluralism', as referring to the simultaneous applicability of various normative systems in a same social field, and 'adopting a legal pluralist perspective' to the study of the simultaneous applicability of norms originating from the same normative (sub)system. In the second part of the chapter, Desmet turns to the relationship between human rights law and other normative orders that are applicable in the same field. She distinguishes two main possible scenarios. In the first one, human rights law and another normative order stand in opposition to each other as regards a particular issue, and hence human rights law may be invoked against the rules of the normative order that violates human rights. In the second one, human rights law and another normative order are aligned on a particular theme, defending similar values, interests or entitlements. In this case, human rights law may be invoked to reinforce the rules of that other normative order. Desmet's analysis of how indigenous legal orders have influenced the emergence and implementation of human rights standards in the domain of indigenous land, territorial and resource rights, demonstrates that in practice, both scenarios may occur at the same time. Despite the apparent alliance between human rights and indigenous law in this area, the overlap is only partial. Indigenous legal orders tend to see nature in a holistic and spiritual way, whereas human rights law reflects an anthropocentric understanding of the connection between men and the environment. Based on this, Desmet challenges any unidimensional characterisation of the relationship between human rights law and other normative orders, even within a particular domain. She argues instead for a nuanced assessment that does justice to what is actually a multifaceted relationship.

In chapter 4, Gómez Isa discusses in detail how this multifaceted relationship played out in one particular case brought by indigenous peoples before the Inter-American Court of Human Rights, ie the famous *Awas Tingni* case (2001). He describes how in the mid-1990s, a poor indigenous community of the Atlantic coast of Nicaragua resorted to the Inter-American system of human rights. They denounced the timber exploitation concession which the government of Nicaragua had granted to a transnational company in their territory without their consent. In this case, human rights law was mobilised by indigenous peoples in alliance with renowned experts and donors from North America, seeking a novel interpretation of Article 21 of the American Convention, which protects the right to property, as including indigenous communal property. The Inter-American Court ruled in favour of the petitioners and identified indigenous traditional practices and customs as the foundation for expanding the scope of this right. This not only implied a flexible interpretation of human rights standards, but also a reconfiguration of indigenous peoples' relationships with space. In the community's understanding, the territory was characterised by porous and fluctuating borders. This stood in contrast with the demand of clear demarcation underpinning the court's view of the right to property and the mechanisms envisaged to protect it. Despite this tension, Gómez Isa concludes that the *Awas Tingni* case constitutes an instance of intercultural dialogue, in which indigenous law informed an inclusive reinterpretation of human rights. An ensuing question is whether this has led to changes in indigenous norms and practices regarding the territory.

In chapter 5, Hoekema brings the reflection on the intercultural interpretation of standards to the national level. He focuses on how international standards are understood within legal pluralism policies embodied in what he calls 'internal conflict rules', ie national legislation and/or case law stipulating the competence of the different legal orders recognised within a state, and which determine how to solve conflicts between them. One such instance of conflict may emerge when one of these legal orders violates the human rights protected by the state. Hoekema takes issue with policies that demand compliance with international standards without adopting an intercultural approach. According to him, such policies may result in Eurocentric human rights discourses that justify the criminalisation of marginalised groups. Hoekema examines how internal conflict rules took shape and were applied in concrete cases in which physical punishments were administered by indigenous justice. These examples from Colombia, Guatemala and Peru illustrate how internal conflict rules may reflect an intercultural interpretation of the right not to be subjected to torture and other cruel, inhuman or degrading treatment or punishment. His conclusion suggests that policies on legal pluralism, and in particular their rules on human rights, constitute a double-edged sword. Depending on how human rights are understood within these policies, they may serve to perpetuate the oppression of marginalised groups, or they may lead to processes of interlegality, in which inclusive definitions on human rights may emerge.

Chapter 6 by Corradi explores precisely this question, but regarding the right to a fair trial. Her chapter discusses the complexities involved in the cross-cultural assessment of whether indigenous procedural norms comply with this right. Based on a case study conducted in Bolivia, she shows that different modes of dispute processing rooted in different forms of social organisation influence how arbitrariness and abuses of power may manifest at the procedural level, and hence which standards of fair trial may be applicable to prevent this. Her analysis indicates that factors such as the aim of the disputing process, and the role of third parties therein, interplay with the relevance and appropriate interpretation of certain elements of this right in different disputing contexts. She also identifies areas of tension and overlap, and reflects on how policies on legal pluralism may address them. Since indigenous justice operates in a context of interlegality, it is necessary to construct spaces for collaborative interaction between authorities representing different legal orders, in which various normative and epistemological frameworks can be combined in the treatment of cases, particularly at grass-roots level.

Part 2 opens with chapter 7, in which Hellum and Katsande examine the gendered dynamics of justice sector initiatives seeking to advance human rights through a legally plural framework. They present two longitudinal case studies from South Africa and Zimbabwe in which individual women and women's rights organisations undertook legal advocacy, legal literacy and legal aid in order to mediate the tension between the principle of gender equality and the plurality of legal orders that regulate women's lives. The study on South Africa investigates how the right to equality embedded in CEDAW, the South African Constitution and the Land Restitution Act was implemented by state and non-state actors involved in different phases of the land restitution process in the Limpopo Province. The study shows that the spaces of operation of human rights organisations opened and then closed in the political shift from a social-justice-based to a market-based land restitution policy. The former allowed human rights organisations to address power structures within communities, and hence gender relations, whereas the latter saw this as a private matter and foreclosed this possibility. The study on Zimbabwe analyses the work of two women's rights organisations in the area of equal inheritance rights. It shows how the breakdown of the rule of law and the politicisation of customary authorities led to situations of legal impunity that curtailed women's options to negotiate their property rights. Both case studies demonstrate that different paradigms of governance, rooted in changing political and economic terrains, affect the bargaining power of individual women and women's rights organisations seeking gender justice. In both cases, the success of the interventions depended not only on these organisations' ability to develop situational and locally appropriate strategies of argumentation, but also on the broader political, legal and economic power structures in which they operated.

In chapter 8, Henquinet illustrates this further. She explains how two transnational aid organisations active in Niger, CARE and UNICEF, negotiate the meaning of women's rights and the scope of their interventions within semi-autonomous social fields. These fields are impacted by competing women's rights discourses endorsed by national legislation and popular religious views of Islam. The context in which these organisations work is characterised by neoliberal policies and the retreat of the state from markets, governance and services. In addition, there is a strong presence of ideas of male guardianship and provision, internalised through popular discourses on Islamic jurisprudence. Henquinet shows that in this setting, the process of implementing equality based notions of women's rights is resisted by drawing on other rights discourses that are rooted in Nigeriens' identities as Muslims. As a result, ideas of equality and independence are set aside in exchange for a discourse that emphasises the improvement of women's status in communal relations, without challenging women's subordinate position in the family. This results in the success of certain women's rights interventions, such as the Quota Law increasing the number of women in public spaces. But at the same time, it leads to the rejection of initiatives to reform family law, the persistence of reservations to CEDAW and the reformulation of programmes on the ground to conform to popular notions of the family that reproduce gender inequalities in the private sphere. Henquinet concludes that in Niger, women's rights are largely conceived outside the realm of global discourses on the liberal subject due to the complex interplay of policies on legal pluralism, a weak state and the prominence of religious networks.

Chapter 9 by Buerger turns towards the examination of how a plurality of norms may be used strategically by actors that decide to mobilise in the name of human rights. She discusses the case of a human rights advocacy campaign conducted by two contiguous low-income communities in Accra, Ghana, which sought the improvement of the drainage stream that divided them. The latter had been historically neglected, leading to serious problems of health and sanitation. Her study illustrates how the plurality of legal orders that characterised the milieu of this human rights campaign influenced the strategies pursued, and how the meaning of human rights was contested in the process. In the course of their advocacy, some members of the youth club involved in the campaign combined a human rights discourse on health and sanitation with patriarchal notions of community obligation embedded in custom. While this increased the number of social networks of which they could make claims, it also raised important questions about what methods were considered acceptable for claiming rights, what values fitted under 'a human rights approach', and who had the capacity to decide. Buerger demonstrates that human rights mobilisation outside the strictly regulated spaces of courtrooms allows for the negotiation of the boundaries of different legal orders, including human rights, making them flexible and unstable. She defines these spaces as 'legal borderlands', highlighting not only the porousness of the borders between coexisting legal orders, but also the way in which individual actors attempt to reshape them for strategic purposes.

Strategic use of different layers of law, and the structures that limit different actors' options with it, is at the core of chapter 10 by Lecoyer. She analyses the women's rights implications of the de facto coexistence of state law and a multiplicity of Islamic discourses regulating the divorce practices of Muslim families in Belgium. Lecoyer explores how state law and global as well as local Islamic normative discourses available to Belgian Muslim families influence women's strategies and experiences with divorce, and affect their legal consciousness. She shows that these discourses are heterogeneous and subject to reinterpretation. Nevertheless, they remain controlled by male religious scholars, who stay largely insensitive to the need to adapt these discourses to the realities of women and contemporary life in a secular context. In exploring women's strategies and experiences with divorce, she shows that besides the options and limits offered by these discourses, other factors enable and constrain women's agency. Having access to several options for marriage dissolution enhances women's ability to pursue their interests, as does the support of the social and family networks of which they are part. Conversely, social pressure rooted in patriarchal views of gender relations appears as the main obstacle to divorce. In this context, some women will refrain from challenging discriminatory practices due to fear of the stigma that is associated with making a marital dispute public in court. Against this backdrop, Lecoyer argues that human rights strategies aiming at enhancing the position of these women need to marry the right to equality and religion. Instead of adopting legislation seeking to regulate the plurality of norms at play, these strategies need to enhance Muslim women's awareness of their rights under all the normative frameworks that apply to them, and their capacity to (re)define them.

Also concerned with individual's experiences with plural law, the last chapter by Truffin and Struelens interrogates the concept of interlegality. They focus on intra-family conflicts involving members of Congolese families and families of Congolese descent living in Belgium. They analyse two typical conflictual situations that individuals from these families face in their adolescence and adulthood: intergenerational tension between youths and their parents, and contradictory models of conjugal relationships produced by diverse fields of state law affecting couples with a migratory background. By adopting an actor perspective, their study shows that egalitarian and hierarchical models of the family are at play both within families and at the level of state law. As a result, it is not possible to allocate either model to a single normative order. Truffin and Struelens depict these complex configurations of normative plurality by the concept of 'inter-normativity', ie a diversity of references and models entwined in a source of norms. The narratives of young people and spouses examined by Truffin and Struelens uncover the tensions, ruptures and continuities that result from family relationships being reproduced in private and public spheres that are characterised by internormativity. In their conclusion, they reflect on the implications of these findings, and in particular what they mean in terms of enhancing the protection of the right to family life. On the one hand, they argue that stereotypes attributing an egalitarian vision of the family to the public sphere and a hierarchical one to the 'Congolese community' lie at the root of the lack of responsiveness of state institutions towards the realities of these families. On the other hand, they question migratory regulations that affect the economy of relationship inside transnational families by granting some members a status on which others depend. As their data indicates, these regulations fuel conflicts within families, which are too high a cost for social cohesion in comparison with the benefits of controlling migration flows.

Overall, the essays in this collection constitute an invitation to continue to think critically about the multiple interfaces between human rights and legal pluralism. At the crossroads of all contributions is a concern with understanding how human rights may become vehicles for social justice.

Part One

Normative Approaches

2

Legal Pluralism as a Human Right and/or as a Human Rights Violation

EVA BREMS

1. THE COMPLEX ARCHITECTURE OF INTERNATIONAL HUMAN RIGHTS LAW[1]

INTERNATIONAL HUMAN RIGHTS law can be analysed in terms of legal pluralism. In public opinion, 'human rights' are often portrayed as a clear and homogenous concept. Yet those who work in the field of human rights know that the reality is very different. A seemingly simple question such as 'show me the list of all human rights' or 'draft me a list of all human rights' is certain to generate as many different lists as there are human rights experts. Indeed, there is no such thing as a single human rights catalogue. Instead, human rights are found in a multitude of highly diverse sources. Even if we leave aside domestic legal sources and focus only on international human rights law, we are dealing with a complex, multilayered reality. The sources and mechanisms of international human rights law can be differentiated along several lines.

In the first place, sources and mechanisms can be categorised on the basis of the *governance level* at which they operate. At the universal level, human rights standards have been set by the United Nations[2] and a number

---

[1] For a more extensive discussion, see Brems (2014).

[2] The main ones are the Universal Declaration of Human Rights (1948), the International Covenant on Civil and Political Rights (1966), the International Covenant on Economic, Social and Cultural Rights (1966), the International Convention on the Elimination of All Forms of Racial Discrimination (1966), the Convention on the Elimination of All Forms of Discrimination Against Women (1979), the Convention against Torture and other Cruel, Inhuman or Degrading Treatment or Punishment (1984), the Convention on the Rights of the Child (1989), the International Convention on the Protection of the Rights of all Migrant Workers and Members of their Families (1990), the International Convention for the Protection of All Persons from Enforced Disappearance (2006), and the Convention on the Rights of Persons with Disabilities (2008).

of specialised agencies such as Unesco[3] and the International Labour Organization.[4] Additional—and largely overlapping in terms of content—standards have been set by regional and subregional organisations, in particular the Council of Europe,[5] the European Union,[6] the Organization of American States,[7] the African Union,[8] the Association of Southeast Asian Nations[9] and the League of Arab States.[10]

In addition, human rights texts can be differentiated on the basis of their scope *ratione materiae*. Comprehensive texts, aiming at a complete list of human rights,[11] coexist with texts that focus on one category of human rights—generally either civil and political rights or economic, social and cultural rights[12]—and single-issue texts.[13]

Furthermore, with respect to their scope *ratione personae*, some human rights instruments are universal, ie applicable to all human beings, while

---

[3] eg Universal Declaration on Bioethics and Human Rights (2005).

[4] eg ILO Convention No 87 concerning Freedom of Association and Protection of the Right to Organise, ILO Convention No 105 concerning the Abolition of Forced Labour, ILO Convention No 111 concerning Discrimination in Respect of Employment and Occupation ILO Convention No 182 concerning the Prohibition and Immediate Action for the Elimination of the Worst Forms of Child Labour.

[5] The main human rights convention of the Council of Europe is the Convention for the Protection of Human Rights and Fundamental Freedoms (1950), known as the European Convention on Human Rights (ECHR).

[6] The main human rights standard set by the European Union is the Charter of Fundamental Rights of the European Union (2000).

[7] The main human rights convention of the OAS is the American Convention on Human Rights (1969).

[8] The main human rights convention of the African Union is the African Charter on Human and Peoples' Rights (1981).

[9] ASEAN Human Rights Declaration 2012.

[10] Arab Charter on Human Rights 2004.

[11] eg Universal Declaration of Human Rights, African Charter on Human and Peoples' Rights, Charter of Fundamental Rights of the European Union.

[12] eg International Covenant on Civil and Political Rights, International Covenant on Economic, Social and Cultural Rights, European Convention on Human Rights, European Social Charter (1961 and 1996), American Convention on Human Rights, Additional Protocol to the American Convention on Human Rights in the Area of Economic, Social and Cultural Rights (1999).

[13] eg Convention Against Torture, International Convention for the Protection of All Persons from Enforced Disappearance, Convention on the Elimination of All Forms of Racial Discrimination, European Convention for the Prevention of Torture and Inhuman or Degrading Treatment or Punishment (1987), Council of Europe Convention on Action against Trafficking in Human Beings (2005), Council Of Europe Convention On Preventing And Combating Violence Against Women And Domestic Violence (2011), Inter-American Convention on the Prevention, Punishment and Eradication of Violence against Women (1994), Inter-American Convention to Prevent and Punish Torture (1985), Inter-American Convention on Forced Disappearance of Persons (1994).

others have a specific target group, eg women,[14] children,[15] persons with a disability,[16] or members of minority or indigenous groups.[17]

Also, a distinction can be made based on the *legal force* of the instruments. While numerous human rights norms—constitutions, treaties, customary law—are binding, human rights have also been included in formally non-binding soft law—eg declarations and resolutions—that may nevertheless have strong moral or political force, and even acquire, in the words of the International Court of Justice a 'normative value'.[18]

Finally, there is a great variety among the *monitoring mechanisms* that accompany binding human rights instruments: these range from judicial control by supranational courts—the European Court of Human Rights, the Inter-American Court of Human Rights, the African Court of Human and Peoples' Rights—to quasi-judicial control—individual complaints examined by expert committees[19]—to other forms of expert control and political control-reporting procedures,[20] special rapporteurs, etc.

While each of these sources is internally coherent and each monitoring body has developed its own broadly consistent case law using its own interpretation tools, the picture as a whole is rather complex. It is a reality of legal pluralism (Berman 2007), which can be experienced as a mega-mall in which rights-holders can go 'forum shopping', thus benefiting from the diversity of norms, yet also as a labyrinth in which they—and their rights—may get lost. It is a polyphony that may produce a rich harmonious sound

---

[14] eg Convention on the Elimination of All Forms of Discrimination Against Women, Protocol to the African Charter on Human and Peoples' Rights on the Rights of Women in Africa (2003).

[15] eg Convention on the Rights of the Child, African Charter on the Rights and Welfare of the Child (1990), Inter-American Convention on International Traffic in Minors (1994).

[16] eg Convention on the Rights of Persons with Disabilities.

[17] eg Declaration on the Rights of Persons Belonging to National or Ethnic, Religious and Linguistic Minorities (1992), Council of Europe Framework Convention for the Protection of national Minorities (1995), United Nations Declaration on the Rights of Indigenous Peoples (2007).

[18] International Court of Justice, *Legality of the Threat or Use of Nuclear Weapons*, Advisory Opinion, 8 July 1996, *ICJ Reports* 1996, 226, at 254, § 70.

[19] eg the individual complaint procedures before some of the UN treaty monitoring bodies: the Human Rights Committee, the Committee Against Torture, the Committee on the Elimination of Discrimination Against Women, the Committee on the Elimination of Racial Discrimination, the Committee on Economic, Social and Cultural Rights, the Committee on the Rights of Persons with Disabilities and the Committee on Enforced Disappearances; also the collective complaint procedure before the European Committee on Social Rights, and the procedures before the African Commission on Human and Peoples' Rights and the Inter-American Commission on Human Rights.

[20] Self-reporting followed by discussion of the report by an expert body may be considered the standard international human rights monitoring procedure on account of its wide use at the global as well as regional levels (Smith 2012: 154).

that strongly gets a message across, yet may also be a cacophony in which we hear a lot of noise—or noises—but cannot distinguish a clear melody.

2. TOWARD AN INTEGRATED PERSPECTIVE OF INTERNATIONAL HUMAN RIGHTS LAW

Academia has a tendency toward specialisation. As the field of human rights law has emancipated, general human rights experts have largely been replaced by experts in, for example, 'children's rights' or 'women's rights' or 'minorities', or experts in the European Convention or the UN system, or in one specific freedom, such as press freedom or non-discrimination, privacy or religious freedom. While this has brought the discipline to a higher level, it has also contributed to creating a fragmented, compartmentalised view of human rights law.

I submit that our interest in the trees should not make us forget to study the forest. I argue that it is highly relevant for scholars of human rights law to study human rights law as an integrated whole: looking at, among other things, issues of consistency and alignment as well as divergence across the different layers of human rights law, at gaps in the overall protection system, and at all kinds of cross-cutting or isolated dynamics. This is relevant both from a bottom-up perspective and from a top-down perspective.

First of all, the study of human rights law as an integrated whole is relevant from the bottom-up perspective of the users of human rights law (Desmet 2014). When I use the term 'users' of human rights law, I mean in the first place the individuals and entities that are the subjects of human rights law, the rights-holders, who are at risk of potential violations, or who have already suffered violations. Yet I include under this term also the public authorities and other duty-bearers under human rights norms, because the point I want to make applies to them as well. The point is that users of human rights law are confronted simultaneously with all of these human rights provisions. To any particular situation, a dozen relevant human rights sources may apply. Hence, in my point of view, it is highly relevant to look at this complex human rights architecture through the lens of its users. This means that we should not just study separate human rights norms or mechanisms, but that we should also pay attention to their simultaneous application, and examine what that implies for the users of human rights law, and how these users deal with that reality of 'internal' legal pluralism.

The study of human rights law is relevant also from a top-down perspective, in the sense that it resonates with some of the central principles of human rights law, in particular the principles of universality and indivisibility of human rights. These two central dogmas of international human rights law appear to plead in favour of an integrated perspective of human rights that takes into account all human rights norms relevant in a particular situation; as well as taking into account the human rights of all rights-holders whose rights are affected by a particular situation. Universality means that all people have all human rights. Indivisibility and interdependence means that human rights are a package deal and that there is no hierarchy within human rights. Together, they require that all human rights should carry the same weight, and that they should be read together, strengthening each other. The reality of human rights implementation is, however, often far removed from these principles: cases involving multiple human rights are routinely examined through the lens of one human right only; and the invoking of multiple norms in a single situation remains the exception rather than the rule.

1.   Inconsistencies within International Human Rights Law: The Case of Legal Pluralism

When one adopts this holistic, integrated view of international human rights law, one cannot escape the finding that there are a number of inconsistencies within international human rights law taken as a whole. Those may be the result of deliberate choice or instead the unplanned result of the uncoordinated growth of international human rights law. They may create opportunities for rights-holders trying to obtain human rights justice, as well as for human rights duty-bearers trying to duck their obligations. And they may carry a number of risks: the risk of suboptimal human rights protection, the risk of unequal standards of protection, and the risk of lack of legal certainty.

One such inconsistency concerns the attitude of international human rights law towards the recognition of legal pluralism, in the sense of an official legal system making room for a system of 'tradition-based law', a term which I intend to cover indigenous law, customary law as well as religious law. As the discussion that follows will show, there is one layer or field of international human rights law that considers state recognition of tradition-based law as mandatory and non-recognition as a violation of human rights (section 3.1 below). And there is another layer or field of international human rights law that considers such state recognition of tradition-based law as a violation of human rights (section 3.2 below). Human rights law as a whole thus at the same time mandates state organisation of legal pluralism and bans it. The remainder of this chapter will discuss the inconsistent attitude of international human rights law as a whole towards legal pluralism as a case study illustrating the dynamics and consequences of the internal plurality that characterises international human rights law. After discussing each of the above-sketched human rights approaches to legal pluralism in turn, we will examine the implications of this normative inconsistency.

2.1. A Right to Legal Pluralism: Indigenous Peoples' Rights

The first approach within international human rights law, mandating recognition of traditional law, and hence mandating the recognition and organisation of legal pluralism by the state, is found in the universal regime governing the rights of indigenous peoples. This is laid down in ILO Convention 169 (1989) concerning Indigenous and Tribal Peoples in Independent Countries and in the United Nations Declaration on the Rights of Indigenous Peoples (2007).

The ILO Convention grants indigenous peoples the right to retain their own customs and institutions (Article 8(2)), and mandates state respect for 'the methods customarily practised by the peoples concerned for dealing with offences committed by their members' (Article 9(1)). Both provisions precondition these rights on compatibility with national law and international human rights. In the same vein, the UN Declaration states that: '[I]ndigenous peoples have the right to promote, develop and maintain their institutional structures and their distinctive customs, spirituality, traditions, procedures, practices and, in the cases where they exist, juridical systems or customs, in accordance with international human rights standards' (Article 34).

At the universal level, and in the specific context of indigenous peoples, there is thus unambiguous recognition of a human right to traditional law. This is a collective human right that belongs to a people as a collective entity (Anaya 2007). It is a fully fledged right, which entails both a freedom from interference as well as a number of positive state obligations. As is common in human rights law, the freedom from interference that this right entails is not absolute. In particular, the drafters of these international texts on indigenous rights have foreseen that there might be situations in which the collective rights of indigenous peoples enter into conflict with individual human rights—which may be the rights of individual members of an indigenous people or of individuals who do not belong to the indigenous people. Both texts give priority to the individuals' human rights in such situations. A number of positive state obligations that have been specifically included in the UN Declaration relate to the implications of a state recognising traditional law next to state law and organising a system of legal pluralism. They include the duty to resolve conflicts between legal systems, and the duty to give due recognition to indigenous law in a number of procedures of state law (Articles 27 and 40 UN Declaration).

In the field of indigenous peoples' rights, human rights norms thus require states to recognise certain realities of legal pluralism and to engage with these realities. It has been argued that this is a significant innovation in international human rights law, as it 'challenges the primacy and sphere of state governing authority in a much more fundamental sense than classic individual rights' (Anaya 2007: 8). This is not a small thing, and its significance is increased by the fact that the UN Declaration on the Rights of

Indigenous Peoples is one of the most recent normative human rights texts at the universal level, and that it was adopted overwhelmingly by the world community.[21]

Yet these novel ideas that challenge the centrality of the state have not—as yet—penetrated all layers of international human rights law. As will be discussed below, in another room of the house of human rights, different standards apply, which not only do not mandate state recognition and organisation of legal pluralism, but which even go so far as to ban it, labelling it a human rights violation.

2.2. A Ban on Legal Pluralism in the Name of Human Rights: The *Refah* Case

This other room or other field is that of the Council of Europe human rights protection system, and more specifically the case law of the European Court of Human Rights, applying the European Convention on Human Rights. The approach of the European Convention system to any human rights matter is an important fact within international human rights law as a whole. The European Court of Human Rights is the oldest supranational human rights court, it has by far the largest body of case law of any supranational human rights body, and it is based in a region with a long democratic tradition. It is therefore not surprising to find that the Court and its case law have become reference points within the global human rights project, also beyond Europe.

When it comes to the European Court of Human Rights' position on state recognition of legal pluralism, the relevant case law is not extensive. There have been a number of cases in which the Court—or the former Commission[22]—dealt with the consequences of legal pluralism, eg cases involving polygamy among immigrants in the UK,[23] Roma marriage in Spain,[24] informal Islamic marriage in Turkey,[25] or the enforcement in an Italian state court of a judgment of a religious tribunal of the Catholic church.[26]

---

[21] The Declaration was adopted with an affirmative vote of 144 states in the UN General Assembly. Only four countries—the United States, Canada, Australia and New Zealand—voted against it, while Azerbaijan, Bangladesh, Bhutan, Burundi, Colombia, Georgia, Kenya, Nigeria, Russia, Samoa and Ukraine abstained.

[22] Until the entry into force of the 11th additional protocol to the European Convention on Human Rights in 1999, the Convention system was based on two bodies, the European Commission on Human Rights (ECmHR) and the European Court of Human Rights (ECtHR). Individuals did not have direct access to the Court, but had to apply to the Commission. The Commission issued decisions on admissibility and reports on the merits of cases.

[23] ECmHR, application no 19628/92, *Bibi v United Kingdom*, 29 June 1992 (dec).

[24] ECtHR, application no 49151/07, *Muñoz Diaz v Spain*, 8 December 2009.

[25] ECtHR (Grand Chamber), application no 3976/05, *Şerife Yiğit v Turkey*, 2 November 2010.

[26] ECtHR, application no 30882/96, *Pellegrini v Italy*, 20 June 2001.

Yet only one case addressed the recognition of legal pluralism and its relationship to human rights as such, the case of *Refah Partisi v Turkey*.[27] This case will be discussed in some detail in what follows, to the extent that it addresses the issue of legal pluralism. It is an important case, as it was adopted by a unanimous Grand Chamber of 17 judges. The case concerned the forced dissolution of a political party, at that time the biggest party in the Turkish parliament, on the ground that it was 'a centre of anti-secular activities'. This accusation relied on three arguments, one of which concerned the allegation that Refah intended to introduce a system of legal pluralism in Turkey. The other arguments concerned the allegation that Refah would—within this context of legal pluralism—introduce sharia law in Turkey and the allegation that Refah members had suggested that they might use violence to reach their political objectives.

In the Refah judgment, the Court held in quite absolute terms that both the concept of institutionalised legal pluralism and sharia law as such violated human rights. Unfortunately, with respect to each of these far-reaching pronouncements, one cannot escape the impression that the Court did not rely on sufficient expert knowledge and that it did not thoroughly think through the consequences of its rulings. Although a lot can be said about the Court's inappropriate statements about sharia law in the Refah judgment,[28] this chapter will focus on what it said about legal pluralism.

The allegation that the Refah party intended to 'set up a plurality of legal systems' was based on two quotations from speeches of party leader Necmettin Erbakan:[29]

> There must be several legal systems. The citizen must be able to choose for himself which legal system is most appropriate for him, within a framework of general principles. ... The right to choose one's own legal system is an integral part of the freedom of religion'.

and

> When we are in power a Muslim will be able to get married before the mufti, if he wishes, and a Christian will be able to marry in church, if he prefers.

Hence the case did not address a situation in which a state actually recognises or organises legal pluralism.[30] Nor was there any concrete plan in

---

[27] ECtHR (Grand Chamber), applications nos 41340/98 41342/98 41343/98 41344/98, *Refah Partisi v Turkey*, 13 February 2003.

[28] The Court stated in general terms that 'sharia is incompatible with the fundamental principles of democracy', and described sharia as 'stable and invariable', and claimed that 'principles such as pluralism in the political sphere or the constant evolution of public freedoms have no place in it' (*Refah* judgment, para 123). These statements are at odds with how (Western) experts of Islamic law describe sharia, eg Otto (2011).

[29] *Refah Partisi v Turkey*, para 28.

[30] Such situations are rare in the Council of Europe Member States. An example, also relating to Islamic law, are the Mufti jurisdictions operating among the Muslim/Turkish minority in western Thrace (Greece).

this sense, as this issue was not included in the party's constitution or programme. Yet what matters for our purpose is that the Court saw sufficient evidence of an intent in this sense, and expressed a clear opinion on the matter. The Court concluded that 'a plurality of legal systems, as proposed by Refah, cannot be considered to be compatible with the Convention system'.[31] In other words, in the eyes of the European Court of Human Rights, legal pluralism is by definition at odds with human rights.

The Court interpreted Refah's point of view in a rather radical way, stating that:

> [It] would introduce into all legal relationships a distinction between individuals grounded on religion, would categorise everyone according to his religious beliefs and would allow him rights and freedoms not as an individual but according to his allegiance to a religious movement.[32]

That is a remarkable starting point, given the fact that neither the application of legal pluralism to all legal relationships nor the categorisation of all individuals can be directly derived from Erbakan's words. Practice shows that where institutionalised legal pluralism exists, it is generally limited to certain parts of the law, usually in the sphere of family law.[33] Moreover it may be organised in such a way that next to tradition-based law, there is a neutral option under state law, which can be opted for by believers and non-believers alike.[34] In addition, the same individual may rely for certain matters and in certain circumstances on tradition-based law, while preferring state law for other matters or at other times. This is the well-known phenomenon of 'forum shopping'.[35] There are, however, systems that assign individuals to ethnic or religious categories without giving them such a freedom of choice.[36] I submit that this is a crucial variable in discussions about the recognition of legal pluralism from a human rights point of view. A mandatory system may offer stronger protection to collective cultural or religious rights, but appears hard to reconcile with individual human rights, in particular with autonomy rights and individual religious freedom, whereas no such a priori conclusion can be drawn with regard to a system that allows for free choice. It is therefore astonishing that the European Court of Human Rights entirely ignores the latter category, and appears to assume automatically that any system of organised legal pluralism must be

---

[31] *Refah Partisi v Turkey*, para 129.

[32] ibid.

[33] This is, for example, the case in India, which recognises several types of religious family law (for Hindus, Muslims, Christians and Parsi). See Solanki (2011).

[34] cf the campaign for the recognition of Muslim personal law in South Africa (conducted amongst others by feminists), in a context that also recognises/regulates customary marriage, in addition to providing for civil marriage. See Amien (2010).

[35] See Hoekema (2008: 3).

[36] In Malaysia, for example, Muslims do not have the possibility to opt for the general legislation that is valid for non-Muslims. See Hussain (2011: 380–81).

a mandatory system. This is especially remarkable given the fact that the quotations from Erbakan that form the basis of the whole discussion seem to emphasise free choice.

In support of its conclusion that setting up a plurality of legal system is incompatible with human rights, the Court advances two arguments. The first argument is about state monopoly of the law as a requirement for human rights protection (section 3.2.1 below). The second argument considers legal pluralism as inherently discriminatory (section 3.2.2 below). In what follows, the validity of these arguments will be critically assessed.

2.2.1. *State Monopoly of the Law as a Requirement for Human Rights Protection*

In the first place, the Court refers to the obligation of a state 'to ensure that everyone within its jurisdiction enjoys in full, and without being able to waive them, the rights and freedoms guaranteed by the Convention'.[37] The Court states that this role of the state would be undermined by a system of institutionalised legal pluralism, because 'it would oblige individuals to obey, not rules laid down by the State in the exercise of its above-mentioned functions, but static rules of law imposed by the religion concerned'.[38]

This argument is problematic. To start with, it is not clear what the Court means by 'enjoy human rights in full'. The Convention rights allow for restrictions and the role of the Court is precisely to distinguish between acceptable and unacceptable restrictions. Restrictions based on religious rules are treated in the same way as other restrictions. What the Court does not take into consideration is that recognising legal pluralism, and in particular making room for religious law in this context, can be one way of striving for the 'full enjoyment of human rights'. Indeed, institutionalised legal pluralism is regularly defended in the name of human rights; these may be collective rights of cultural or religious groups, but also individual rights, in particular the right to live according to the prescriptions of one's religion.[39] From that perspective one might say that the organisation of legal pluralism does indeed fit within the state's role as 'guarantor of individual rights and freedoms'.

In the Court's reasoning, moreover, there appears to be no room for a scenario in which rules of religious law are in conformity with human rights. Yet the practice of legal pluralism shows that there is no basis for the idea that the recognition of legal pluralism would automatically imply an abdication of the state's obligation to protect human rights. Most individuals

[37] *Refah Partisi v Turkey*, para 119.
[38] Ibid.
[39] cf Meerschaut and Gutwirth (2008: 433).

obey the rules of a number of non-state organisations, both in their private life and in their professional life. This does not undermine human rights, because human rights have been included in constitutions and international conventions, and are therefore on the top of the hierarchy of legal norms, which gives them priority over other rules. One of the reasons for a state to opt for the recognition of legal pluralism is precisely because it allows a state to enforce this priority. Recognition opens the door to regulation of normative orders that exist on the state's territory regardless of recognition. Practice shows that a wide range of techniques are used by states to control the substance as well as the impact of sharia or other tradition-based legal systems in a context of legal pluralism. State law can restrict the spheres of law or the types of disputes to which sharia can be applied. It can codify sharia and in this exercise do away with discriminatory rules through amendment or interpretation. The state can also make secular judges responsible for the application of sharia rules, or it can provide an appeal procedure before state courts.[40] The Court rightly states that:

> Turkey … may legitimately prevent the application within its jurisdiction of private-law rules of religious inspiration prejudicial to public order and the values of democracy for Convention purposes (such as rules permitting discrimination based on the gender of the parties concerned, as in polygamy and privileges for the male sex in matters of divorce and succession).[41]

Yet it misses the mark when it assumes that this can be realised only by rejecting the recognition of legal pluralism. Instead the opposite is true. Throughout the world, tradition-based legal systems are applied on a large scale regardless of recognition. This means that there are cases in which an important goal such as the fight against discrimination may be better reached through recognition and control than by ignoring the reality of (unofficial) legal pluralism.[42] There can be no doubt that a state party to the European Convention that opted for the recognition of legal pluralism would be obliged to amend the religion- or tradition-based law it would recognise so as to render it compatible with human rights. This may be compared to what happens when a state allows the private sector to organise issues such as education, healthcare or security. Privatisation of these human-rights-sensitive services is not automatically at odds with human

---

[40] For examples, see Otto (2011)

[41] *Refah Partisi v Turkey*, para 128.

[42] The Court's case law with respect to Turkey offers an example: the case of *Şerife Yiğit v Turkey* (see above) concerns the disadvantages suffered in the sphere of social rights by a widow whose Islamic religious marriage was not recognised by the state authorities. This case illustrates that despite its lack of recognition, Islamic law is applied in Turkey in the sphere of family law. It also shows that discrimination of women results not necessarily—or not only—from the application of religious law, but may be the result of the state's lack of recognition of religious law. The same point is made with respect to South Africa (Amien 2010).

rights, yet it requires the state to provide guarantees for human rights protection via, amongst other things, the legal instruments that govern such privatisation and through the exercise of control (De Feyter et al 2005). However, rather than giving states guidance on how to address the reality of legal pluralism in a way that optimises human rights protection, the Court chooses to present a caricature of legal pluralism that ignores the reality on the ground.

2.2.2. *Legal Pluralism as Inherently Discriminatory*

The other argument of the Court considers legal pluralism as inherently discriminatory. The Court states that such pluralism discriminates among individuals as regards their enjoyment of public freedoms and that it is not capable of maintaining

> a fair balance between, on the one hand, the claims of certain religious groups who wish to be governed by their own rules and on the other the interest of society as a whole, which must be based on peace and on tolerance between the various religions and beliefs.[43]

This is another example of the Court not taking into account the possibility that the institutionalisation of legal pluralism might be organised on the basis of individual free choice. It seems untenable to hold that there is discrimination against persons who choose to rely on Islamic law rather than state law, especially since such choice is the expression of their religious freedom, which is itself a Convention right.[44]

Assuming that the balancing between religious rights and other human rights in a context of legal pluralism leads to different levels of human rights protection within the same state, the question arises whether this is unacceptable in principle, as the Court maintains. In that respect it is useful to point out that other, widely accepted, institutional arrangements lead to the same result, ie different levels of human rights protection because of different legal regimes applying within a state. One can think in particular of the impact of federalism on the enjoyment of human rights. It is not uncommon in federal states that individuals enjoy different levels of human rights protection depending on where they happen to live. Same-sex marriage used to be allowed in some US states but not in others, and the same holds

---

[43] *Refah Partisi v Turkey*, para 119.
[44] cf the Court's statement in the 'face veil ban' case of *SAS v France* (Grand Chamber), 1 July 2014, para 119: 'The Court takes the view, however, that a State Party cannot invoke gender equality in order to ban a practice that is defended by women—such as the applicant—in the context of the exercise of the rights enshrined in those provisions, unless it were to be understood that individuals could be protected on that basis from the exercise of their own fundamental rights and freedoms.'

for the death penalty. Likewise, teachers can wear an Islamic headscarf in some German *Länder* but not in others. Foreigners migrating to Belgium have to take mandatory integration classes in Flanders, but not in Wallonia. Moreover, powers in a federal system are not by definition based (only) on territorial criteria. In Belgium, some inhabitants of Brussels are part of the Flemish community, others of the French community. If the Flemish parliament decides to ban religious dress in schools, while the French Community assembly allows such dress, children and teachers in Brussels would enjoy different levels of protection of their religious freedom depending on the language of their schooling. Would the European Court of Human Rights in that hypothetical situation also maintain that 'such a difference in treatment cannot maintain a fair balance between, on the one hand, the claims of certain [linguistic] groups who wish to be governed by their own rules and on the other the interest of society as a whole, which must be based on peace and on tolerance between the various [linguistic] communities'?[45]

Given the continuum between federalism and legal pluralism,[46] an a priori rejection of the recognition of legal pluralism on grounds of discrimination is not tenable unless one also rejects all types of federalism in which the power of the federated entities impacts on fundamental rights protection.

2.2.3. *Opposite Approaches to Legal Pluralism*

While the reasoning of the European Court of Human Rights in the *Refah* judgment is vulnerable to criticism, it has undeniably strong authority. As a fairly recent judgment, which was adopted by a unanimous Grand Chamber, it is not likely to be overruled in the near future. Hence international human rights law taken as a whole includes two diametrically opposite approaches to state recognition and organisation of legal pluralism. Within the universal system for the protection of indigenous peoples' rights, state recognition and organisation of legal pluralism is mandatory as a matter of human rights law. Yet within the regional system of the Council of Europe, state recognition and organisation of legal pluralism is considered to be by definition a human rights violation, at least if the broad statements of the Court in the *Refah* judgment are to be taken at face value. In what follows, we will examine how to deal with this internal inconsistency of international human rights law.

---

[45] *Refah Partisi v Turkey*, para 119
[46] It is submitted that federalism and legal pluralism are not two entirely different things, but rather are part of a continuum of group-based rights concerning cultural/religious identity and self-determination. For example, for Kymlicka, both federalism and the recognition of tradition-based family law are types of self-government rights, which he considers to be one of three types of group-differentiated rights for cultural groups (Kymlicka 2005). It has to be acknowledged, however, that federalism is not always an expression of self-determination of cultural groups.

2.3. Dealing with Inconsistency

Can international human rights law at the same time mandate the recognition of legal pluralism and oppose it? Do such internal contradictions threaten the sustainability of international human rights law and undermine its force and credibility? In what follows, several lines of arguments that may be advanced to soften or nuance the normative contradiction we observed will be examined on their merits.

2.3.1. European Exceptionalism

One way of reconciling the apparently contradictory norms might be to state that Europe does not participate in the global consensus in favour of the recognition of legal pluralism. However, this point cannot be sustained if one looks at the positions of Council of Europe Member States with respect to the universal norms on the rights of indigenous peoples. Among the 22 states that ratified ILO Convention 169, there are four Council of Europe Member States (the Netherlands, Denmark, Norway and Spain). As for the UN Declaration, most Council of Europe Member States were among the large majority that voted in favour at the UN General Assembly. None was among the four dissenters and two states (Azerbaijan and Russia) were among the 11 abstentions.

Hence it is clear that the internal contradiction within international human rights law cannot be characterised as a divergence between a universal standard and a European standard. At least as far as indigenous peoples' rights are concerned, the Member States of the Council of Europe are part of the global consensus that supports a collective right to state-organised legal pluralism.

2.3.2. A Pragmatic Users' Perspective

Another way of solving the matter might be to focus on the fact that the universal norm applies specifically to indigenous peoples and does not take a position on the recognition of legal pluralism beyond that specific context. As there are not so many issues concerning indigenous peoples in Europe,[47] and as these issues seem so far not to have included claims for the recognition of indigenous law, one might argue that in practice, at the level of the human rights users, actual conflicts between contradictory norms of international human rights do not occur. However, this position may be carrying pragmatism a little too far for most tastes. Moreover, even within its

---

[47] This is linked to the fact that there are not so many indigenous peoples in Europe. Yet there are some, in particular the Sami in Scandinavia, the Nenet in Siberia, the Komi peoples in the Urals, and the Circassians in the North Caucasus.

pragmatic logic it may be problematic, as it relies on ostrich politics. Indeed, one should not exclude the possibility that any of Europe's indigenous peoples might in the future claim recognition of some of its indigenous law. If the Sami of Norway claim recognition of their indigenous law, the Norwegian state would be legally bound under ILO Convention 169, and politically bound under the UN Declaration, to grant that claim. Yet at the same time, it would be prohibited from doing so on the basis of the European Convention on Human Rights, as interpreted by the European Court of Human Rights in its *Refah* judgment.

2.3.3. *Drawing a Line Between Religion and Culture*

As a third option, one may consider a restrictive reading of the *Refah* ruling, focusing on the fact that the case is about religious law. The European Court of Human Rights manifestly does not want to make room for religious groups to have their own norms, but, so the argument would go, it might think differently about norms based on culture and tradition as is the case for indigenous peoples. In terms of legal interpretation, that would be a stretch and a twist, as the Court's arguments—relying on the importance it attaches to the state monopoly of the law and of equal protection of the human rights of all citizens— apply prima facie regardless of whether one deals with norms of religious or cultural origin. Yet such restrictive interpretation is not unthinkable, as the language of the Court does refer to religion. However, from an anthropological perspective, drawing a clear line between cultural and religious norms would be hard to sustain. This is so on the one hand because 'religious' rules are strongly intertwined with tradition and culture, and on the other because indigenous norms often carry spiritual and religious meanings. Hence an approach that relies on a black-and-white dichotomy between religion and culture would misrepresent reality and would therefore be viable only by resorting to manipulations that are not compatible with legal certainty.

2.3.4. *Distinguishing Minority, Majority and Indigenous Peoples' Claims*

Another distinction that could be made between the rights of indigenous peoples and the *Refah* case is that the latter deals with the rights of the majority population in Turkey. It may be argued that the claim for the accommodation of the cultural particularities of a minority group that has known a history of discrimination and whose traditions may be threatened with disappearance is much stronger than that of the members of the majority culture or religion. This does indeed seem to be the overall tendency in international human rights law, in particular in the field of culture, where the right to live according to one's culture appears to be entrenched only for minorities. Moreover, the overall layout of international human rights law also shows that among minority peoples, indigenous peoples are singled out for special protection to an extent that goes much beyond what is provided for minorities in general. Hence it might be argued that it is coherent to restrict the right to recognition of legal pluralism to indigenous peoples only. However, upon closer scrutiny this argument is quite problematic. In the first place, this distinction does not have a basis in the *Refah* judgment, which makes claims of a general nature. It could in principle have argued that the accommodation of Muslim personal law in Turkey would be undesirable because it might affect the large majority of the population.[48] But it did not do so. Even if we place this fact between brackets and work with the hypothesis that in a future case based on an indigenous claim the Court might wish to distinguish that case from *Refah*, it might be difficult to do so on the basis of presumed unique characteristics of indigenous peoples. While there are good reasons to differentiate between the rights of indigenous peoples and other peoples with respect to those aspects that relate to the distinguishing characteristics of indigenous peoples—in particular their relationship to their lands—such good reasons do not support all differentiations existing today. When it comes to claims for the recognition of tradition-based law, one cannot get around the similarities between indigenous law and customary law of minority—or indeed majority—peoples.[49] Would it then not be discrimination, as well as an affront to the principle of universality of human rights, to grant rights to recognition of legal traditions only to indigenous peoples? By way of justification for such unequal treatment, reference to a history of discrimination will not do, as many minorities that are not indigenous peoples have suffered similar histories, and as in many cases majority peoples would likewise be able to argue that their legal traditions were suppressed during colonialism.

3. CONCLUSION

When we analyse international human rights law as an integrated whole and focus on its pluralist nature, one approach may be seen as concentrating on drawing normative conclusions from such analysis, with a goal of optimising human rights protection. From that perspective, I conclude that the normative contradiction highlighted in this chapter is indeed problematic,

---

[48] It could have argued, for instance, that this might create pressure to opt for Muslim personal law rather than civil law: cf its arguments with respect to the Islamic headscarf in a university context, in *Leyla Şahin v Turkey* (Grand Chamber, application no 44774/98, 10 November 2005) para 115.

[49] cf Glenn's category of the 'chtonic legal tradition', which includes both the law of indigenous peoples around the world, and customary law in Africa and Asia (Glenn 2004).

as it cannot be explained in a coherent manner. Moreover the exploration of this contradiction pointed to an area that remains unresolved, namely the position of the universal human rights system vis-à-vis the recognition of legal pluralism in other situations than that of indigenous peoples. Currently, human rights law at the universal level is silent about this matter. As universal human rights law does not include obligations on the part of states to recognise customary or religious law in their rules on minority rights or religious freedom, there is no ground to claim that a right to such recognition currently exists. Neither is there a ground to claim that such recognition would be considered a violation of human rights.

A universal human right to the recognition of legal pluralism appears unrealistic and probably undesirable. Yet, as such a right has been recognised for one category of peoples, international human rights discourse should be able to offer persuasive arguments justifying such privileged treatment. Moreover, looking at international human rights law as an integrated whole, the position of the European Court on Human Rights on this issue is a problematic one, both because it is grounded on arguments that are not persuasive and because it creates contradictory obligations for some states. Should this position spread to the universal level—for all situations except those involving indigenous peoples—this would be even more problematic, as it would lead to blatant unequal treatment of similar cases. Ultimately, it appears important that all actors that play a role in the human rights enforcement machinery are well aware of the fact that they do not operate in isolation, but rather are part of a global project. Within this global project of universal human rights protection, reflection is needed about the demarcation and the rules of the game to create a sustainable room for divergence and a space for bottom-up dynamics.

3

Legal Pluralism and International Human Rights Law: A Multifaceted Relationship

ELLEN DESMET[1]

1. INTRODUCTION

THIS CHAPTER ANALYSES some characteristics of the relationship between international human rights law and the concept of legal pluralism at two levels. The first part provides some theoretical reflections on the linkages between human rights, international human rights law and legal pluralism. The use of the term 'legal pluralism' in relation to ever-smaller bodies of law, such as international human rights law itself, then leads to some reflections as to where this process may bring us. A distinction is proposed between 'legal pluralism', as referring to the simultaneous applicability of various normative systems in a given social field, and 'applying a legal pluralist perspective' to the study of the simultaneous applicability of norms originating from the same normative (sub)system.

The second part of the chapter further explores the relationship between legal pluralism as a social phenomenon and international human rights law on the basis of a concrete issue, namely the land, territorial and resource rights of indigenous peoples. How does the empirical fact of legal pluralism interplay with the emergence and implementation of human rights standards in the domain of indigenous land, territorial and resource rights? It will be also highlighted that the relationship between substantive provisions in international human rights law, on the one hand, and norms of other legal orders,

[1] Assistant Professor at the Human Rights Centre, Ghent University, Belgium. This research has been funded by the Interuniversity Attraction Poles Programme initiated by the Belgian Science Policy Office, namely the IAP 'The Global Challenge of Human Rights Integration: Towards a Users' Perspective' (www.hrintegration.be). I am grateful to Giselle Corradi, Eva Brems, Lourdes Peroni, Valeska David and the participants of the workshop 'How Does Legal Pluralism Interplay with the Promotion of Human Rights?', held 2–3 May 2013 at Oñati, for their useful comments on earlier versions of this chapter.

on the other, may go in various, parallel or opposing, directions. In this way, the richness and variability of possible relations between various normative orders are illustrated, defying any unidimensional characterisations of normative orders as regards a particular issue—for instance, of human rights law as supporting indigenous land and resource claims 'all the way'.

2. ABOUT LEGAL PLURALISM, HUMAN RIGHTS AND INTERNATIONAL HUMAN RIGHTS LAW

2.1. Legal Pluralism in Sociolegal Scholarship

Franz von Benda-Beckmann (2002: 72) has noted that there is 'little uniformity in the conceptualisation of ... legal pluralism'. This is partly because the concept of legal pluralism has been employed across various disciplines, including anthropology, sociology and legal science (ibid: 73). In the sociolegal literature, the concept of legal pluralism is most commonly understood as referring to 'a situation in which two or more legal systems coexist in the same social field' (Merry 1988: 870) or, in a similar vein, 'the coexistence of different normative orders within one socio-political space' (von Benda-Beckmann 1997: 1). These normative orders may coexist independently from one another, each with their own basis of legitimacy. This has been named 'strong' legal pluralism (Griffiths 1986) or 'wild' legal pluralism (von Benda-Beckmann 2006: 59), standing in contrast to 'weak' legal pluralism (Griffiths 1986). In the latter case, the functioning of a certain normative system is dependent upon its recognition by another normative order—often, but not necessarily, the state legal system.

De Sousa Santos prefers the expression 'plurality of legal orders' over 'legal pluralism', because the latter term has in his view a normative undertone and seems to imply that there is something 'inherently good, progressive or emancipatory' about legal pluralism, which he contests (de Sousa Santos 2002: 89). As an example, he refers to the repressive legal orders established by paramilitary groups in territories under their control. Other authors, working on gender issues, have preferred the term 'legal pluralities', considering that this term 'best evokes the fluid, multilayered, contradictory and transnational forms of legal ordering that shape women's life prospects today' (Sieder et al 2013: 1) or 'plural legalities' (Hellum et al 2007). Notwithstanding the different denominations, they all refer to a multiplicity of forms of normative ordering that simultaneously apply to a particular social field. In that sense, they do not fundamentally seem to differ from one another, even though the term legal pluralism may evoke somewhat more the impression of 'discrete', 'separate' legal orders, whereas the notions of 'legal pluralities' and 'plural legalities' emphasise more the fluidity and intersection of these forms of ordering. In the latter vein, de

Sousa Santos (2002: 437) has coined the term 'interlegality' to indicate 'different legal spaces superimposed, interpenetrated and mixed in our minds, as much as in our actions'.

2.2. Legal Pluralism, Human Rights and International Human Rights Law

Legal pluralism and human rights are at first sight 'strange bedfellows', as Mégret (2013: 69) has noted: human rights are inherently normative in nature, whereas the concept of legal pluralism usually refers to a social fact of multiple legal orders coexisting in the same sociopolitical space. Legal pluralism and human rights are thus not 'conceptual analogues' (Provost et al 2013: 1).

I understand one of the objectives of this volume to be to try to describe and explain under which circumstances human rights may be realised in a world characterised by the simultaneous applicability of multiple normative systems in a given social field. As will be illustrated below regarding indigenous land, territorial and resource rights, the relationship between human rights and legal pluralism is ambivalent and context dependent: a legally plural situation on the ground may contribute or not to the realisation of human rights, depending on the specific circumstances and the interpretation and application of both human rights standards and other norms.

A key role in the realisation of human rights is—or should be—played by international human rights *law*, ie the codification of human rights in international legal instruments. From a human rights perspective, international human rights law is an important vehicle for the protection and promotion of human rights, one that has been specifically designed for and is supposed to be exclusively dedicated to this goal. This does not imply that the application of international human rights law is the only way of realising human rights. Human rights may also be respected, protected and fulfilled through the functioning of other legal systems, such as state law, other branches of international law (eg international humanitarian law or international criminal law) or non-state legal orders. Non-legal ways to enhance human rights include the use of media, political action and social mobilisation. Human rights may thus have considerable impact even when they are not mobilised as 'law' (Merry et al 2010).

From a legal pluralist perspective, international human rights law is one of the legal orders that is applicable today in practically every social field.[2]

---

[2] Quane (2013: 677) notes that 'when viewed in conjunction with a state's national law, the very existence of international human rights law represents a particular form of legal pluralism'. In her exploration of the relationship between international human rights law and legal pluralism, she seems to limit herself to a 'weak' conception of legal pluralism (cf Griffiths 1986), namely aiming to 'explore the extent to which a state's acceptance *de facto* or *de jure* of religious and/or customary law within its territory is compatible with the requirements of international human rights law' (Quane 2013: 677–78).

Tamanaha (2008: 397–400) has broadly identified six systems of normative ordering: official or positive legal systems; customary normative systems; religious normative systems; economic/capitalist normative systems; functional normative systems and community/cultural normative systems. He considers 'human rights' as one type of official legal systems, next to, among others, state law and European Union law. Given his characterisation of official legal systems as 'linked to an institutionalised legal apparatus of some kind; ... manifested in legislature, enforcement agencies, tribunals' (ibid: 397), I submit that he actually intends to refer to human rights *law* instead of human rights as such.

The place of 'human rights (law)' in the scheme of Tamanaha as one type of official legal system already points to the fact that normative systems usually consist of different subsystems. This can be observed at various, and ever smaller, levels. For instance, official legal systems can roughly be divided into international law, regional law (eg of the European Union, the African Union and the Organisation of American States), national/federal state law, and various lower levels of official law depending on the state structure (eg provincial law and municipal law). International law itself also consists of multiple subsystems. International human rights law is, then, one of these subsystems, next to, among others, international humanitarian law, international criminal law, international environmental law, and international trade and investment law. Often, various subsystems of international law will apply concurrently, such as international environmental law and international investment law (see eg Onana 2012).

International human rights law is not a uniform system either. It is itself multilayered, consisting of a global system (United Nations) and various regional human rights systems, and has diversified towards specific categories of people (women, children, persons with disabilities, migrant workers, minorities, indigenous peoples, etc) and themes (torture, discrimination, etc) (Brems 2014). In recent years, the concept of 'legal pluralism' seems to be increasingly used also to refer to this diversity *within* a particular legal system or subsystem (see eg, as regards international law, Burke-White 2004). According to Twining (2010: 513), in the literature on global legal pluralism, the term 'pluralism' has moreover 'sometimes been extended to encompass other referents', such as the proliferation of actors in international relations, and the diversification of supranational courts and tribunals as well as norm-creating agencies.

2.3. The Smallest Constitutive Element?

The use of the concept of legal pluralism to refer to normative diversity within ever-smaller bodies of law as well as to other referents brings us to the question of where this process may lead us. Is it possible, desirable and/or necessary to identify a smallest constitutive element to be able to speak of 'legal pluralism' in an analytical sense? Without wanting to essentialise the concept or being picky about labels, I would argue that this tendency of opening up the concept of legal pluralism very widely may lead to vagueness or confusion as to the characteristics that are generally associated with it, at least in sociolegal scholarship. In this sense, I concur with Twining (2010: 513) when he notes:

> If 'legal pluralism' merely means more than one legal phenomenon without limit on the kinds of phenomenon referred to, it is doubtful whether it is a useful concept and whether the heritage of mainstream socio-legal literature on legal pluralism up to 1990 is very helpful in interpreting these very varied topics.[3]

One of the most commonly shared distinctive features of legal pluralism within the sociolegal literature is the simultaneous applicability of different normative 'orders' or 'systems', as referred to above. A legal system in the analytical sense has been described by von Benda-Beckmann (1997: 8) as 'the totality of legal phenomena generated and maintained in a given social unit'. He continues:

> I speak of an empirical legal system when the *same basis of ultimate validity* is asserted for a body of law. Thus we can speak of state law, religious law, or traditional law, when state, religion or tradition refer to the ultimate basis on which the validity of the legal conceptions is grounded and which unifies the set of sources of valid law. (ibid, emphasis added)

Different legal systems thus originate in different sources of authority and are consequently often characterised by other underlying principles (eg legal certainty, reciprocity, harmony). This may lead to diverse ways of decision-making (eg democratic, autocratic, consensual) and of conflict resolution (eg conflict avoidance, mediation, adjudication). It was these fundamental disparities between legal systems as well as their interaction that triggered the interest of legal anthropologists.

Various authors have noted, however, that the requirement of a 'system' should not be interpreted as a *conditio sine qua non* or in a too restrictive manner, in order to be able to speak of legal pluralism. According to von Benda-Beckmann (ibid): 'Apart from such "system" law, in which the systems are named, there may be also "unnamed law", law not attributed to a system but, for instance, to the asserted self-regulatory autonomy of people.' Tamanaha (2008: 399) has noted in relation to community/cultural normative systems that '[i]n its thinnest manifestation (which can nonetheless exert a powerful influence), the norms that bind and define the community may not be definite or reiterated enough to be considered a "system" in the same sense that that applies to the other categories'. This suggests that

---

[3] And specifically with respect to human rights: 'The idea of "pluralism" applied to ... the proliferation of human rights means little more than diversity' (Twining 2010: 516).

the conceptualisation of 'system' should not be too strict, in order not to exclude such more fluid or vague community/cultural normative systems.

Not only do various norms within a certain legal system share their 'basis of ultimate validity' (von Benda-Beckmann 1997: 8), within the subsystem of international human rights law, these norms also share the objective of promoting and protecting human rights. There is no universally accepted understanding or definition of 'human rights': human rights mean different things for different people and the particular interpretation of the content of certain rights will vary with the context and situation. But at least there is some consensus on basic tenets and principles relating to, for instance, the goal of human dignity, the protection of the right to life and the prohibition of torture. Certain rules of other normative systems may be grounded, however, in fundamentally different aspirations, such as the perpetuation of a patriarchal society, the dominance of a particular religious worldview, or monetary gain. The potential clash between different systems of normative ordering will thus be greater when analysing the interaction between two normative orders that do not belong to a same 'mother' order than when looking at issues that relate to the diversity and divergence within a certain normative (sub)system, such as international human rights law.

If one, however, broadens the conceptualisation of legal pluralism towards the simultaneous applicability of legal norms that originate within the same '(sub)system', then one comes on a ground with which doctrinal lawyers are also familiar, be it mostly in relation to state or supranational law: that of conflicting rules within one system. Since such rules belong to the same system, there is no clash between the ultimate authority and fundamental principles in which these rules are grounded. Mechanisms, institutions and rules have been devised within normative systems to deal with this kind of conflict. In state law, for instance, a hierarchy of norms has been established, and principles such as *lex posterior derogat legi priori* and *lex specialis derogat legi generali* are applied. In international law, the distinction between hard law and soft law may moreover be relevant (Hespel et al 2012). In addition, in customary normative systems, rules of prioritisation or principles that facilitate or indicate how to arrive at a decision in the case of conflicting rules will often be in place. An example constitutes the principle within the Andean community that harmony is the ultimate goal of dispute resolution or management (Drzewieniecki 1995: 8).

An overly broad conceptualisation of legal pluralism thus does not seem particularly useful for analytical purposes. It may therefore make sense to distinguish between 'legal pluralism' (as referring to the coexistence of different normative systems or other bodies of law, such as unnamed law, in a particular social field) and 'applying a legal pluralist perspective' to the study of the simultaneous applicability of various norms within one legal (sub)system. Applying a legal pluralist perspective then implies drawing on the insights of the field of legal pluralism to explain the dynamics and manage the internal plurality of a particular (sub)system of law. Oomen (2014), for instance, has employed insights from the field of legal pluralism to increase our understanding of the multilayeredness of human rights law.

3. INDIGENOUS LAND, TERRITORIAL AND RESOURCE RIGHTS

In what follows, the relationship between international human rights law and legal pluralism is further analysed in the concrete domain of the land, territorial and resource rights of indigenous peoples. Two main scenarios may be analytically distinguished. First, as regards a particular issue, international human rights law and another normative order may stand, to a greater or lesser extent, in opposition to each other. Here, human rights law can be invoked against those rules of the other normative order that seem to violate human rights. Second, human rights law and another normative order may be aligned on particular themes, defending similar values, interests and rights. In this case, human rights law and the other normative order may be mutually reinforcing. This second scenario seems to have received less scholarly attention, as research more readily focuses on conflicting legal systems than on reciprocally supportive systems (see also Twining 2009: 27). In practice, the two scenarios will often occur together, in that standards of international human rights law and another legal order may strengthen each other on a particular issue (scenario two) to the detriment of norms originating within one or more other legal orders (scenario one). The extent to which international human rights law is supported or challenged by another normative system will also depend on the interpretation that is given to both human rights standards and the other norms involved.

Without denying the possible presence and impact of a variety of other forms of normative ordering in a concrete situation, such as religious law, project law (see eg Weilenmann 2009), or other branches of international law, the remainder of this chapter mainly focuses on the interplay between three legal orders: local (indigenous/customary) law, state law and international human rights law. These normative orders are among the most relevant ones to assess the interplay between international human rights law and legal pluralism in the domain of indigenous land, territorial and resource rights. The selection of and principal focus on the three levels of local, national and international may be justified by referring to the distinction made by de Sousa Santos (1987: 287) of 'three different legal spaces and their correspondent forms of law: local, national and world legality'. He notes that these legal orders often have the same object of regulation, here the rights of indigenous peoples to their lands, territories and natural resources. In his symbolic cartography of law, de Sousa Santos links these three legal orders to three different 'scales': 'Local law is a *large-scale legality*. Nation state law is a *medium-scale legality*. World law is a *small-scale legality*' (ibid). He illustrates this distinction with the example of a labour conflict. Within a local legality such as a factory code, the prevention and management of labour conflicts stand central and are regulated in great detail, similar to when a large cartographic scale is used. Within national state labour law, the labour conflict is only one aspect of a broader reality of industrial relations. Within the world legality of, for instance, international franchising, the labour conflict becomes a minor, almost negligible detail. Because of their different scale, these different legal orders thus create different legal realities, based on the same social object. However, 'in real socio-legal life the different legal scales do not exist in isolation but rather interact in different ways' (ibid: 288).

3.1. International Human Rights Law 'versus' Other Normative Orders

In the first scenario, international human rights law is invoked against norms or practices grounded in another legal order that appear to constitute human rights violations. Since states are the primary duty-bearers in international law, state law should, or at least could, be an important vehicle of implementation of human rights. Frequently, however, it is state law that goes against human rights, even though implicitly, subtly or at a lower legal level than the constitutional one, where fundamental rights and freedoms are formally entrenched (see eg Desmet 2011b).

As such, international human rights law has been used by indigenous peoples against actions grounded in the state legal system, such as the unilateral establishment by the state of protected areas situated in their ancestral territories. This drawing upon international human rights law to contest state conservation has been a gradual evolution. To start, during the past decades, international human rights law has become the primary vehicle for indigenous peoples to claim recognition of and respect for their rights at the international level. This was not always the case: the turn to human rights by the indigenous rights movement was prompted by a rejection at the international level of their claims of self-determination (Engle 2011). Moreover, within the human rights framework, attention to the potentially negative consequences of externally induced conservation initiatives has only recently increased (Campese et al 2007). In contrast to the general relationship between human rights and the environment, the particular link between human rights and nature conservation appeared later on the radar of the human rights community. Only in the past few years have violations of indigenous peoples' human rights been found to be explicitly caused by the establishment of state-protected areas, and this both within the African and the Inter-American human rights system.

A landmark case on the relationship between indigenous rights and nature conservation is the *Endorois* decision, adopted in 2009 by the African

Commission on Human and Peoples' Rights.[4] The Endorois, a semi-nomadic indigenous community of about 60,000 people, had for centuries been living in the Lake Bogoria area in Kenya. In 1973, the Kenyan government superimposed a protected area, the Lake Hannington Game Reserve (later renamed the Lake Bogoria Game Reserve), on their ancestral lands. This gazettement led to the forced eviction of the Endorois, without appropriate compensation. Moreover, their access to the Lake Bogoria area, necessary for their pastoral lifestyle and cultural integrity, was denied. After recognising the Endorois as an indigenous people, the African Commission found a violation of the Endorois' right to practise religion (Article 8), the right to property (Article 14), the right to culture (Article 17(2) and (3)), the right to dispose freely of their natural resources (Article 21) and the right to development (Article 22) of the African Charter on Human and Peoples' Rights.[5] The Endorois case has been most commonly applauded because it is the first case in which the African Commission has pronounced on the definition of indigenous peoples and on their rights to land and natural resources. Moreover, it is also the first time that an international tribunal has found a violation of the right to development, since the African Charter is the only international treaty enshrining a right to development (Ashamu 2011: 302). I would like to stress, however, that this is also the first supranational case in which violations of indigenous peoples' rights were directly linked to and caused by externally induced nature conservation initiatives, namely the creation of a protected area by the state on indigenous territory and the subsequent forced eviction.

In August 2010, the Inter-American Court of Human Rights, in its turn, issued its first judgment in a conservation-related case regarding indigenous peoples, namely *Xákmok Kásek Indigenous Community v Paraguay*.[6] In 2008, a private nature reserve was declared for a period of five years, partially on land claimed by the Xákmok Kásek Indigenous Community. The creation of the protected area took place without consulting the members of the community or taking into account their territorial claims (§80). It prevented the community members from carrying out their traditional activities on that land, such as hunting, fishing and gathering, and impeded the expropriation and occupation of the land under any other condition (§82). The action on unconstitutionality filed by the community to redress the situation

---

[4] *Centre for Minority Rights Development (Kenya) & Minority Rights Group International on behalf of the Endorois Welfare Council Case*, African Commission on Human and Peoples' Rights, Communication 276/2003, 27th Activity Report (November 2009).

[5] African Charter on Human and Peoples' Rights (adopted 27 June 1981, entered into force 21 October 1986) (1982) 21 ILM 58 (African Charter).

[6] *Xákmok Kásek Indigenous Community Case* (Merits, Reparations, and Costs Judgment), Inter-American Court of Human Rights Series C No 214 (24 August 2010). In the case of *Salvador Chiriboga v Ecuador*, the Court addressed the relationship between protected areas and the right to property of *non-indigenous* persons. *Salvador Chiriboga Case* (Preliminary Objection and Merits Judgment), Inter-American Court of Human Rights Series C No 179 (6 May 2008).

did not achieve any result. Consequently, the Court found a violation of the rights to communal property (Article 21(1)), judicial guarantees (Article 8(1)) and judicial protection (Article 25(1)) of the American Convention on Human Rights,[7] in relation to Articles 1(1) and 2 thereof, to the detriment of the members of the Xákmok Kásek Community. The contribution of Rodolfo Stavenhagen, the former UN Special Rapporteur on the Rights of Indigenous Peoples, is noteworthy. In his expert testimony, he stated:

> [T]he said declaration as a protected wooded area could constitute a new and sophisticated mechanism adopted by the private owners of land claimed by indigenous communities 'to obstruct the land claims of the original peoples ... using legal mechanisms and even invoking purposes as virtuous as the conservation of the environment.' (§ 169)

In two other cases concerning the impact of protected areas on the rights of indigenous peoples, judgments of the Inter-American Court are pending. In its merits report on the case of the Kaliña and Lokono peoples, the Inter-American Commission concluded that the State of Suriname violated the Kaliña and Lokono peoples' property rights by 'establishing and maintaining the Wia Wia, Galibi and Wane Kreek Reserves ... without conducting a consultation process aimed at obtaining their free, prior and informed consent according to Inter-American standards'.[8] Similarly, although with less weight attached to the conservation initiative, in the case of the Garífuna Community of Triunfo de la Cruz, the Commission concluded that the State of Honduras had violated Article 21 of the American Convention, because it had failed to ensure the effective participation of the community and its members in measures affecting their territory.[9] One of these measures was the establishment of the Punta Izopo National Park, which restricted access to the area and consequently prevented the community from carrying out its traditional cultural practices (§ 264). A third case concerning the adverse consequences of the establishment and management of a protected area without carrying out proper consultations, namely in relation to the Garífuna Community of Cayos Cochinos, was declared admissible by the Inter-American Commission in 2007.[10]

---

[7] American Convention on Human Rights (adopted 22 November 1969, entered into force 18 July 1978), 1144 UNTS 123, OAS Treaty Series No 36 (1969) (American Convention).

[8] *The Kaliña and Lokono Peoples* (Suriname) (Merits Report), Inter-American Commission on Human Rights Report No 79/13, Case 12.639 (18 July 2013) § 167(3).

[9] *Garífuna Community of 'Triunfo de la Cruz' and its members* (Honduras) (Merits Report), Inter-American Commission on Human Rights Report No 76/12, Case 12.548 (7 November 2012) § 266, see also § 294(2). The Garífuna people are the result of cultural syncretism between indigenous and African peoples. They have asserted their rights in Honduras as an indigenous people; their indigenous character was not contested by the state in this case. Therefore, the Inter-American Commission analysed the case taking into account the Inter-American jurisprudence on indigenous peoples' rights. ibid §§ 190–91.

[10] *Garífuna Community of Cayos Cochinos and its members* (Honduras) (Admissibility Decision), Inter-American Commission on Human Rights Report No 39/07, Petition 1118-03

International human rights law can also be invoked against state law without having recourse to judicial avenues, for instance in negotiation processes with the local or national government. An example constitutes the categorisation process of a provisional protected area, the Güeppí Reserved Zone situated in the extreme north of the Peruvian Amazon. In this case, the ancestral habitants of that area, the Airo Pai, successfully invoked their right to be adequately consulted, which led to a new consultation round more in accordance with international human rights standards (Desmet 2011a: 600–10).

3.2. International Human Rights Law in Alliance with Other Normative Orders

The second scenario relates to situations in which international human rights law and other normative orders find themselves 'on the same line', and may thus be mutually reinforcing in a legally plural world. Again, this may be the case for human rights law in relation to any other normative system. A common perception is that local (indigenous/customary) law—as often based on 'traditions'—tends to fit uneasily with international human rights standards. There are various areas, however, where customary and community normative orders are in line with or endorsed by current international human rights law. This is to a large extent the case for the land, territorial and resource rights of indigenous peoples, which have been recognised in international human rights law as based on customary normative systems. This is evident from Article 26 of the UN Declaration on the Rights of Indigenous Peoples,[11] the jurisprudence within the Inter-American and African human right system, and—especially as far land and territorial rights are concerned—from ILO Convention 169 (Articles 13–15).[12] Regarding indigenous land, territorial and resource rights, it is most often state law that stands in contrast with both international human rights and indigenous/customary law. Peruvian state legislation, for example, only awards limited lots of *land* to peasant and native *communities*, instead of recognising the *territories* of indigenous *peoples*. This approach contains two fundamental

(24 July 2007). A part of the original complaint, concerning acts of physical aggression by soldiers in charge of monitoring the environment on the archipelago of Cayos Cochinos, was broken down into a separate petition, which was declared admissible in 2013. *Jesús Flores Satuye and Others* (Honduras) (Admissibility Decision). Inter-American Commission on Human Rights Report No 93/13, Petition 1063-07 (4 November 2013).

[11] UN Declaration on the Rights of Indigenous Peoples, UN General Assembly Res 61/295 (13 September 2007).
[12] Convention (No 169) Concerning Indigenous and Tribal Peoples in Independent Countries (adopted 27 June 1989, entered into force 5 September 1991) International Labour Conference (ILO Convention 169).

flaws. First, the Peruvian constitution does not recognise the legal subject of indigenous 'peoples', but only attributes rights to 'communities' (comparable to villages).[13] This has implied a fragmentation of the Peruvian indigenous peoples into various legal persons (Desmet 2011a: 372–77). The Airo Pai people, for instance, are divided into four officially registered native communities and one village that has not been legally recognised. Second, the Peruvian legislation does not incorporate the concept of 'territory', which goes beyond the concept of land and 'covers the total environment of the areas which [indigenous peoples] occupy or otherwise use'.[14] Only limited lots of land are given in title to the peasant and native communities (Desmet 2011a: 378–88). The land titles of the four Airo Pai native communities cover only a fraction of their ancestral territory. Peruvian state law qualifies the remainder of the Airo Pai territory, which includes their ancestors' cemeteries and various historically and culturally important sites, as 'state land'. Such an approach goes against both international human rights law and the customary normative systems of the peoples concerned.

There thus seems to be a shift in alliance, at least as far the rights of indigenous peoples are concerned. Whereas international law historically has served to legitimise the colonisation of indigenous peoples, supporting the efforts of the nation states involved in this endeavour, international human rights law has become increasingly receptive towards accommodating indigenous peoples' claims, which are based on their customary normative orders (Anaya 2004). From the perspective of state duty-bearers, this raises additional concerns, as now the pressure comes from two sides: from below (via customary norms and institutions) and from above (via international human rights obligations). Other authors have made similar observations regarding the potential association between local (indigenous/customary) law and international human rights law. Colchester (2011: 38), for instance, has observed that: 'Indigenous peoples are now practised at invoking international law to support reforms of State laws so they recognise indigenous peoples' rights *in line with countries' international obligations and in ways respectful of their customary systems*' (emphasis added). As concerns economic, social and cultural (ESC) rights, and more specifically subsistence rights, Gómez Isa (2011: 60) has written that: 'Some local cultural practices ... have a great potential for the realization of subsistence rights in local settings.' He adds that more empirical research is needed regarding the extent to which 'local cultural practices and social arrangements in the socio-economic domain ... constitute a positive input for the local realization of ESC rights' (ibid).

---

[13] Constitution of Peru 1993, Art 89. The peasant communities (*comunidades campesinas*) are mostly found in the Andes and coastal region, the native communities (*comunidades nativas*) in the Amazon.
[14] ILO Convention 169, Art 13(2). See also below.

Nevertheless, it must be emphasised that despite their overall alliance, international human rights law and customary normative orders (the latter, of course, also being internally diverse) generally do not completely coincide in their approaches to indigenous land, territorial and resource rights. Indigenous peoples generally approach nature in a holistic and spiritual way. The Indigenous Peoples' Earth Charter was drafted in the margin of the 1992 UN Conference on Environment and Development at Rio de Janeiro as a response to the dominance of conservationists at the event. In the Charter, indigenous peoples express their vision: 'Our territories are living totalities in permanent vital relation between human beings and nature. Their possession produced the development of our culture. Our territorial property should be inalienable, unceasable [*sic*] and not denied title' (§ 32). They define their territory as including 'space (air), land and sea' (§ 34). The Charter of the Indigenous and Tribal Peoples of the Tropical Forests of 1996 declared that:

> Our territories and forests are to us more than an economic resource. For us, they are life itself and have an integral and spiritual value for our communities. They are fundamental to our social, cultural, spiritual, economic and political survival as distinct peoples.

State legal systems, in contrast, usually adopt a diametrically different approach, whereby legislation compartmentalises the natural environment, dividing it into different sectors, including the land surface, subsoil resources, the water and the forests. These natural resources are then subjected to divergent finalities (ranging from strict conservation to large-scale exploitation) and to different legal regimes, which are designed and monitored by various—often rivalling—ministries and departments, at different levels (national, provincial, local). Moreover, state legislation traditionally focuses on (first) the economic and (second) the environmental value of natural resources, attaching less importance to cultural-spiritual dimensions. Such fragmentation of the natural environment negates the holistic vision of indigenous peoples.

Even though international human rights law generally recognises indigenous land, territorial and resource rights in line with customary normative systems, from the perspective of indigenous peoples, it does not go 'all the way'. Article 15(2) of ILO Convention 169, for instance, explicitly envisages the possibility that 'the State retains the ownership of mineral or sub-surface resources or rights to other resources pertaining to lands' of indigenous peoples. Indigenous peoples must then (only) be consulted before any exploration or exploitation is undertaken, and they should participate in the benefits of such activities. With respect to water, von Benda-Beckmann (2009: 125) has pointed to the fact that local customary water rights may be very extensive, whereas the human right to water only covers a small part of these customary water rights, namely the access to clean drinking water.

He concludes: 'In the domain of natural resource management and land and water rights, local people(s) claiming human rights may end up with less than they would have, had they based their economic and social claims on their own law' (ibid). The overall alliance between international human rights law and indigenous customary orders must therefore be nuanced.

4. CONCLUSION

This chapter analysed some features of the relationship between legal pluralism and international human rights law, first at a conceptual level, then in the concrete case of indigenous land, territorial and resource rights. Given that the term 'legal pluralism' seems to be increasingly employed in relation to smaller bodies of law, it was suggested to maintain a distinction between a situation of 'legal pluralism' (as referring to the coexistence of different normative systems in a certain social field) and 'applying a legal pluralist perspective' when studying the simultaneous applicability of different legal norms originating from the same legal (sub)system. The chapter continued with exploring the relationship between international human rights law and other normative orders in the domain of indigenous land, territorial and resource rights. It was shown that a detailed analysis of the interrelation between substantive norms of different normative orders is necessary, so as to be able to adequately assess the relationship between these orders. Even within one domain, no overly broad statements can be made as to the alliance or opposition between various normative orders.

4

Human Rights, Cultural Diversity and Legal Pluralism from an Indigenous Perspective: *The* Awas Tingni *Case*

FELIPE GÓMEZ ISA

1. INTRODUCTION

THE CULTURAL DIVERSITY and plurality of legal orders prevailing in the Global South should not be seen as a threat to a universal concept of human rights, but as an enriching input for it. The progressive recognition of indigenous peoples' rights in the last decades is forging, sometimes with difficulties, a more open and dynamic conception of human rights. By opening the door to indigenous conceptions of law, justice and dignity, the Inter-American Court of Human Rights is decisively contributing with its progressive jurisprudence to an increasingly multicultural approach to human rights law. The culmination of this complex and somewhat contradictory process took place with the adoption of the United Nations Declaration on the rights of indigenous peoples in September 2007, a clear example of an attempt to balance indigenous conceptions of dignity with the very basics of international human rights law.

The aim of my chapter is to analyse how the Inter-American Court of Human Rights conceives the challenging relationship between indigenous legal orders and the protection and promotion of human dignity. This so-called *multicultural jurisprudence* is paving the way for a more inclusive conception of human rights, a conception enriched by local ways of framing and understanding human dignity. I will illustrate my main findings with the analysis of the *Awas Tingni* case (2001), a very relevant example of how global human rights standards are applied to local realities and, in turn, how this application also influences the development and implementation of international human rights law. I will analyse not only the final decision by the Inter-American Court, but also the process by which the indigenous community took the decision to bring the case before an international forum.[1]

2. HUMAN RIGHTS AND DIVERSITY: TOWARDS AN INCLUSIVE UNIVERSALISM[2]

2.1. Exclusion of Indigenous Peoples from Human Rights Instruments

The origin of human rights dates back to the liberal revolutions of the eighteenth century, in particular the French Revolution and the French Declaration of the Rights of Man and of the Citizen (1789). Since then, Western culture, which is based on Modernism and the Enlightenment, has sought to transform those human rights, which arose in a specific context, into genuinely universal human rights. However, in the opinion of Fariñas, this assumption of universality stems in reality from a 'Western myth, an *a priori* or a legitimising fiction which conceals aspirations of domination and world hegemony'.[3] What is described as universal is in fact only an attempt to universalise a particular conception of human rights, which is legitimate but necessarily specific. That specific conception has been based on a political liberalism which is markedly individualist, and on the importance given to civil and political rights to the detriment of economic, social and cultural rights. If we truly want to achieve a universal conception of human rights, the Western viewpoint cannot be accepted uncritically. Instead a process of dialogue must be opened in which different worldviews, including that of indigenous peoples, are able to put forward their own specific approach to human rights. Human rights must be reconceptualised as multicultural if they are to become a genuine common language of humanity. If that does not happen, and they continue to be conceived, as they have been, as universal, 'human rights will always be an instrument of Samuel Huntington's "clash of civilisations", that is to say, of the struggle of the West against the rest' (De Sousa Santos 2009).

The other great foundational document containing an avowedly universal conception of human rights is the *Universal* Declaration of Human Rights (emphasis added), adopted in 1948 by the United Nations General Assembly. The adoption process was completely monopolised by states, in

---

[1] The case may be seen as an interesting example of the 'localisation of human rights' (De Feyter et al 2011).

[2] On the thought-provoking concept of 'inclusive universality', see the pioneering work by Brems (2001).

[3] See Fariñas Dulce, MJ, 'El Dios Universal y los Derechos Humanos', *El País*, 25 October 2004, 16.

particular those dominating the international arena after the Second World War,[4] and failed to take account of local realities and different ways of dealing with the protection of human dignity in those local arenas. Admittedly, some non-European states participated in the negotiations leading to the Universal Declaration, but they did not question the main assumptions of the liberal Western tradition which permeated the prevailing human rights culture at the time. Essentially, the seminal human rights document of the twentieth century sought to offer 'universal legitimacy to a doctrine that is fundamentally Eurocentric in its construction. ... Non-Western philosophies and traditions—particularly on the nature of man and the purposes for political society—were either unrepresented or marginalised' (Mutua 2002).

Several Latin American countries played a very active role during discussions of the Declaration,[5] yet this did not mean that the views of indigenous peoples were on the table.[6] In fact it was quite the opposite; indigenous peoples were not taken into account at all when the underlying philosophy and content of the Declaration were being discussed and negotiated, even though the Declaration aspired to be nothing less than universal. As Chief Wilton Littlechild of the Cree Nation noted in his speech before the United Nations Human Rights Council on the 60th anniversary of the Universal Declaration of Human Rights:

> In 1948 Indigenous Peoples were not included in the Universal Declaration. We were not considered to have equal rights as everyone else. Indeed we were not considered as human nor as peoples. ... Indigenous peoples simply did not benefit from the rights and freedoms set forth in the Universal Declaration. (Littlechild 2009)

Indigenous peoples continued to be absent from the principal international treaties that went on to develop the provisions of the Universal Declaration. In this respect, Clavero has referred to indigenous peoples as the 'absent humanity', because they have been systematically excluded from the processes of discussion and adoption of the major international instruments of human rights protection (Clavero 1998). In particular, neither the International Covenant on Civil and Political Rights (ICCPR, 1966) nor the International Covenant on Economic, Social and Cultural Rights (ICESCR, 1966) contain a single mention of the rights of indigenous peoples, even

---

[4] The leading role of the most powerful countries and the subordinate position of the countries and societies from the South is, from the very outset, inherent to and characteristic of the process leading to the emergence of international law. A critical analysis of international law as hegemonic discourse and a source of domination can be found in Rajagopal (2003).

[5] On the role of Latin American countries in the process of debating and adopting the Declaration, see Glendon (2003).

[6] It should be remembered that in May 1948, several months before the Universal Declaration of Human Rights was adopted, the American Declaration of the Rights and Duties of Man, in which there was no mention whatsoever of indigenous peoples, was adopted by the Organization of American States (OAS).

though both refer expressly to the rights of peoples to self-determination in their common Article 1.[7] The only way open for some indigenous demands has been through the recognition, in Article 27 of the ICCPR, of the rights of people who belong to ethnic, religious and linguistic minorities.[8] Indigenous peoples and their rights are subsumed under the category of *minorities*, and the Human Rights Committee, the body that oversees the correct implementation of the ICCPR by states, has settled several cases involving indigenous peoples under the umbrella of Article 27 of the Covenant. Needless to say, this situation is far from satisfactory. First, indigenous peoples have persistently sought not to be confused with minorities. Despite sharing some characteristics stemming from their position as minorities in relation to the dominant society, even when in some contexts indigenous people are in the majority, in reality they are two very different realities which require specific protection.[9] Furthermore, the rights enshrined in Article 27 of the Covenant are individual rights, rights that are conferred on 'persons belonging to such minorities', even though they are exercised 'in community with the other members of their group'. By contrast, indigenous peoples are demanding collective rights, whereby the holder is not the sum of the individuals who belong to a particular group, but the same group considered collectively.

2.2. From Invisibility to Gradual Recognition

Although the International Convention on the Elimination of all Forms of Racial Discrimination (CERD) was adopted in 1965, it was not until the 1990s that the Committee for the Elimination of Racial Discrimination began to pay particular attention to the discrimination suffered by indigenous peoples (Álvarez Molinero 2009). In order to tackle the specific nature of the discrimination affecting indigenous peoples, in 1997 the Committee adopted its General Recommendation XXIII. In the opinion of the Committee, this discrimination has structural causes and is rooted in the historical injustices that have affected indigenous peoples, particularly the fact that they were deprived of their lands and resources by colonists, private

---

[7] Art 1 is common to both Covenants: 'All peoples have the right of self-determination. By virtue of that right they freely determine their political status and freely pursue their economic, social and cultural development.' For a long time the orthodox interpretation of this right has been that the only peoples who could claim self-determination were those subjected to colonial domination, not those peoples who live under democratic states which respect their singularity. For an analysis of the evolution of the right to self-determination, see Xanthaki (2007).

[8] As Art 27 sets forth: 'In those States in which ethnic, religious or linguistic minorities exist, persons belonging to such minorities shall not be denied the right, in community with the other members of their group, to enjoy their own culture, to profess and practise their own religion, or to use their own language.'

[9] On the conceptual distinction between minorities and indigenous peoples, see: Meijknecht (2001), Pentassuglia (2014) and Thornberry (2002).

business and states. Other essential aspects of the endeavour to reverse the patterns of discrimination against indigenous peoples are respect for their cultural identity, languages and traditional ways of living; the promotion of economic and social development that is sustainable and compatible with their cultural characteristics; their effective participation in public life; and that decisions affecting them should not be made without their informed consent.[10] As a result of this growing attention by the Committee to the discrimination affecting indigenous peoples, it must be recognised that indigenous peoples are now increasingly using the different mechanisms provided by the Committee (Álvarez Molinero 2009).

An international treaty which paid special attention to the indigenous reality, probably because it was drawn up in the mid-1980s, when the International Labour Organization (ILO) Convention 169 concerning Indigenous and Tribal Peoples in Independent Countries was also being discussed, is the Convention on the Rights of the Child (1989). In particular, there are two provisions which expressly refer to indigenous minors and their rights. Article 29 of the Convention establishes that the child's education should be oriented towards instilling respect 'for his or her own cultural identity, language and values' and preparing 'the child for responsible life ..., in the spirit of understanding, peace, tolerance, equality of sexes, and friendship among all peoples, ethnic, national and religious groups and *persons of indigenous origin*' (emphasis added). As can be seen, the Convention explicitly calls for the cultural identity of minors, including indigenous people, to be respected, and for friendship and tolerance among all peoples to be promoted. But the most interesting article is number 30, which states that:

> In those States in which ethnic, religious or linguistic minorities or persons of indigenous origin exist, a child belonging to such a minority or who is indigenous shall not be denied the right, in community with other members of his or her group, to enjoy his or her own culture, to profess and practice his or her own religion, or to use his or her own language.

In other words, this provision recalls Article 27 of the ICCPR, as it recognises the indigenous child's *individual* rights to have his or her own cultural life, profess his or her own religion, and use his or her own language, which are rights that a child can exercise 'in community with other members of his or her group'. It is obvious that this is an improvement, given that indigenous minors are expressly mentioned, but the recognition of their rights remains rooted in an individualistic conception of those rights. It is not until the adoption of ILO Convention 169 in 1989 and, above all, the United Nations Declaration on the Rights of Indigenous Peoples in 2007 that genuinely collective rights, one of the main demands of indigenous peoples, appear.

---

[10] CERD Committee, 'Indigenous Peoples', General Recommendation No 23, UN Doc A/52/18, Annex V, 18 August 1997, paras 3–4.

As has been demonstrated, the reality of indigenous peoples was not taken into account when human rights were first devised, and the main human rights instruments which were approved after the Second World War were completely blind to their demands. This situation began to change in the 1980s when the growing visibility of indigenous peoples meant that more account was taken of them, and this led to a gradual questioning of one of the main tenets of human rights—their universality. The challenge was how to accommodate indigenous demands within a conception of human rights from which such peoples were absent. Moreover, some elements of the indigenous worldview appear to clash with certain aspects of the orthodox conception of human rights. We are at an interesting point when we need to move towards developing a conception of human rights that is more open to diversity and other forms of understanding human dignity.[11] Ultimately, it is a question of opening the doors to an inclusive universality in which, through sincere and open intercultural dialogue, it is possible to determine the minimum requirements for a transcultural conception of dignity.

2.3. The Need for an Intercultural Dialogue

Internationally, indigenous peoples have made significant gains by appropriating the human rights discourse to convey their demands and claims.[12] It is significant that indigenous peoples see the rights discourse as having the potential to become a tool for defending their dignity. Obviously, this acceptance of human rights as a framework for debate means that indigenous peoples themselves will need to be willing to open their worldviews to comparison with international human rights standards. This can only be done on the basis of respect and a thorough knowledge of indigenous reality and in the context of a sincere and open intercultural dialogue.

It is very difficult, if not impossible, to consider human rights as an abstract idea, given that its meaning(s) must necessarily be conceived as contextual and relative. Such an idea of human rights is essentially contingent, dynamic and open to evolution, change and continuous transformation (Goodale 2007). In that respect, 'rather than seeing universality and cultural relativism as alternatives between which a definitive choice must be made, the tensions between these positions should be seen as part of the continuous process of negotiation between local and global norms which is constantly changing and inter-relating' (Cowan et al 2001).

---

[11] See generally O'Connell (2008).
[12] The most illustrative example is the UN Declaration on the Rights of Indigenous Peoples, UN Doc GA Resolution 61/295, 13 September 2007. A detailed analysis of this document can be found in Allen et al (2011).

For human rights to resonate in local arenas, the voices of those who are 'different' must be heard and understood (Twinning 2009). If universal norms and principles are to be applied in local contexts, they need to undergo a complex process of *contextualisation*, of adaptation to local circumstances. Contextualisation and adaptation involve the *cultural translation* of global ideas, such as human rights, into local frameworks of meaning and signification. Anthropologist Salle Engle Merry has studied in detail both the challenges and potential of these translation processes. First, the ideas and institutions of human rights 'need to be framed in images, symbols, narratives and religious or secular language that resonate with the local community'. They also need to be 'tailored to the structural conditions of the place where they are deployed, including its economic, political, and kinship systems' (Merry 2006). The local, in this case the indigenous, and the global, the internationally proclaimed human rights, 'coexist and intermingle in the contemporary multicultural process of the production of universal values and norms' (Baxi 2006). In this respect, there is a constant creative tension between global processes for developing human rights norms, in which indigenous peoples have participated with some success in recent decades, and local processes for owning those norms so that they have some degree of local relevance. For human rights to become meaningful and play a relevant role, 'they need to be translated into local terms and situated within local contexts of power and meaning' (Merry 2006: 1). A fundamental role in this delicate process is that of the so-called *cultural intermediaries* or *translators*, actors who navigate between local and global spaces and who have the ability to deal with and understand key aspects of local worldviews.[13] These intermediaries are usually individuals, groups and organisations who move easily between local and global spaces; for example, new indigenous leaders who, in contact with transnational organisations working for the defence of indigenous rights, and with activists and academics, have helped to forge alliances so that indigenous demands can be conveyed to transnational discussion and standard-building spaces such as the United Nations.[14] In this context, the process of adopting the United Nations Declaration on the Rights of Indigenous Peoples (2007), which took over twenty years, is a prime example of how productive such alliances can be between actors with local legitimacy and those involved in global processes that take account of local realities.

---

[13] In the second part of this study, we shall see the essential role played by anthropologists who are experts in indigenous matters in making the Inter-American Court of Human Rights understand the fundamental elements of the indigenous world views which were relevant for the *Awas Tingni* case. For a critical view of their role, see Ariza (2009).

[14] For some interesting reflections on these new indigenous leaders, see especially Bengoa (2007).

2.4. Towards an Open and Dynamic Concept of Culture

First of all, there is a need to take a critical approach to one's own culture, starting from the assumption that all cultures are incomplete. As De Sousa Santos writes in this regard, 'the recognition of weaknesses and the reciprocal lack of completeness is a *conditio sine qua non* for intercultural dialogue' (De Sousa Santos 2009: 111). In any case, one objective difficulty in trying to establish a dialogue with Western culture about human rights and democracy is precisely its lack of cultural modesty. Western modernity is so proud of having 'discovered' human rights that it has serious difficulties in embarking on a dialogue which might question some of the essential premises of its conception of human rights (Mutua 2009). Its belief that it owns the copyright on human rights and democracy means that Western culture is not predisposed to a genuine dialogue. In turn, the openness and flexibility required of the Western conception of human rights must also be present in the indigenous peoples who wish to embark on this process of dialogue.

One of the main obstacles standing in the way of this cultural opening-up that seeks to give legitimacy to the global human rights discourse is the tendency to invariably see local cultures and practices as obscure, static and contrary to universal human rights. These arguments are based on a very narrow and limited conception of culture, often based on Western cultural arrogance (not to mention ignorance), which risks stigmatising and demonising some cultural practices by saying that they are barbarous and contrary to progress and civilization (Mutua 2009: 155). Instead, when an effort is made to fully understand local realities, which by definition are complex, the conception of culture becomes much more malleable and heterogeneous, hybrid and dynamic. Culture is closer to being a hybrid concept rather than an essentialist one. According to some anthropological studies which have questioned certain assumptions inherent in the politically correct human rights discourse, 'culture is not a totalizing influence, but a field that is constantly in transformation' (Keck and Sikkink 1998: 211). Culture is permeable, open to both internal and external influences in a constant process of evolution and questioning. According to this conception, culture is a resource for change, not just an insurmountable barrier for universal human rights (Merry 2006: 9). Some local cultural practices, based on community values and a basic sense of solidarity, social justice and complementarity between group members, have enormous potential for the realisation of fundamental human rights. Much work remains to be done in determining to what extent certain cultural and community practices and arrangements (from traditional indigenous knowledge with regard to health and food security to community land-holding systems and traditional methods of conflict resolution and indigenous justice) constitute positive elements for an all-embracing conception of human rights and their realisation. Essentially, the aim of the whole process of transposing and adapting global human rights to local scenarios is not to call into question the universal nature of the core content of human rights but to enrich that core with views from below.

3. THE *AWAS TIGNI* CASE: LOCALISING HUMAN RIGHTS[15]

Natural resources have become strategic both economically and geopolitically. Many of these resources (oil, minerals, etc) are located in territories inhabited by indigenous peoples, whose land is depository of a vast part of the earth's biodiversity (Szablowski 2007). Accordingly, a great number of conflicts have emerged between states, transnational companies and indigenous peoples, since these peoples have a rather different vision of what *development* really means (Gómez Isa 2015).

In the mid-1990s, a poor and isolated indigenous community of the Atlantic coast of Nicaragua resorted to the Inter-American system to denounce the Nicaraguan government's timber exploitation concession which was given to a transnational company in a territory inhabited by the Awas Tingni community without this community's consent. After a long and difficult judicial process, the judgment by the Inter-American Court on Human Rights (2001)[16] set a far-reaching precedent for the multicultural interpretation of the right to property when applied in indigenous scenarios. Through an 'evolving' method of interpretation, as termed by the Inter-American Court itself, it went beyond strictly formal criteria when interpreting the nature and scope of the right to land and natural resources of indigenous peoples. Fortunately, the Inter-American Court has continued deepening its progressive jurisprudence in recent cases such as *Yakye Axa, Moiwana, Saramaka, Sawhoyamaxa, Xákmok Kásek* and *Sarayaku*.

3.1. Role of External Stakeholders

The *Awas Tingni* case is a clear example of the important role to be played potentially by *transnational activists*[17] in their attempt to bring local causes to the global institutional arena of human rights in order ultimately to generate structural changes not only within the legal and political systems in

---

[15] This part of the chapter is based on the findings of a research project on the process of implementation of this emblematic judgment. The team of the project conducted 28 interviews with relevant stakeholders and with members of the Awas Tingni community in Nicaragua between 2011 and 2013. The results of this research can be found in Gómez Isa (2013).

[16] Inter-American Court on Human Rights, *The Case of the Mayagna (Sumo) Awas Tingni Community v Nicaragua*, Series C, No 79, 31 August 2001.

[17] See generally Tarrow (2006).

question but also in the international mechanisms that defend human rights themselves (Aylwin 2011; Rodríguez-Piñero 2004). What was initially a typical case of the defence of environmental rights undertaken by the influential conservationist non-governmental organisation the World Wildlife Fund (WWF) evolved into a landmark case of the defence of the rights of an indigenous people to their ancestral lands and territories in the face of the interests of governments and transnational companies. It is true, of course, that in this case the role of external agents or stakeholders has been absolutely decisive. Without their aid, it would have been unthinkable for a group as tiny and isolated as the Awas Tingni community even to dream of the possibility of suing the state before an international court for appropriation of its ancestral lands without its consent.[18] The *Awas Tingni* case would never have happened without the assistance of the Indian Law Resource Centre (ILRC) and without monies from US foundations, which were instrumental in funding the very expensive strategy involved.

3.2. Defining Strategies

One of the salient aspects regarding actions undertaken in defence of the human rights of vulnerable groups has to do with choosing the strategies that are best adapted to each specific case. We must bear in mind that instances of violation of the territorial rights of indigenous groups tend to be tremendously complex, involving interests and stakes of the most varied nature. Thus, in general, these cases call for different and complementary strategies. As a renowned expert in the issues involving indigenous communities of the Caribbean coast of Nicaragua, and specifically in those concerning the Awas Tingni community says, 'it is important to remember that these types of cases involve a juridical strategy, of course, but much more than that alone'.[19] In the *Awas Tingni* case specifically, it is true that the legal aspects predominated in the strategy in place. There were attempts to combine legal and political strategies, but it soon became apparent that the limitations were too great. Accordingly, the ILRC, a Washington-based organisation that defends the rights of indigenous peoples, provided the legal team headed by international law professor James Anaya with logistical and financial support. It was of course decisive that Armstrong Wiggins, a significant ILRC member, was the Centre's person in charge of the Central American region. Wiggins, a Miskito Indian who had been profoundly involved in the defence

[18] The Community members were unaware of the existence of the Inter-American system for the protection of human rights until the appearance of the team of advisors led by James Anaya and Armstrong Wiggins.
[19] Interview with Myrna Cunnigham, former President of the UN Forum on Indigenous Issues, Bilwi, Nicaragua, January 2012.

of the territorial rights of the indigenous communities along the Caribbean coast within the context of the Sandinista wars, had a very clear grasp of the political implications of the recognition of the territorial rights of indigenous communities. He understood the repercussions this would have on the consolidation and intensification of autonomy in the Caribbean coast of Nicaragua. Nevertheless, the attempts to link the different strategies did not have the desired effects, resulting ultimately in the withdrawal of both the ILRC and Armstrong Wiggins from the *Awas Tingni* case in 2002. This breakup was due not only to the fact that the ILRC and the legal team did not see eye to eye, but even more to the reservations of the Mayangna Indians, who believed that Wiggins's vested interests included supporting the Miskitos instead of defending the interests of the Awas Tingni community.

The fact is that the legal strategy upheld before the Inter-American Commission on Human Rights, initially, and then before the Inter-American Court of Human Rights, was not only very well structured but also very adroitly developed. The aim was, of course, to win the lawsuit, thereby setting a precedent that would contribute to add to the number of cases in international practice and thus increase the protection guaranteed to indigenous peoples universally. Here the real driving force was James Anaya, the author of one of the first reference works in the field (Anaya 1996). Professor Anaya had broad experience in defending the rights of Native Americans in the United States of America. The legal team was tasked with convincing both the Inter-American Commission on Human Rights and the Inter-American Court of Human Rights that the case could well fit within the American Convention on Human Rights. This was no mean feat, since the Convention does not mention indigenous peoples, and, what is more, neither the Commission nor the Court had previously admitted any case related to the rights of indigenous peoples to property, lands and territories. The fact is that this strategy, at the end of the day and after an outstandingly creative and courageous legal campaign, was a fruitful one indeed. Ultimately, both the Commission and the Court were to accept each and every one of the novel positions defended by the legal team.

The legal strategy was complemented by a working strategy involving the media, whereby case details were made available to media representatives in order to raise awareness in Nicaraguan society in general and among political leaders more specifically, as well as more broadly at an international level.[20] While during the initial stages of the case it was difficult to convince the more conservative members of the Nicaraguan press that attention should be paid to the situation in which indigenous peoples found

---

[20] The case was so important that it was actually covered by the *New York Times*, 'It's Indians vs Loggers in Nicaragua', *New York Times International*, 25 June 1996, A5.

themselves, things changed upon the issuing of the sentence by the Inter-American Court. This ruling made the headlines both on the Caribbean coast as well as in Nicaragua at large: the media covered it in articles and editorials, different universities held conferences on the issue, and there were awareness-raising workshops. The truth is that this strategy, together with other political factors we will be discussing below, has greatly contributed to changing how Nicaraguans in general perceive the Caribbean coast, and more specifically how they view the indigenous peoples who inhabit that part of the country.

One final strategic aspect that is also essential has to do with the understanding that this case is only a part of a much broader process in which other indigenous communities similar to the Awas Tingni community are involved. We must underscore the relevance of approaching this case from the perspective of *accompanying* the community: the case must be conceived as an instrument to strengthen the community's capacity and its social fabric (Beristain 2009). A consequence of this approach is the great importance regarding the acquisition of skills throughout the process.[21] As we know, court cases—especially those that are eventually heard by international courts—have their own internal logic, their own dynamics and their own pace (a pace that is difficult to understand if you are a victim, since victims aspire to a relatively prompt righting of the wrongs done to them). Not only are expectations regarding the speedy issuing of a sentence made more realistic, but also those long waiting periods, the time during which 'nothing happens', are used to strengthen the relationship with the community, to foster its internal dynamics and to hone those skills perceived to be necessary. The truth is that the need for skills is one of the aspects underscored by most of the persons interviewed for this research project. Thus, the Awas Tingni legal team did not limit itself to providing legal expertise, but likewise provided training in the skillset needed to carry out activities in the fields of human rights, negotiation and conflict resolution, and in participative mapping activities involving the Geographical Positioning System (GPS). One of the community's local advisors underscores that 'one of the absolutely essential elements is the bolstering of the community's capacities'. This capacity-building must involve basic aspects such as leadership and community cohesion, managing development projects or the appropriate management of economic funds.[22]

---

[21] It is important to bear in mind that there are risks implicit in taking legal action, because a broad base of persons in the community must be able to follow and indeed participate in the process whereby their rights are defended. As the case advances and progresses, its technicality and complexity grow, in such a way that only some few elite groups will be able to feel involved and committed with the proceedings (Wainright et al 2009).

[22] This is yet another serious problem, since the members of the Awas Tingni community do not have any tradition or know-how of managing money, which paves the way for corruption, graft and the inappropriate use of said funds.

3.3. The Case Before the Inter-American Commission on Human Rights

Once the Awas Tingni community took the decision to internationalise its vindication, the legal team led by James Anaya tackled the elaboration and argumentation of the petition to be filed before the Inter-American Commission on Human Rights. The gist of the petition was rooted in the interpretation of Article 21 of the American Convention on Human Rights.[23] What the petitioners sought was that the right to ownership of property that is described in said Article 21 be interpreted in the light of the norms that stem from the rights of indigenous peoples as enshrined in international human rights law,[24] including the draft American Declaration on the rights of indigenous peoples that was, at that point in time, under discussion within the Inter-American Commission itself. As the draft states:

> [I]ndigenous peoples have the right to the recognition of their property and ownership rights with respect to lands, territories and resources they have historically occupied, as well as to the use of those to which they have historically had access for their traditional activities and livelihood.[25]

Thus, what was sought was that the right to property described in Article 21 of the American Convention include also the right to communal property of the indigenous peoples. This being the core argument, the petition requested the revoking of the concession by the government of Nicaragua to the company SOLCARSA and the implementation of a legal framework to ensure the demarcation and titling of the lands of the Awas Tingni community.

3.3.1. Documentation and Mapping of the Awas Tingni Community Demands

A very relevant aspect in the preparation and elaboration of the legal basis for this case was the documentation and analysis of the data that would vouch for the legitimacy of the claims on the territories maintained by the Awas Tingni community. It was essential to have a reliable historical, ethnographic and geographic study of the community's relationship with the

---

[23] Art 21, under the heading 'Right to Property', declares in para 1 that: 'Everyone has the right to the use and enjoyment of his property. The law may subordinate such use and enjoyment to the interest of society.' As we can see, this is classical wording, typical of the texts drafted describing the right to property as a right of an individual nature that is included in most international human rights documents.

[24] Art 14.1 ILO Convention 169 (1989) concerning Indigenous and Tribal Peoples in Independent Countries establishes that: 'The rights of ownership and possession of the peoples concerned over the lands which they traditionally occupy shall be recognized.' Also, Art 15.1 declares that: 'The rights of the peoples concerned to the natural resources pertaining to their lands shall be specially safeguarded.'

[25] Art 18.2 Proposed American Declaration on the Rights of Indigenous Peoples, Approved by the Inter-American Commission on Human Rights on February 26, 1997, at its 1333rd session, 95th regular session.

lands it claimed, and with this aim in mind James Anaya got in contact with Theodore Macdonald of Harvard University's Weatherhead Center for International Affairs. Macdonald, an anthropologist, had worked with Anaya previously in advising Miskito Indians during the peace negotiations with the Sandinista government in the mid-1980s. It was with this objective in mind that Macdonald spent a number of weeks in Awas Tingni in 1995 and 1996. His fieldwork there was undertaken jointly with two distinguished members of the community, Jamie Castillo and Charlie Mclean.

In any case, they were not starting from scratch, since the community itself was fully aware that history bound them to their territory, and they knew the limits thereof. It is fitting here to bring to mind the document approved by the community in 1992 that was titled *Luchando por Mayangna Sauni* (*Fighting for Mayangna Sauni*) and its accompanying map that served to illustrate the geographic boundaries of their lands. This map served as the foundations for Macdonald's work. He was able to prepare a report on the historical patterns of the use of the territory by the Awas Tingni community[26] thanks to the ongoing assistance he received from members of the community and his use GPS for mapping.[27] One of the more revealing details in Macdonald's report referred to the fact that, historically, the limits of the territory used by the Awas Tingni community have fluctuated, and sometimes have overlapped with the territorial limits used by other neighbouring communities.[28] In other words, the territorial limits of use between indigenous communities are not by any means completely fixed and pre-established boundaries, but rather are 'porous borders' (Anaya et al 2009: 127). As Carlos Martín Beristain points out: '[F]rom the indigenous peoples' perspective, territorial limits are not drawn like a straight line, but rather depend on customary use, on their ecology or on their traditional or symbolic value' (Beristain 2009: 440).

This issue of the drawing up of maps of indigenous territories on the basis of geographic, legal or technological criteria—the standard approach in a Western scientific setting—actually poses some interesting questions regarding its potential impact on the way communities perceive themselves and their borders, as well as on their assessment of their relations with the neighbours.[29] This, indeed, has been one of the most controversial issues in the

---

[26] See Macdonald (1996).

[27] See Anaya et al (1995).

[28] See especially Alistar Nicaragua (2003: 5).

[29] Gender issues are also very important and influence the communities' mapping decisions and how they contribute data to expert land-surveyors and geographers. Wainright and Bryan's suggestion—that when the time comes to prepare a map or a cartographical rendering of the patterns of territorial use in any given community, 'it is the spaces where *men* hunt, fish, or log wood ... that are taken into account' (emphasis added)—is interesting. This process of exclusion is known as 'gender territorialisation' (Wainright and Bryan (2009: 161).

Awas Tingni case, since the determination of the precise lines of demarcation in Macdonald's map and ensuing judicial actions have perhaps contributed to intensifying the traditional conflicts with neighbouring Miskito communities, thus making intercommunity collaboration even more difficult (Bryan 2009). Ultimately, Macdonald's undertaking was but a process calling for great abstraction in which a specific community had to be positioned and defined within a physical space and in accordance with geographical, technological and legal criteria that are beyond the interest and control of the community's view of the world. We must not lose sight of the fact that the map's main virtue was to provide support to the Awas Tingni community's claims as upheld before the government of Nicaragua and before national and international legal authorities as well. It is in this vein that Joe Bryan describes the map as 'a little machine for producing conviction' (Bryan 2005: 16). Generating this conviction, in accordance with technical criteria, needed much more than reinventing the map that the community had drawn up. Ultimately, it called for 'a comprehensive reconfiguration of space, producing a very different version of the Awas Tingni community, its members, and its rights' (ibid: 21).

3.3.2. *Request for Precautionary Measures by the Inter-American Commission*

Despite the attempts made by the Inter-American Commission on Human Rights to ensure that the parties reached an amicable solution, the government at no point expressed the slightest intention of revoking the logging concession made to SOLCARSA or of acknowledging the legitimacy of the land claim made by the Awas Tingni community. It was in this setting that the Commission took an unprecedented measure, and in October 1997 it requested of the State of Nicaragua that it take precautionary measures 'to suspend the concession granted by the Government to the company SOLCARSA to carry out forestry-related activities in the lands of the indigenous Awas Tingni community'.[30] In fact, this step taken by the Commission was 'extraordinary; it was the first time that the Commission requested the taking of precautionary measures in a case unrelated to offences against life and physical integrity' (Anaya et al 2009: 130).

The request for these precautionary measures, together with the lobbying by civil society and the media, forced the government to revoke the SOLCARSA concession in February 1998. Despite the revocation, the gist of the issue was still unresolved. In fact, the Awas Tingni community, like most other indigenous communities peopling the Atlantic coast, had not succeeded in having its territory demarcated and titled. Worse yet, there

---

[30] Case 11.577 corresponding to the indigenous Awas Tingni community, 30 October 1997.

was no clear indication that the government of Nicaragua was resolved to right this situation. In view of which, and after verifying the Inter-American Commission's failed attempts to have the parties reach an amicable solution, the Commission finalised its investigations and sent a confidential report to the government of Nicaragua[31] upholding its opinion that Nicaragua had not taken the necessary measures to guarantee the rights of the Awas Tingni community to communal property and to natural resources. The Commission gave the government a two-month period, at the end of which it was to report back on the measures implemented to respond to the recommendations issued. Nicaragua's response to the recommendations in question underscored that the government had indeed revoked the concession to SOLCARSA, referring also to the 1996 creation of the National Commission for the Demarcation of the Lands of the Indigenous Communities along the Atlantic Coast,[32] and to its intention to approve a law for the demarcation and titling of lands belonging to the communities of indigenous peoples' along the Atlantic coast.[33] But the Inter-American Commission was not satisfied with this essentially generic response by the government of Nicaragua. The legal counsel of the Awas Tingni community informed the Commission of the government's lack of determination to put an end, once and for all, to the precarious nature of the rights to property of the indigenous communities along the Atlantic coast. Thus, in June 1998, the Commission finally decided to take the case to the Inter-American Court on Human Rights. This was a momentous decision, since at the time the Commission submitted very few cases to the Court (Anaya et al 2009).

3.4. The *Awas Tingni* Case Before the Inter-American Court

The case submitted by the Inter-American Commission on Human Rights to the Court was based, essentially, on the legal position upheld by the group of lawyers representing the Awas Tingni community. As we have seen, the position also served as the basis for the confidential report sent by the Commission to the government of Nicaragua. As for the government of Nicaragua, it availed itself of three arguments, basically, to negate the validity of the claims defended by the Awas Tingni community. The first of these tried to stymie one of the central tenets upheld by the

[31] Report No 27/98, 3 March 1998.
[32] Decree 16-96, 23 August 1996, *Diario Oficial La Gaceta*, no 169, 6 September 1996.
[33] A transcript of the Government of Nicaragua's response to the recommendations contained in the Inter-American Commission's confidential report is included in the 'Complaint of the Inter-American Commission on Human Rights, submitted to the Inter-American Court of Human Rights in the case of the Awas Tingni Mayangna (Sumo) Indigenous Community against the Republic of Nicaragua' (2002) 19 *Arizona Journal of International and Comparative Law* 36.

community, since the government maintained that 'the lands reclaimed by the Awas Tingni community have not been in their possession since the time of their ancestors',[34] because the community had only occupied the land where they currently resided since the 1940s. The second argument refers to the fact that 'the lands reclaimed by the Awas Tingni Community affect the rights of other communities that are in possession of legitimate communal titles'.[35] And finally, the third argument endorsed by the representatives of Nicaragua posits that the magnitude of the territory reclaimed by the Awas Tingni community is not proportional to either the concept itself of communal lands or to the population of the community, which consists of few members. Therefore, as expressly set forth in the official response made by Nicaragua to the suit,

> the number of acres claimed—approximately 150,000—is out of proportion, absurd and irrational. In absolute terms, that number surpasses the amount of land needed for the existence of the community and is based on a fickle and partial *Ethnographic Study* that did not take into account the physical presence of other communities.[36]

As mentioned above, one of the more problematic aspects of the *Awas Tingni* case had to do with this community's conflictive relations with its neighbours, of Miskito heritage, and with the lack of a clear drawing out of the limits or borders between the different indigenous territories. The claims set forth by the Awas Tingni community sparked misgivings among the Miskito groups, which led to growing tensions between the communities and ultimately resulted in hostility and acts of violence. The government, irresponsibly enough, encouraged these hostilities, in the belief that this was a way of distracting attention from its ultimate responsibility for the essential issue, namely the solution of the territorial conflicts in which most indigenous communities of the Atlantic coast are mired (Alvarado 2007: 629). The Awas Tingni community and its advisors attempted to appease and convince the neighbouring Miskito communities that the Awas Tingni struggle could well bear fruit for all of the indigenous communities of the Atlantic coast. Legal representative María Luisa Acosta and Miskito Indian Armstrong Wiggings were instrumental at this point. Wiggings, who was then working for the ILRC and who was familiar with the realities of life for the Miskitos and Mayangnas, contributed in a special way (Anaya et al 2009: 133). However, while tensions were repressed for the duration of the proceedings before the Inter-American Court, things worsened considerably after the Court ruled in August 2001. In fact, this has been one of the main

[34] 'Reply of the Republic of Nicaragua to the Complaint presented before the Inter-American Court of Human Rights in the case of the Mayangna Community of Awas Tingni (submitted October 21, 1998)', ibid 109.
[35] ibid 113.
[36] ibid 120.

obstacles contributing to the slowing down of the implementation of the decision.

3.4.1. *The Hearing Before the Court: Something to Remember*[37]

One of the most important events that took place during the case was the public hearing held at San José de Costa Rica, the seat of the Inter-American Court of Human Rights, in November 2000. Significantly, a number of persons testified as to the territorial claims made by the Awas Tingni community. Anthropologist Charles Hale, who was sworn in as an expert witness during this hearing, said that it was an 'unprecedented' event, since the representatives of the government of Nicaragua had perforce to hear out the claims upheld by a tiny indigenous community in a setting as solemn as that of the Inter-American Court (Hale 2006: 96).

The first aspect to highlight regarding the public hearing at the Court was its duration itself: this was the first time the Court agreed to a public hearing for an entire three days (Raisz 2008: 42). We must not lose track of the fact that this was the first case of this nature—a complex and controversial issue involving the territorial rights of indigenous peoples—to be heard by the Inter-American Court. The complexity of the issue at hand called for essential explanations to clarify the concept of the relevance of land to the worldview of indigenous peoples (Anaya et al 2002: 10, 11). This is indeed one of the most relevant aspects of the *Awas Tingni* case, since throughout the entire three days of hearings, the seven judges who compose the Court saw and heard leading members of the Awas Tingni community[38] and some of the world's salient experts on the rights of indigenous peoples[39] explaining to the members of the Court

> the scope and depth of the relationship existing between the Awas Tingni Community and its territory ... and the powerlessness of Nicaragua's legal system and official institutions to formally recognise the constitutional right of indigenous peoples to the possession of their lands and territories, and provide the necessary content and duties to that right. (Wiggins 2002:11)

---

[37] This is an expression borrowed from Armstrong Wiggins, who said that 'the court hearing was *something to remember* for the record of the struggle of indigenous peoples on the Atlantic Coast' (emphasis added) (Wiggings 2002: 11).

[38] Jaime Castillo, Charlie Mclean and Wilfredo Mclean made their statements before the Court. But they were not alone: a further thirty members of the community were bused from Nicaragua to the Court's seat, a fact which is of tremendous importance from the point of view of the community's 'appropriation' of the case. See Anaya et al (2009: 134).

[39] Theodore Macdonald, Rodolfo Stavenhagen, Guillermo Castilleja, Galio Gurdián, Brooklyn Rivera, Humberto Thompson, Charles Hale, Roque Roldán and Lottie Cunningham participated as expert witnesses in the hearing. See 'Transcript of the Public Hearing on the Merits, November 16, 17 and 18, 2000, at the Seat of the Court' (2002) 19 *Arizona Journal of International and Comparative Law* 129–305.

On the other hand, we must stress the important symbolic value of a hearing of this nature, a session before the entity that protects and guarantees human rights within the framework of the OAS. As Carlos Martín Beristain points out, the hearing may well be a venue that will generate, in the hearts of victims, 'the satisfaction of being heard and acknowledged and taken into account' (Beristain 2009: 67), which in turn may transform it into a tool of reparation, since the fact itself that 'the State is mandated to both hear and be judged impartially has tremendously restorative implications' (ibid: 69). This is definitely the impression we had after interviewing members of the community: they consider that having been able to confront the state of Nicaragua before the Inter-American Court has generated, in the community's heart and mind, a feeling of dignity and empowerment. This is of tremendous importance to groups as vulnerable as indigenous peoples have traditionally been: their self-esteem and dignity have not always flourished.

3.4.2. The Decision by the Court

We must acknowledge that the sentence issued by the Inter-American Court of Human Rights in the *Awas Tingni Community v Nicaragua* case of August 2001 has set a very promising precedent for future legislation and for the rights of indigenous peoples to their lands and natural resources within the broader international legal system. The Inter-American Court's interpretation of the right to property in this landmark case is and will continue to be a challenge to the traditional interpretation of the right to property as it currently stands in the more relevant legal instruments dealing with international human rights. What is more, this novel and courageous jurisprudence has been followed and intensified by the Inter-American Court in other cases also involving indigenous peoples defending their ancestral territories. The most salient of these cases are *Yakye Axa, Moiwana, Saramaka, Sawhoy-amaxa, Xákmok Kásek* and *Sarayaku*, among others.[40] The Court followed what it termed an 'evolutive method' in its interpretation of the law, accepting the use of different developments in the field of human rights that have surfaced in contexts other than the Inter-American system. This decision allowed the Court to go beyond the limits set by strictly formalist criteria on interpreting the meaning, nature and reach of the right of indigenous peoples to be title-holders of their territories and natural resources. Despite

---

[40] The jurisprudence developed by the Inter-American Court on indigenous peoples' land rights has also had an influence beyond the Americas, a far-reaching example of what can be considered as a cross-fertilisation of regional human rights systems. The African Commission on Human and Peoples' Rights has used the rationale followed by the Inter-American Court in the Endorois Case, *The Centre for Minority Rights Development and Minority Rights Group International (on behalf of the Endorois Welfare Council) v Kenya*, Communication 276/2003, African Commission on Human and Peoples' Rights, 2010.

the fact that Article 21 of the American Convention on Human Rights of 1969 does not explicitly make reference to the right to collective property of indigenous peoples, the Court's interpretation is that this provision includes not only the traditional and orthodox notion of the right to own property as a right of an individual nature, but also that the aim is to protect communal property belonging to the indigenous community as a whole, in accordance with established traditions and customs. As a result of this progressive and challenging interpretation, the Inter-American Court reached the conclusion that the Awas Tingni community's right to own property had been violated by Nicaragua since the government of Nicaragua had granted the concession to exploit the land to a logging company without the community's consent and without demarcating, titling and including in the land registration office the ownership of the community's territory, as set forth both in the constitution of Nicaragua of 1987 and in the Statute of Autonomy of the Autonomous Region of the Northern Atlantic (RAAN), also of 1987.

The second innovative feature of the decision taken by the Inter-American Court has to do with the predominantly collective dimension granted to indigenous peoples' right to property. This is at loggerheads with the classical interpretation of human rights within the Western context. Thanks to the testimonials of Awas Tingni community leaders and of world experts in the field of the rights of indigenous peoples, during the Court hearings that took place in San José de Costa Rica, the highest judicial body of the OAS reached the conclusion that 'among indigenous peoples there is a communitarian tradition regarding a communal form of collective property of the land, in the sense that ownership of the land is not centred on an individual but rather on the group and its community'.[41] Along these same lines, the Court maintained that 'the close ties of indigenous people with the land must be recognized and understood as the fundamental basis of their cultures, their spiritual life, their integrity, and their economic survival',[42] underscoring the cultural and spiritual meaning that the land has for the worldview of indigenous peoples. Accordingly, the Court also defended the intergenerational dimension of the protection of the indigenous peoples' right to communal property. As the Court stated: '[F]or indigenous communities, relations to the land are not merely a matter of possession and production but a material and spiritual element which they must fully enjoy, even to preserve their cultural legacy and transmit it to future generations.'[43]

Another important point in the Court's ruling is related to the ultimate foundation of indigenous peoples' right to own property. In the Court's eyes, this is not rooted in the state's recognition of that right, but rather is based on the traditional practices and customs of the indigenous communities

---

[41] Inter-American Court on Human Rights (n 16) para 149.
[42] ibid.
[43] ibid.

themselves. To quote the Court: '[A]s a result of customary practices, possession of the land should suffice for indigenous communities lacking real title to property of the land to obtain official recognition of that property, and for consequent registration.'[44]

For all of the above reasons, the Court declared that Nicaragua had violated the right to property of the Awas Tingni community. As a consequence, Nicaragua was mandated to establish the boundaries of the territory of the Awas Tingni community and other indigenous communities of Nicaragua, and then proceed to the demarcation and titling of the lands.

Despite the vast difficulties that the Awas Tingni community has had to overcome in order for the decision to be enforced (in fact, the community received the deed of ownership of the lands in question in December 2008, nearly eight years after the ruling), it is a fact that the verdict paved the way to a progressive and far-reaching development in the domain of the rights of indigenous peoples to ownership of their lands and territories and to an empowerment of indigenous peoples in general, who now feel they can stand up to defend their rights. However, there continues to be a huge distance between the official declarations and legal recognition of rights of indigenous peoples and the bitter reality they must face every day in the fierce struggle for access to valuable natural resources.

4. CONCLUSIONS

Although the classical and orthodox conception of universal human rights has essentially been based on Western liberalism, in recent decades indigenous reality and diversity have gradually shaped and articulated a multicultural interpretation of human rights.[45] Indigenous peoples have appropriated the rights discourse, turned it into a useful tool for defending their claims and furthermore sought to enrich it with new ideas, proposals and paradigms stemming from their own worldviews. We are at a key moment in the always complex process of intercultural dialogue which must give birth to new perspectives, new concepts and new legal instruments, such as the recently adopted United Nations Declaration on the Rights of Indigenous Peoples, on which indigenous peoples undeniably had a significant influence (Regino Montes et al 2009). To a great extent, this landmark document is the result of a fruitful dialogue between different views on human dignity and human rights. The concept of human rights is sufficiently open and flexible to be able to incorporate new demands and new claims that

---

[44] ibid, para 151.
[45] In part this has also occurred in Europe because of the presence of minorities and new groups resulting from immigration. See Ruiz Vieytez (2006).

contribute to enriching and expanding it. This is a clear-cut example of what some scholars refer to as *inclusive universality* (Brems 2001).

A demonstration of this new and dynamic approach to human rights has come from the progressive case law on indigenous rights developed by the Inter-American Court of Human Rights. It has proved to be very sensitive and open to recognising indigenous views and frames of meaning when applying basic standards relating to the right to property. The decision on the Awas Tingni case has set a very promising precedent for the evolution of the rights of indigenous peoples to their traditional lands and territories under both international and domestic law. The interpretation given by the Inter-American Court to the right to property in this emblematic case poses a significant challenge to the orthodox interpretation of this right and paves the way for a multicultural approach to it, thus contributing to its enrichment.

5

Taking the Challenge of Legal Pluralism for Human Rights Seriously

ANDRÉ HOEKEMA

1. INTRODUCTION

'L EGAL PLURALISM AND development', or more generally 'the role of development actors in the justice sector',[1] are domains in which standard policies have recently started to change somewhat. Some scholars and some development activists have explored new ways to reconcile development and policies on legal pluralism (Harper 2011a,b; Tamanaha et al 2012). The official endorsement of legal pluralism by states is no longer perceived as just a stumbling block in development or as a hindrance to the aspirations of human rights. Furthermore, in terms of land tenure, the usual development-oriented approach of providing untitled land-holders with individual private property titles has sometimes been replaced by consideration of other ways to legalise land holdings, including the option of recognising local communal land tenure institutions.[2] In terms of the recent wave of developmental goals such as good governance, promoting the rule of law, furthering access to law for the poor, keeping order and preserving local cohesion and peace, there is now more interest in officially endorsing

---

[1] The first quote is the title of a volume edited by Tamanaha et al (2012), the second is the subtitle of Corradi (2012).

[2] I refer to my publication 'If Not Private Property, Then What?' in Otto and Hoekema (2012). Let me define this institution of community-based or communal ownership of land as a *complex of values, practices and procedures developed and enforced within a specific non-state community or people, regulating legitimate control and management rights as well as use, transaction and inheritance rights over a variety of forms of land like arable land, grazing areas, trees, forest, reserve lands, waters, etc, thereby combining rights in the hands of individuals, families, clans and the community itself or its authorities, often in the form of rights that with regard to a specific piece of land overlap in time or place.*

non-state communitarian systems of doing justice and keeping order.[3] Finally, the collective rights in the hands of indigenous people all over the world will eventually oblige states to assign full legal competence to local indigenous authorities and their ways of keeping order among their people.[4] All these innovations mean aiming for the recognition of existing non-state forms of law, local law, customary law,[5] and declaring them equally legally valid as state law, ie instituting official ('formal') legal pluralism.

Many of these non-state forms of law are embedded in local communities that manifest (sometimes only partly) a *distinct* way of seeing man, nature and the supernatural, ie a different 'cosmovision' and way of life.[6] This goes hand in hand with challenges, such as how to build these *distinct* ways of local authorities regulating land tenure conflicts and administering justice in the state political and legal order? How best to officially recognise extra-legal local law and/or how to recognise 'community-based' land tenure? There are many problems to be solved in this endeavour. Particularly important is the notorious problem of how to bring local decisions and procedures in line with universal human rights. This in turn is part of the more general need to define the limits of these local laws and local decisions vis-à-vis state law. In other words: how to coordinate these local systems with state law? This is the topic of what I have called internal conflict rules,[7] which I define as

> legal rules, at the national level, that define the scope and limits as well as personal and material competence of an officially recognized, distinct, community-based

---

[3] See, for instance, Chirayat et al (2005: 3), who stress that up until recently official development efforts in terms of justice reform normally only had official state justice in mind and not local justice. But this picture is changing.

[4] The ILO Convention 169, for instance, obliges states to recognise and implement legal pluralism characterised by the presence of law administered by indigenous peoples, as does the Inter-American Court of Human Rights. See the case of the *Mayagna (Sumo) Awas Tingni Community v Nicaragua*, Inter-American Court of Human Rights, 31 August 2001, and also the case of the Saramaka people in *Surinam versus Surinam*, Inter-American Court of Human Rights Series C No 172 (28 November 2007). The same admonition comes from the non-binding UN declaration on the rights of indigenous peoples (2007).

[5] Problems with this term are well known, as it suggests static, only slowly changing principles and rules that are supposed to exist since time immemorial. It also suggests a subordinated, supplementary position under official law. I prefer the term 'local law'.

[6] I am dealing with legal pluralism engrained in the juxtaposition of state law and the law of distinct communities. This means I am not referring to 'functional communities' whose members to a greater extent share the outlook and commonly accepted perceptions of the world and social life with the dominant society, particularly the dominant elite. So I exclude in this chapter the norms medical professionals develop among themselves or the conventions and norms developed in branches of industry such as the garment industry.

[7] Others, like Woodman (2012: 139), call these rules meta-rules. I prefer 'conflict rules' because they fulfil the same task as 'conflict rules' in international private law and in public international law regarding the possible harmonisation of conflicting norms and decisions from different legal regimes. To distinguish them from international private and public law rules, I have added the term 'internal' (or: domestic).

jurisdiction and/or of an officially recognized, community-based authority to manage the land.[8]

These rules also establish the procedures to solve problems of 'mixed' cases and conflicts over jurisdiction between this indigenous justice and the official one.[9] These internal conflict rules cover a variety of conditions imposed on local law and justice. For instance, it is often found that an internal conflict rule restricts the competence of communitarian justice to 'minor cases'. Or the conflict rules order that everyone can always appeal from a local assembly to a state court. Yet another rule says that local authorities have to lay down their decision in writing. Sometimes the conflict rule stipulates that the use of local justice is not obligatory and that local people can address a state court as well. An often-imposed major rule is the one saying that the local decisions and procedures shall not violate internationally accepted human rights, or even shall not contravene 'the Constitution and the Laws of the Republic'. The latter rule, the one referring to the Laws of the Republic, is a form of cultural imperialism, as it almost takes away with one hand what was granted with the other, namely official space offered to local communities to practise their own forms of administering justice. But even restricting the conflict rule to the need, for instance, to respect 'the Constitution' or perhaps even only 'the human rights enshrined in the constitution and/or in international treaties ratified by the state' could also raise the question if the local community will respect this condition or will feel obstructed in their attempts to rule themselves in their own way.

Although such empirical questions are important to study, there are, to the best of my knowledge, hardly any studies addressing the question of the impact of conflict rules on the way local justice is done. Partly, this is due to the notorious absence of official internal conflict rules (see the next section). Therefore, I have to step back and raise questions about the process of producing conflict rules and speculate about the conditions under which these rules do *not* have the tendency to forbid distinct forms and norms of administering justice. As to the matter of imposing human rights limits, remarkably often it is assumed that local justice *as a matter of course* should respect human rights, while the content of these rights is not interrogated further. Local justice therefore has to adapt itself rapidly to 'universal' but often 'Western' notions. True, in the multiple forms of local justice there are

---

[8] Although I call these conflict rules 'legal', these official rules are not to be approached from the legal point of view but taken seriously only to the extent that they are implemented in reality and have some real impact on the way conflicts between local legal orders and state legal orders are managed. Sometimes these conflict rules have no official standing at all but manifest themselves in practice such as the tendency by official authorities not to step in when a local justice assembly leads to imposing a corporal punishment on a convict. This condoning stand means that we have come across a 'de facto' conflict rule that has no official legal status.

[9] Or, in the land rights case, conflicts between the new land management powers of local communities and state competences.

elements that are clearly a violation of human rights in almost every, even intercultural, interpretation. And as to the 'automatic imposition' of this restriction, it is true that the automatism is being questioned now more than before. Corradi (2012) devotes her study to human rights interventions in legally plural Africa. She shows on the one hand that non-state practices of doing justice are dominant in many of those countries and that these local practices occasionally achieve official recognition. On the other hand, however, she also shows that the imposition of human rights restrictions is often done unilaterally, top down, without sufficient knowledge of the various local institutions and without entering into a serious dialogue with these local actors.[10] This conclusion is persuasive, but more scholarly attention is necessary to the theme of how to make human rights interpretations more inclusive and what this inclusive interpretation would entail.

Other scholars plead for an interpretation of human rights restrictions in a culturally sensitive, intercultural way. Inksater (2006), discussing corporal punishments, uses the term 'transformative juricultural pluralism'.[11] We also read about 'the inherent elasticity of human rights', their 'inherent indeterminacy' and 'unavoidably plural' interpretation (Kinley 2012: 53, 55, 63). Pimentel (2010), dealing with the widespread world of South Sudan customary courts, discusses the need for cultural sensitivity in any intervention in the local administration of justice. But quite often, these discussions remain very general: it is quite rare to come across an intercultural analysis of the meaning of human rights *on the basis of concrete rights* such as what 'corporal punishment' means or how to evaluate judging someone without an official defender.[12] Such a resort to concrete rights and finding out what these might mean in a distinct culture and the administration of justice therein is the only way to progress towards a sound cooperation between local justice and the state legal order, but only a few scholars have undertaken this kind of analysis. One of the very few is Inksater (2006) about corporal punishment. This scarcity means that the challenge of legal pluralism to the deployment of human rights is not taken up sufficiently seriously. I do hope, however, to break novel ground by discussing concrete examples of corporal punishment[13] in the light of human rights.[14] Before doing so

---

[10] Chiayath et al lay the same stress on the need not to approach local justice systems with top-down uniform requirements, but to create 'mediating institutions wherein actors from both realms can meet ... to craft new arrangements that both sides can own and enforce' (Chiayath et al 2005: 25, 26).

[11] An intercultural interpretation of human rights, even of any law, is sometimes required in official coordination rules (= internal conflict rules) or their drafts.

[12] But see chapter 5 in this volume.

[13] The term 'corporal punishment' in itself already means using a specific way of framing physical sanctions. This may not do justice to the way in which these sanctions are experienced by those involved (eg the cleansing dimension may be more relevant than the punishment).

[14] There are many other aspects of local justice that will be perceived almost automatically as a violation of elementary strands of justice but could be and have to be discussed in an intercultural dialogue on the basis of concrete cases, eg gender inequality, 'property grabbing'

in section 4 below, I want to discuss the problems mentioned briefly in the introduction, namely the scarcity of official internal rules (section 2) and the calling of the requirement of not violating 'the human rights' as 'natural' (section 3).

2. DO WE ENCOUNTER INTERNAL CONFLICT RULES AT ALL?

Are there examples of internal conflict rules at all, except the usual abstract reference to non-violation of human rights and respect for the minimum standards of justice?[15] There are hardly any, at least not in the sense of going into detail. Lately, in states such as Sierra Leone, Bolivia, South Africa and Liberia, conflict rules conditioning the official recognition of some elements of local customary justice have indeed been at issue. But politically speaking, this topic is so sensitive that legislative discussions about the issuing of internal conflict rules often get bogged down. However, *drafts* of coordination rules are available in countries such as Colombia and Ecuador. Sometimes conflict rules are developed by a court, national or international. The most famous example is the Constitutional Court of Colombia. This is the only court in the world that has engaged head on with the official abstract conflict rule (Article 246 of the 1991 Constitution), saying that to be legally valid, local indigenous justice decisions should not violate the Constitution or 'the laws of the Republic'.[16] The clause of not violating *national law* was an easy one for the Court. They argued that if this restriction is taken literally, one could just close down local justice (and drive it underground). So the Court left this clause out of consideration. The requirement about not violating the Constitution, however, was widely discussed, particularly the chapter about the fundamental rights.

Their most controversial contribution lies in the way they almost did away with the usual requirement that local indigenous decisions should not

---

of widows, accountability and 'objectivity' of local justice, or the practice of offering one's daughter as compensation for a tort such as a wrongful death (Pimentel 2010: 18). Again, although in recent years many of these aspects of local justice have been researched, eg Harper (2011a,b), Ubink (2011a,b), I have not come across an interculturally oriented debate about the need, justification and wisdom of striking these practices down without further ado.

[15] I have been looking for detailed conflict rules, not just the kind that only delivers an abstract message such as the ILO 169 Art 8 rule saying that local decisions should be 'compatible with fundamental rights enshrined in the national legal system and with the internationally recognized human rights'. This is an abstract message that glosses over the important question of what fundamental rights are covered by it.

[16] This Court has the competence to check lower juridical sentences and decisions, also from the indigenous justice system, in terms of respecting human rights. This is called *tutela*. So it is not an ordinary appeal court, it is what Pimentel (2010: 23) calls 'collateral' review. The composition of this court is another important problem. It would be best to provide for both state judges from the dominant society and judges from distinct communities.

contravene individual fundamental rights as set out in Article 12 prohibiting torture and treatments or sanctions that are cruel, inhumane or degrading. The Court's justification that they would not keep local justice bound by the usual catalogue of human rights merits our attention: 'In a nation where cultural diversity is recognized, no world view can prevail over the other, let alone attempt to dominate' (in verdict T 496 of 26 September 1996). This is an almost unheard-of acceptance of the diversity of the constituent nations of Colombia and their right to be different (Assies 2003; Hoekema 2003). However, the Court retains a hard core of essential human rights which have to be respected by local authorities: the right to life, the right not to be enslaved, the right not to be tortured[17] and finally the right not to be judged in ways that are unforeseeable for the accused. Under this latter 'due process' clause, for instance, arbitrary and capricious ways of administering criminal justice and/or sentences will be struck down. The Court acknowledges, however, that not every novelty in procedure or material rules can be grounds for annulling local decisions. The Colombian situation is unique also in the sense that through the work of the Court, a long list of principles and concrete rules has been produced that can fully qualify as internal conflict rules.[18]

The picture showing the near absence of internal conflict rules is to some extent different in the matter of legalising local tenure arrangements. For instance, the new land laws of Tanzania (Hoekema 2012) grant power to villages to manage and regulate the land according to customary law. These official land laws are very detailed and contain many internal conflict rules.[19] But in other examples of legalisation of local land tenure arrangements, internal conflict rules are deficient or completely missing.[20]

3. HUMAN RIGHTS AND OTHER LIMITING CRITERIA ARE OFTEN DEFENDED AS 'NATURAL'

As I mentioned above, there seems to be a consensus that restrictions on local justice concerning 'human rights' are only natural and obvious. Remarks such as 'obviously local justice shall have to live up to principles of fair play and refrain from using corporal punishments' are rather common.

[17] But torture is not easily assumed. For example, whipping survives the constitutional test. See the discussion below in section 4.
[18] See Pimentel (2011) for a systematic overview of the main principles that could be used to order the relations between national (state) jurisdiction and local jurisdictions.
[19] But the level of detail is such that in practice implementation possibly will not occur or only haphazardly.
[20] In my article, 'If Not Private Property, Then What?' (Hoekema 2012) I discuss a variety of these coordinating attempts and note many weak spots and missing links in the set of internal conflict rules that is in place.

Human rights are often referred to as limits without discussing which rights, in what interpretation and why so. Pimentel (2010), for instance, in dealing with the relation between customary courts and state courts in South Sudan, claims that it is necessary to recognise customary courts to provide people with access to justice, but he does not question the overall limiting role of human rights and does not discuss a culturally sensitive interpretation of these rights. This contrasts with his keen eye for the possible consequences of restrictions such as the need for codification of local law that tend to undermine the distinct character of this law and make it 'the property of the state' (Pimentel 2010: 19). Another example can be found in an in itself interesting IDLO paper, in which Wojkowska and Cunningham (2009) describe and analyse possible justice reforms through which customary systems may be recognised as part of the official legal order. But when it comes to a possible elaboration and discussion of internal conflict rules (in my terms), the authors gloss over this problem. Or, rather, they take for granted a great many limits imposed on and restrictions of the recognition of local institutions. The point of departure of these comments often is based on a gloomy and critical image of the quality of a local administration of justice. But this does not justify a complete omission of at least the possibility and perhaps the need to develop a set of concrete, culturally sensitive internal conflict rules.

What Pimentel observed about the possible impact of a conflict rule requiring codification of local law refers to the impact conflict rules might have on local life, on local power relations, on the empowerment of the community as such, on changes in the position of local authorities within the communities and in the position of minorities within a distinct community, on the external relations between local communities and the national society.[21] These are all different specific themes to consider and to evaluate before calling 'natural' the requirement that local justice should respect all the usual human and fundamental rights. Such empirical studies are very scarce but I venture a speculation. Each one of the following list of conflict rules, if officially required and in practice enforced, will have a strong effect on the local justice arrangements and change them into something different:

— to respect internationally guaranteed human rights;
— to refrain from what is called—without definition and discussion— corporal punishment;
— to provide legal professional representation to the accused;

---

[21] All these possible impacts have to be studied in the broader context of a host of further circumstances such as the general relations of power between a dominant elite and distinct local groups, the internal power struggles and rifts, the role of a possible fight for exploitation of natural sub-soil resources, and so on.

— to give the community members a choice either to go to the traditional system or to opt for the state judge;
— to require that the local rules and practices be put in writing and the cases noted in a register;
— to restrict the community's administration of justice to minor cases.

This list produced is not the fruit of a morbid phantasy but paraphrased from various studies, such as Wojkowska's UNDP report of 2006, 'Doing Justice: How informal Systems Can Contribute'.[22] We have to confront the question of whether or not implementation of one or more of such restrictive conflict rules is directly or indirectly pushing the community into becoming something else.[23] For some outsiders, and perhaps for some insiders, this means something positive: the community is at last forced to adopt the traits of a modern rule-of-law society. Others are not so sure. They ask whether that customary order, indeed the life of the community as such, can still be called *indigenous* after having lived under the new and very tight recognition regime for some time (ICHRP 2009: 31, 32).[24] We see here intriguing questions arising about legal empowerment on the community level. While some groups or fractions of the community may be empowered through the imposition of such requirements to stand up for a better position within that community—a matter very much in the mind of the writers of the ICHPR report just quoted—it may well be that instead the community eventually loses opportunities to develop, reconstruct and externally defend its indigenousness.[25] It might, for instance, not be able to ward off mining projects and other forms of encroachment on its territory.

Let me refer briefly to a study by Herrera (2011) about the way in which Mayan communitarian ways of doing justice were officially recognised in the Mexican state of Quintana Roo. The list I gave above describes accurately the existing list of conflict rules imposed on the Maya justice arrangements. It is required, for instance, that the Mayan judges have to act in strict compliance with human rights, otherwise their decision is invalid because it is illegal, and this rule is fairly strictly enforced (Herrera, 2011: 174).

---

[22] The same tendency to claim a generous use of requirements, conditions and restrictions for recognising local justice is to be found in a 'Justice for the Poor Program' report by Stephen (2006).

[23] Van Cott (2003: 25) asks what the linking of this informal justice system to the state system might mean. She underscores the authority, flexibility and dynamism of the local system that flows from its uncodified character and suggests: 'Is this authority, flexibility and dynamism lost if community authorities become agents of the state?' The question is raised, but she could not really explore and study it.

[24] Presuming the regime will be implemented!

[25] The case of the introduction of local mediation-like institutions or alternative dispute resolution (ADR) platforms is different. ADR is not about respecting indigenous norms, culture and institutions, but about quick and efficient problem-solving. Therefore, ADR does not raise intriguing questions about recognising 'separate' legal orders and 'loss of state power'.

Moreover, indigenous justice is not obligatory for the Mayan people; it is defined as an alternative only (ibid: 183). The local judges only have jurisdiction in minor cases (ibid: 41–44), etc. But I repeat, it is not clear if even the sum of these conflict rules really dooms the traditional local ways of doing justice. It seems that Mayan traditional authorities do cunningly use their limited powers, and it might well be that the Mayan people feel they benefit from this development, and that their communities are in a better position to defend and develop their distinctive identity, as Herrera predicts (ibid: 39, 149).

This Mexican case perhaps partly contradicts my gloomy speculation about the alienating impact of such a strict series of conflict rules on the local community. It teaches the important lesson that only a longitudinal study can provide some answers. When considering the situation of legalisation of land tenure and recognition of the local right to adjudicate land tenure conflicts, more research exists about the impact of conflict rules on local life, as in Tanzania.[26]

4. HOW TO PROMOTE INTERCULTURAL REFLECTION ON SPECIFIC HUMAN RIGHTS?

In what follows, the core of my chapter, I want to elaborate on the topic of intercultural dialogue, co-operation and reflection about how to mutually respect a diversity of worldviews, cultures and laws while at the same time not forgetting the need to accommodate or to harmonise the one with the other, ie to develop commonly agreed conflict rules. My main material comes from confrontations between (quasi-)legal state professionals and local communitarian authorities. Another important source of the vicissitudes of intercultural reflection is to be found in the myriad of ways in which local authorities and their followers *within their own communities* discuss their own practices and consider the need to take on board some

---

[26] Take the case of women and land in rural Tanzania. Is local practice changing for the better *because of the new land laws*, meaning that in matters of land tenure, women fare better 'because of' this rule and its socialisation on the ground? To investigate this, we need to study concrete events of, for example, the inheritance of land by women, particularly widowed women, as well as internal opposition against discriminatory practices, possible pressure groups, the presence of a local NGO or CSO working together with women's groups to pressure the traditional authorities and the village council, etc. Only along these lines could we get an impression of the ways in which women in these villages are empowered. Moreover, we would have to know the general context of the situation as well as the 'baseline situation' (how local life functioned before the recognition came) so as to be able to gauge whether or not some more general tendencies are already working towards a better local legal and social position of women quite apart from any possible effect of the conflict rule I quoted. Such empirical longitudinal evaluative research is very scarce, however.

of the values and norms of 'the other side', for instance human rights.[27] Through these dialogue and co-operation efforts both the state administration of justice and the local one will adapt itself in some aspects to the other. This mutual adaptation process can be called: a process of interlegality or hybridisation of legal orders. Interlegality is not a legal normative requirement but a factual social process of mutual adaption and learning by both sides from the other system of doing justice, and in the course of that learning process taking over some elements from the other. Whether this happens or not is a question of the facts.

I concentrate my attention to a human right already mentioned various times above as a typical example of a human right that often is taken as a 'natural' restriction on local justice: corporal sanctions or the right not to be subjected to torture and other cruel, inhumane or degrading treatments or punishments (the title of a relevant convention on this matter). I want to discuss this matter through the lens of an intercultural interpretation of this right. First I present a concrete case dealt with by the Colombian Constitutional Court, then two cases from Mayan justice in Guatemala. Finally, I consider the way the so-called *Rondas Campesinas* in Peru co-operate with the official police.

4.1. Colombia

In its verdict T 523 (15 October 1997), the Colombian Constitutional Court evaluated physical sanctions imposed by local justice.[28] A high-ranking member of an indigenous community had been tried according to the ceremonies and procedures of the Paeces (the Nasa, as they call themselves), an indigenous people living in central Colombia. He was accused of

---

[27] On this matter, internal discussions and initiatives from within confronting the matter of how to adapt a local community and its law and administration of justice to the times of today, including notions of human rights, the IDLO volumes already mentioned give a wealth of material. More specifically, for instance, Ubink (2011a,b) and Hinz (2012) tell the story of deliberations and results of local authority initiatives to improve the position of women in local government, to do away with discriminatory inheritance rules ('property grabbing' of widows) and to engage women in the justice administration, as well as to assemble and partly change and write down local law. Internal dynamics in local distinct communities are often impressive. Another detailed internal study about customary justice, a study concentrating on internal notions of fair play and how they develop, is done by d'Engelbronner-Kolff (2001). Many other studies document attempts of, for example, local women groups, youth groups, new kind of leaders, etc, to step back from some of the cherished local ways of doing things and borrow elements from the dominant society and international law. I previously described many somewhat older examples in my article 'A New Beginning of Law among Indigenous Peoples' (Hoekema 2003).

[28] I summarise the way in which the court dealt with physical punishment, leaving aside all the other important aspects of the case. I follow the clear commentary on this case by Willem Assies, 'Indian Justice in the Andes' (Assies 2003).

having spread false rumours suggesting that the then mayor of the town of Jambaló, the capital of a specific, indigenous, self-governing territory but also a municipality in Colombian public administrative law, had links to the then notorious paramilitary forces. As could be expected in those violent times of civil war, the mayor was shortly afterwards murdered by the FARC. After investigation by various Paez authorities, the case was tried in at least two assemblies, and finally the punishment was announced. The matter was seen as a very serious disturbance to the harmony of the Paeces, and the sanctions imposed were heavy: expulsion from the community, loss of his political rights in the community and 60 lashes with a whip. The first two lower courts to discuss the writ for *tutela*[29] had judged the whipping as torture and declared it in violation of internationally accepted human rights. The Constitutional Court quashed this qualification, however. On the basis of expert opinion—delivered by the legal anthropologist Esther Sánchez upon request[30]—the Court said that the whipping, 'while introduced in the colonial times, as a practice had got a specific meaning in the Paez culture. The Paez (Nasa) perceive it as a stroke of lightning that mediates between light and dark and as a form of purification.' Deliberating about the legality of this sanction, the Court stressed the tension this case manifests between the views of the majority society and those of the Paez.

> Whereas the former punishes because a crime has been committed, the latter sanctions to re-establish the order of nature and to dissuade community members from committing crimes in the future. Whereas the former rejects corporal punishment as a violation of dignity, the latter considers it a purifying element that helps the convict to feel liberated.[31]

The Court then argued as they had previously in case T 349 (see below) that 'in a society that claims itself as being pluralist, no world view[32] can be unilaterally imposed'. In view of the Constitution, 'the indigenous world views merit maximal respect'. Then the Court repeated the human rights minima that can never be violated legally: the right to life and the protection from slavery and torture (plus a kind of due process requirement).

What about torture then? The Court discussed international treaties and decisions, such as the Convention against Torture and Other Cruel, Inhuman and Degrading Punishment, and some sentences of the European

---

[29] On *tutela*, see n 17.

[30] Her expert report can be found in her book (in Spanish): *Justicia y pueblos indígenas de Colombia* (Bogotá, Universidad National de Colombia UNIJUS, 1998). See generally Esther Sánchez's frequently crucial expert opinions about aspects of indigenous cultures, sometimes most delicate and misunderstood practices, in her PhD thesis (Sánchez 2006).

[31] This is the most fundamental difference between Western-style criminal procedure and sanctions and indigenous ones. The matter is analysed impressively and in depth in *Dancing with a Ghost*, by Rupert Ross (2006). It is well proven by many studies that the difference is there, but in real life the situation is often not black and white.

[32] *Cosmovisión*.

Court of Human Rights. It then declared that the flogging is not physically damaging as it is done on the lower part of the legs. Neither is it humiliating as its goal is not to expose the convict to public disgrace but to purify him and re-establish harmony in the community. In conclusion: no 'torture' was found in the sense of human rights.[33]

In T 349, along more or less the same lines, the Court did not deem the sanction of *cepo* to be a violation of the human right not to be tortured. This sanction—tying a person to a pillory—involves forcing a person into a rather uncomfortable position by tying him to stocks for a series of nights while he has to do community work during the daytime. In this case this was ordered for a long period (three years), but the local justice decisions were not quashed by the Court as invalid.

4.2. Guatemala

We have two studies of criminal cases in which whipping was practised in conformity with the procedures of communitarian justice, and ultimately at state level this practice was indirectly recognised as a legitimate punishment. Both cases come from Mayan justice in Guatemala. Padilla (2008) has amply described a case from 2002 and has even produced a documentary film about the story, *Seis Años* (Six Years). Rachel Sieder (2011) describes a case from 2006. Both cases come from the region around Santa Cruz del Quiche, in the Quiche department, which is a typical majoritarian Mayan zone of the country.

Characteristic for the situation of 2002, and still valid to some extent in 2006, is the fact that Guatemala had passed through a horrible and extremely violent civil war, ending after 36 years with a peace treaty in 1996.[34] Because of the massive displacements of populations, the militarised regime and the terror that had reigned in all the villages, the local indigenous institutions had disintegrated, including Mayan structures of justice. Around 2002, in these rural parts, there were cases of mob justice, lynching and burning to death of people suspected of theft, aggression, murder, etc.

---

[33] Likewise it was established that the fact that the suspect was not defended by a lawyer did not violate his 'right to defence' because 'this right can be respected also by other means than the ones enumerated in national and international law'. In this case a community member with good knowledge of the local customs offered to conduct the defence. Also, the accused could speak freely in the Assembly and did so as a matter of fact in the second one. The two tribunals involved earlier had declared the procedure invalid because the right to an independent defence has been violated. (It is known from studies of indigenous justice that in other cases family members come forward, while there are many other means to bring the version and background of the accused to the fore.)

[34] I refer to the very useful sketch of the broader context in the articles by Sieder (2011, 2013).

At the same time, responsible people tried to 'reinvent' the traditional Mayan forms of justice and to set up social movements in various places, the *defensorias* Mayas, to try to bring local justice back to peaceful ways in tune with the ancient values and forms of Mayan justice. Official state agencies as well as the official police either had no serious presence in these areas or were still corrupt and/or very contemptuous of the Mayan population, calling them barbarians. The 2002 case showed all these distorted circumstances, but ended after more than two years with a surprising recognition of the existence and validity of Mayan justice, including corporal punishment. Nevertheless, the position of Mayan justice continues to be very weak as there is still no firm and unambiguous constitutional recognition and many official (semi)legal authorities still do not recognise or even completely ignore Mayan justice.[35]

In the 2002 case, a group of five young males violently threatened the owner of a pick-up truck, Mr Yat, took hold of the truck and disappeared with it. Some police activity followed, and parts of the truck were found in the house of one of the perpetrators, Fransisco ('el Chico') Velasquez. The rest of the truck was found by the victim himself with the help of some of his colleagues. Mr Yat, after a horrendous odyssey visiting bureaucratic agencies, some in the far distant capital, finally obtained an order from a judge in Santa Cruz ordering the return of the remains of his truck (at that point held in legal custody). But the same odyssey did not help him to persuade a prosecutor to arrest Velasquez and bring him before a judge. Meanwhile, people from the local *defensoria* Maya stepped in, contacted Velasquez, got him to offer some money to Mr Yat to pay a part of the damage, and finally got him to name of the other four and commit himself to participate in traditional Maya proceedings. One of the other four, Felix, was notorious for earlier criminal acts, and the *defensoria* leaders, knowing about the absence and lack of interest of state authorities, feared a 'spontaneous' lynching and therefore worked hard to persuade community authorities to join hands and together organise a Mayan procedure to try all five of the men. The main element of this procedure is the organization of a public assembly, which took place on 13 May 2002. An assembly is a way of presenting suspects to a general audience—often consisting of many hundreds of villagers—interrogating them, urging the criminals to confess and repent, and finally discussing with the public what to do with them. At some moments during the session, cries to lynch them were heard, but the leaders of the assembly kept order and assuaged the crowd. All five suspects were present.

---

[35] Art 66 of the Constitution of 1985 contains a weak wording of this recognition. A new constitution with stronger rights for the (majority) of Maya and other indigenous peoples was turned down by a referendum held in 1999. Around 1997 Guatemala also ratified ILO Convention 169, but implementation is erratic.

Velasquez confessed his part of the crime and called upon the other four to speak the truth. All but one (Felix) confessed too, and showed repentance. After a long discussion, it was decided to have them pay damages to Mr Yat and to whip them ritually with nine strokes. The whip is made of cypress branches, not of leather as some members of the audience would have wanted. The suspects were allowed to keep their clothes on and were hit nine times on the back and the legs. The leaders had foreseen the turmoil that the case could evoke and had the assembly filmed in its entirety. Also, they had already warned some official authorities to come after the conclusion of the assembly. Because one suspect did not confess and repent his deeds, by tradition Mayan justice could not fulfil its goal of ritually cleansing the perpetrator, forgiving him and making him ready to resume his place as a loyal member of the community. All this is needed to restore the broken harmony. The five were therefore transferred to the national authorities, who were strongly urged not to take measures against Velasquez because he had confessed from the beginning and had helped decisively to clear up the case.[36] This handing over of the suspects to state justice if not everyone confessed fully had been decided upon earlier between the *defensoria* people and state officials. During the audience, the assembly authorised this step.

Television played a crucial negative role in what followed. Parts of the filmed transcript got into the hands of some reporters, in particular the whipping and the transfer of the five to the official state authorities, and these fragments were shown on the TV news with the comment that state authorities had come forward just in time to save the five from a lynch mob. Police and state legal officials of various levels saw the TV news, believed the story completely, and firmly adopted a view of barbarians at work and proud state officials saving the accused and the rule of law. The film of the entire assembly, revealing the real facts, had been offered to the prosecutor, but this official refused to accept it because 'we cannot use "extrajudicial proof"'. It is not surprising that all suspects were almost immediately set free by order of the judge in charge, with the exception of Velasquez, in view of the fact that he had confessed so loudly.[37] The judge remarked that what the Mayan authorities had done (detention of suspects, whipping them, etc) did not conform to the procedural requirements of the constitution and the criminal procedural code, while 'confession forced by torture' is clearly

---

[36] All five were handed over, not just Felix, because according to the leader of the *defensoria* and president of the meeting, state justice would need the declaration of all members of the group to get the facts straight (Padilla 2008: 161).

[37] The detention of Velasquez is difficult to understand because a confession in the local assembly, as we have seen, is judged 'extrajudicial' and therefore furnishes no basis for a valid proof. But he had already confessed before the Mayan assembly took place. Perhaps this confession was deemed correct in terms of state criminal procedure. The local authorities had urged especially that he be set free, a request that was completely negated.

violating human rights. The judge instead urged the prosecutor to prosecute the assembly leaders responsible for all these 'illegal' steps, and she chastised the way the Mayan authorities had tried 'to hide their atrocities' behind the smokescreen of the 'application of customary Mayan law'.

After this decision to release everyone except Velasquez, many people, both Maya and non-Maya, started to feel uneasy about the course of events, the fate of Velasquez, and the appalling way Mayan justice had been ignored and labelled. Padilla then interviewed various participants in this drama, and made a penetrating film of the case using parts of the documentary of the assembly session (Padilla 2008). The case was reopened. Another prosecutor, versed in indigenous law, persuaded a judge to order the arrest of Felix and the others. Felix went as far as to commit himself also to pay part of the damages, but another judge set him free on the basis of purely state procedural rules. Meanwhile, the new prosecutor organised a session in his office with all the suspects present along with their lawyers or representatives. They all were willing to pay but were urged by their defence not to confess. This strongly violates Mayan ways because the most important thing in any local procedure is to obtain a full confession from the suspect, full repentance and a firm commitment not do such acts again, before the accused can resume his place in the community. Some months later a session was called by the tribunal that still had to decide what to do about Velasquez, who was still in jail. The prosecutor introduced then and there the right of indigenous peoples to have their own system of justice recognised on an equal footing with the state justice (ILO Convention 169). As he had been judged and punished in the assembly and had finally promised to pay damages to Mr Yat, legally Velasquez could not be sentenced here because he had already been sentenced by official Mayan justice. The tribunal, however, passed over this point of view and sentenced Velasquez to six years in prison. On appeal, the appellate judge ratified this sentence, saying that indigenous authorities do not have any jurisdictional competence.[38] Eventually, however, this view was completely reversed in cassation by the highest court, the Corte Suprema de Justicia. This Court ordered the liberation of Velasquez on 7 October 2004 because he had been tried by Mayan justice, which has an official position in Guatemala through ILO Convention 169, and it is a human right that nobody will be officially tried for the same act twice (*no bis in idem*). Although Mayan justice was disqualified many times throughout this case as a violation of human rights or even barbaric, Velasquez was finally saved from prison by the application of a human right, *ne bis in idem*. The fact that this principle was used unconditionally implies the full recognition of the legitimacy and legal validity of

---

[38] In an interview, she talked about the Maya and their way of life in the most racist and contemptuous terms.

the Mayan procedure and decisions, including the whipping. This sentence by the Supreme Court is the first official legal recognition of the existence and validity of Mayan justice. As the whipping had been part of the local procedure, this Mayan form of corporal punishment is indirectly recognised as legitimate, even on the state level.[39]

In 2006, four years later, the antagonistic relations between state justice and local justice had improved a bit towards at least certain forms of informal co-operation, as Sieder describes on the basis of a similar criminal case (Sieder 2011). Again a pick-up truck was stolen and had its valuable parts removed. The case stayed firmly in the hands of the local Mayan authorities, who convened an assembly. Again cries were heard about lynching, and one of the three suspects did not confess. There was no doubt, however, who the perpetrators were because immediately after the theft, local Mayan authorities had interviewed witnesses and had uncovered all the details. After the usual assembly hearings, the whole audience was urged to decide the kind of sanction to apply, which shows the role of consensus in these procedures. The fact that 'everyone' is present is important as it improves the accountability of the procedure and the decisions (ibid: 58). The three had to pay damages for the truck, after which another Mayan element was played out: the need for the perpetrators to confess and show repentance, a kind of public shaming as Sieder calls it. This shaming ritual was executed in a particular way because the Mayan authorities felt that a 'show' of their practice of doing justice in front of a non-Mayan public—the dominant elite—would help to reinforce the position of indigenous justice within the dominant society. The next day in front of the cathedral of the capital, Santa Cruz, an assembly was staged after the three men had been led through the streets with the tires of the stolen truck around their necks. Mayan authorities were present and announced with megaphones to the general public all that had happened. Then, after this meeting, many hundreds of people made their way back to a village nearby where the final assembly was to be held. Here ritual beatings with thin branches were administered, a ritual known as *xik'a'y* that has a long standing in Maya traditions, though it has also raised internal discussions. The three had to take off their shirts, kneel and stretch out their arms. Everyone, even their parents, were invited to hit them, after which the local Maya authorities administered the beating one after the other. That was the end of the matter, and there had no appeal to or intervention by state authorities.

---

[39] I have read about another burglary case in Mayan justice in the area of Totonicapán in which official professionals informally accepted the validity of the local decisions, referred back the case of three suspects who had just escaped from lynching to be tried by the indigenous authorities, and in a subsequent state trial released the arrested suspects because of the *ne bis in idem* principle. See Harper (2011a: 81) and Hessbruegge and Ochoa Garcia (2011).

Sieder describes how within the Mayan leadership and among the common people this practice is leading to discussions about the justification of *xik'a'y*. Meanwhile the whipping did not lead to any action or comment from outsiders. Local Mayan authorities were not persecuted as was the case before. A kind of de facto recognition of indigenous local law is gaining strength, including the whipping procedure

4.3. Intercultural Dialogue: A Peruvian Case

The discussion is still ongoing in Colombia, in Guatemala and elsewhere—a form of intercultural discussion about the crucial question of what limits to the recognition of distinct forms of administering justice can and should be accepted within the main, dominant institutions; in other words, what the limits of formal legal pluralism should be, particularly (but not only) in terms of human rights. If an intercultural interpretation of law and human rights in official law is ordered like in Bolivia, the local communities may take the lead in claiming that specific aspects of their ways of doing justice have to be exempted from standard constitutional restrictions. An interesting case about such intercultural 'discussion' from Peru was studied by Piccoli (2009a,b, 2010, 2011).

In Peru, the *Rondas Campesinas*, which function in many rural communities, have obtained official jurisdiction to deal with local conflicts. However, the competences of these committees are hobbled by the internal conflict rules that are in place. This Peruvian setup of formal legal pluralism is plagued not only by the usual political antagonisms but also by severe legal ambiguities and endless legal professional debates or, if you wish, sabotage. Let me begin with an initial legal nicety. In relevant legislation the competence of these *Rondas* is expressed in terms of 'solving conflicts'. Do 'conflicts' also cover 'crimes', or are crimes still the exclusive domain of the police and other state authorities? The famous Article 149 of the Constitution about the jurisdictional competences of specific communities and therefore recognition of a form of proper justice in the countryside assigns these competences to two types of communities, native and agrarian ones.[40] The *Rondas* are assigned the competence of 'helping' the communities to keep order. This suggests that they do not have competences of their own. Moreover, these two types of communities are the product of specific historical circumstances and do not cover all rural villages and communities.

---

[40] 'Comunidades campesinas y nativas' in the Spanish original. The translation of *campesinas* by agrarian is dubious. These *communidades campesinas* are for the most part communities in the mountainous area, often the villages that in the old days were under the authority of a big landowner (*hacendado*). The 'nativas' are mostly communities of Indian population in the low Amazon region.

While the *Rondas* also function in places not officially recognised as one of the types mentioned in Article 149, the question is: what source do they base their competence on? It may be that some claim they are indigenous and are then covered by ILO Convention 169 (ratified by Peru). But the meaning of 'indigenous' in Peru is not clear. People in the mountains often consider this qualification as pejorative. Moreover, it is well known that in some sectors of the country, including Cajamarca department, the majority of the population is mixed. The list of tricky legal political pitfalls is endless. For example, Article 8 of the ILO Convention 169 stipulates that the decisions taken by the local justice system should be 'compatible with fundamental rights enshrined in the national legal system and with the internationally recognized human rights'.

In reality, this need not disturb the customary functioning of local justice, but it will almost certainly lead to arbitrary and erratic inroads by some authorities. Earlier in the 1990s, there were indeed hundreds of arrests of *ronderos* (eg for cattle theft) after they had dealt with in the local way (detention, whipping, etc). People administering local justice were charged with having exceeded their competence, illegal detention and having imposed physical sanctions. But although no changes have been made to the legal framework, those arrests now seem to have subsided. The antagonisms have partly disappeared, replaced by forms of co-operation between the two distinct forms of doing justice. Take, for instance, the fate of corporal punishment. Part of the routine functioning of the *Rondas* is the use of physical sanctions to urge people to confess and also sometimes as a punishment (whipping, doing nightly exercises, bathing in very cold water). Piccoli describes how in some districts the police co-operate with the *Rondas* in procedures against suspected cattle thieves and how police officials condoned physical sanctions to extract a confession. This kind of de facto co-operation is a regular event; police officers participate in local assemblies in which a suspect is judged. One of the effects of such joining of forces is the promotion of exchanges among *Rondas* and police officers about the legitimacy and moral significance of each other's methods and norms. Interlegality is in the making: *ronderos* discuss corporal punishment among themselves and gradually step back a bit, because they do not want to raise too much trouble in the outside world. Hence, police officers, judges, *ronderos* and (other) community leaders are working out a permanent place for non-state justice by institutionalising real co-operation between de facto equally autonomous but distinct forms of doing justice. It is true that such co-operation is the product of individual, perhaps charismatic personalities, and not necessarily the fruit of a more general trend. But the lesson is clear: restrictive conflict rules can be put aside by good personal relations. Piccoli concludes that a real intercultural dialogue takes place in the margins of the official way to define the position of local justice as strictly subordinate to the official system. We may come to the conclusion that analysing the internal conflict rules and their legal position is one thing, but it is quite another to take into account the fact that conflict rules, even of the restrictive type, will not be the last word in how local jurisdictions and the state justice system become open, however slightly, towards each other's way of doing justice. In a way this is a sobering conclusion for all of us who want to study the possible effects of conflict rules on the way local justice is performed. Life, or if you wish the broader social context, is always stronger.

5. SOME MORE GENERAL CONCLUDING REMARKS

These cases show how local customary arrangements are not static; they are changing all the time. We also saw that official human rights sometimes get interpreted in line with distinct cultural practices and 'cosmovisions', either on the official state level or more informally, in daily practice. Hence both the interpretation of the meaning of human rights and the 'customary' forms of local justice are dynamic phenomena. It is as Kinley (2012: 57) wrote: '[T]he most serious road block to reconciling customary law … and human rights law lies in viewing each as monolithic and unbending.' But 'both are evolving and both impact on each other'. The latter point refers once more to the very important notion of interlegality.[41] As I said, interlegality is purely a matter of an empirical social process of mutual learning and one has to see whether this happens at all. However, interlegality can probably be promoted by deliberately engaging in an intercultural dialogue. Obviously, this dynamism is influenced by a host of contextual and local circumstances, as well as by elements such as poverty, lack of resources, abysmal differences in power between the local and national strata of a society, etc.

Harper (2011a) provides us with many good examples of these contextual elements that I have not and could not address here. She analyses the situation in post-war East Timor, where a sophisticated, Western-style legal order was introduced, and concludes: 'This society did not have the human resources or institutional capacity to operate a sophisticated legal system and resisted the introduction of unfamiliar concepts such as the rule of law and human rights' (2011a: 124–25). It is a matter for practitioners to 'find an appropriate balance between minimum standards, tolerance of cultural

---

[41] This process of giving and taking has manifested itself clearly in a Colombian Paez (Nasa) *resguardo* where the highest authorities of the territory punished local village authorities for only very lightly sanctioning someone who had killed a person suspected of being a witch. The highest authorities said and wrote down in a written sentence: it is unacceptable that a village community approves of the killing of a village member only on the argument that that person is a witch, this is violating his right to life and thereby violating human rights (1999). Human rights are here taken up (partially) as part of the local legal order of the Paeces. See Sanchez (2000).

difference and socio-economic realities' (ibid). Development programmes that call for local law to be generously respected, and at the same time urge local law to be compatible with internationally accepted justice standards and human rights, are not only the fruit of arrogance but also of ignorance and even cultural imperialism.

Through the empirical cases I presented, it transpires that after having obtained some form of recognition for their local authorities and ways of administering justice—formal legal pluralism—a new struggle starts for the communities involved, a struggle to obtain a genuine form and space for exercising (semi)autonomy in important matters. Moreover, the often very restrictive conflict rules sometimes make the scheme a sham from the beginning or at very least pose severe problems that need to be overcome within the communities. Nevertheless, opportunities are sometimes seized in some places, and new, more respectful relations between these communities and the dominant state are starting to grow. The challenge of legal pluralism for human rights is sometimes taken seriously.

6

Indigenous Justice and the Right to a Fair Trial

GISELLE CORRADI

1. INTRODUCTION

WHEN A STATE endorses legal pluralism and gives official status to more than one legal order, it is often confronted with the task of guaranteeing that all these legal orders comply with human rights. This is frequently the case in postcolonial settings, where next to the legal institutions inherited from former colonial powers, indigenous or customary legal orders are also part of the state architecture for justice provision. As with all legal orders, indigenous law may advance human rights in certain areas, but undermine them in others. At the same time, these legal orders are embedded in historical, cultural and socioeconomic contexts that differ in several respects from those that gave rise to human rights law. For these reasons, evaluating whether indigenous law complies with human rights standards and taking measures for the protection of human rights in legally plural jurisdictions are not straightforward tasks. One issue that has been identified as crucial in this respect is the way in which human rights are interpreted and whether such interpretation adopts a cross-cultural approach (An Na'Im 1992; Eberhard 2002; Sousa Santos 2002). This is one of the legacies of the well-known 'universality debate', which, amongst others, showed that human rights need to be understood in flexible ways in order to respond to diverse realities and be seen as legitimate across different contexts (Brems 2001; Donelly 2007, 1984). In addition, comparative legal scholars have demonstrated that indigenous and customary legal orders do not operate in the same way as the civil and common law traditions that lie at the basis of many state legal orders (Glenn 2000). In other words, one needs to take legal diversity into account. Therefore, assessing the relationship between indigenous legal orders and human rights requires understanding the context in which these legal orders operate as well as their logic, ie their underlying rationales, values, principles and ways of reasoning, which inform particular norms and practices (An-Na'Im 1992; Sanchez Botero 2004).

This chapter examines how this applies to the right to a fair trial. Previous cross-cultural studies on the right to a fair trial remark this right has been generally understood in a monocultural way, by implicit reference to legal orders of Western origin (D'Engelbronner-Kolff 2001; Padilla Rubiano 2012; Sanchez Botero 2004). The case law of the Constitutional Court of Colombia can be said to constitute an exception. In determining whether the right to professional legal counsel applies to indigenous justice, the Court highlighted that this form of representation is alien to indigenous practices, and that in a plural society, respect for cultural diversity entails no such imposition.[1] The Court maintained that:

> [Indigenous] judgments should be carried out in conformity with the norms and procedures of indigenous communities, taking into account the specificities of each sociopolitical form of organisation, as well as the characteristics of its legal order.[2]

According to the Court, '[W]hat is required is the fulfilment of those steps that the accused can foresee, and respect for those traditional practices that serve as the basis for social cohesion.'[3] However, the Court provides no guidance on how to evaluate the extent to which indigenous norms and procedures are compatible with fair-trial guarantees. In that regard, some authors argue that a few elements of this right ought to be respected by all legal orders, such as the possibility to defend oneself, the presumption of innocence, the impartiality of the judge, the legitimacy of the procedures and the possibility to appeal (Padilla Rubiano 2012: 92).

Based on a case study conducted in the Aymara indigenous municipality Curahuara de Carangas, in the Bolivian highlands, this chapter identifies a number of elements of the right to a fair trial that raise questions of interpretation when applied to disputing institutions such as those operating in this locality.[4] The chapter is divided into three sections. Following this introduction, the second section presents the backdrop of the case study. It

---

[1] Constitutional Court of Colombia, sentence T523 of 1997
[2] ibid, introductory paragraph (my translation from Spanish).
[3] ibid.
[4] This case study is based on fieldwork carried out in Bolivia in October 2012 and January–March 2013. In Curahuara de Carangas, 41 semi-structured interviews were conducted with indigenous leaders, state justice providers, religious leaders, social workers and litigants. These interviews focused on the procedures followed within indigenous justice forums, the relationship between these and other justice providers available in this town, and how such forms of articulation worked in practice in a number of cases. Four focus group discussions were organised (one with female litigants, two with youngsters aged between 15 and 16, and one with current indigenous authorities) about local perceptions of the different dispute-processing mechanisms available in Curahuara de Carangas. This was complemented by observations at two monthly meetings between indigenous and municipal authorities, and a desk-based literature review on Andean culture, indigenous justice and legal pluralism in Bolivia. In addition, 27 semi-structured interviews were conducted in La Paz and Sucre with representatives from the government, civil society organisations, international organisations and local experts. These interviews dealt with the national legal framework regulating legal pluralism and indigenous

discusses the main characteristics of the justice landscapes in which disputes are handled in Bolivia, including the accessibility of state and indigenous disputing forums and the relationship between these legal orders in law and practice. The third section zooms in on the case study. First, it describes the main features of the indigenous disputing institutions operating in Curahuara de Carangas. And second, it scrutinises the relationship between fair-trial standards and the procedures followed by these disputing forums. Finally, the conclusion reflects on how areas of tension between the former and the latter may be addressed.

2. THE JUSTICE LANDSCAPES OF BOLIVIA

Bolivia constitutes an interesting context in which to examine the relationship between human rights, indigenous law and legal pluralism for several reasons. First, indigenous legal orders play a significant role in regulating social relations within indigenous groups, which constitute the majority of the population (Ministerio de Justicia y Derechos Humanos de Bolivia 1999; Red Participacion y Justicia 2010; Santos Sousa and Exeni Rodriguez 2012).[5] Since the first colonial encounters about five hundred years ago and until recently, these groups and their institutions have been treated as inferior by colonial and postcolonial legal and political regimes, although the models that sustained this repression have changed over time.[6] Despite these policies, indigenous legal orders continued to operate at grass-roots

justice in Bolivia, as well as the controversies that surround it and how these issues relate to human rights. Insights on these topics were also gathered by participating in a three-day panel at the Congress of the Latin American Network of Legal Anthropologists in Sucre from 24 to 26 October 2012, which counted an overwhelming presence of indigenous leaders who presented and debated their views on the subject.

[5] According to the national census of 2001, 62% of the population self-identified as indigenous, whereas the census of 2012 shows a lower percentage of 41%. According to both censuses, the biggest ethnic groups are the Aymara and the Quechua, which together represent about 90% of the indigenous populations of Bolivia, living mainly in the highlands and the valleys. The remaining 34 indigenous groups inhabit the Bolivian lowlands.

[6] Under Spanish colonial rule, a segregationist model was instituted in which 'peninsulars' and 'Indians' were governed by differentiated legal regimes. This allowed indigenous authorities to administer justice amongst indigenous populations according to their practices and customs, but only in minor cases, while serious cases had to be handled by the Spanish authorities. Upon independence at the beginning of the nineteenth century, *criollo* elites, following 'civilising' discourses and the theory of legal monism, embraced an assimilationist model in which the entire population was subjected to a single body of law, the administration of which was the exclusive faculty of the judiciaries of the newly constituted states. By the mid twentieth century, concerns over the widespread poverty and marginalisation of indigenous populations led to the introduction of an integrationist model, in which indigenous institutions would be protected as long as these populations were not fully integrated into the life of the nation. This model, which framed the 'Indian problem' in terms of class, saw indigenous culture as temporary and bound to disappear as socioeconomic measures would integrate these sectors of the population into modern life (Yrigoyen 2002).

level, often in a clandestine way, perpetuating a situation of unofficial legal pluralism. This can be partly explained by the legitimacy of these institutions, and partly by the minimal presence of the judiciary throughout the national territory (Albo 2012; Yrigoyen 2002).

The forms of justice practised by these groups today vary, as has the way in which these practices evolved throughout history in response to contact with colonial and postcolonial state law (Albo 2012; Cottyn 2014). In most regions, they constitute the most accessible form of justice for indigenous populations, particularly in rural areas (IACHR 2007; IIDH 2006; Red Participacion y Justicia 2010). 'Ordinary justice', as state justice is called in Bolivia, presents serious problems in terms of physical access, capacity and credibility due to the small budget allocated to the judicial branch (ibid). According to existing studies, state justice covers only 42% of the territory and is unevenly distributed, extending mainly to urban areas, ie the capital cities of each department (Red Participacion y Justicia 2010).[7] In addition, it cannot muster sufficient personnel to meet the needs of the population, which translates into serious case backlogs. Moreover, state justice has the reputation of being corrupt and discriminatory towards indigenous peoples (ibid). By contrast, indigenous legal orders operate at the most local levels of social organisation and involve extensive community participation (Fernandez Osco 2000; Ministerio de Justicia y Derechos Humanos de Bolivia 1999; Santos Sousa and Exeni Rodriguez 2012). At the same time, these legal orders present their own challenges. For example, their efficacy diminishes in the case of disputes that reach beyond the level of the community (Albo 2012). From a human rights perspective, these challenges also include reports that in some cases corporal punishments may be administered, the fact that women are often discriminated against, and the existence of procedures that contravene fair trial guarantees (Coordinadora de la Mujer 2009; Ministerio de Justicia y Derechos Humanos 1999).

A second reason why Bolivia constitutes an interesting setting for the purposes of this study is that in recent years the country underwent a remarkable shift in its policies towards indigenous legal orders. The history of denial, exploitation, discrimination and exclusion that until recently characterised state–indigenous relationships generated profound distrust of the state among indigenous peoples, as well as demands for inclusion (Goodale 2009). During the last decade of the twentieth century a number of factors converged, such as a return to democracy, the crisis in the legitimacy of state institutions, the organised mobilisation of indigenous peoples, and the development of international law and jurisprudence framing indigenous demands in terms of human rights. This led to the adoption of constitutional reforms throughout the region that recognised the multicultural composition

[7] The territory of Bolivia is divided into nine departments, which are further subdivided into provinces and municipalities.

of society, and, to varying degrees, indigenous law and legal pluralism (Sieder 2002; Van Cott 2002; Yrigoyen 2002). In the case of Bolivia, these transformations first crystallised in the Constitution of 1994, which recognised the right to apply customary law in indigenous communities as an alternative form of justice, subject to the Constitution and the laws of the state (Article 171). But it was only with the adoption of the Constitution of 2009 that indigenous justice and legal pluralism were granted a more solid status. Bolivia's current constitutional recognition of indigenous legal orders is actually among the few in the world to reflect the standards that international human rights law establishes with regard to this matter.[8] The Bolivian Constitution grants indigenous communities the right to administer indigenous law according to their 'cosmovision' (Political Constitution of the Bolivian State 2009, Article 30(14)), while it stipulates that state and indigenous law have the same hierarchy, and that both legal orders are expected to comply with human rights (Political Constitution of the Bolivian State 2009, Article 179).

This new framework for the relationship between state and indigenous law generates unprecedented opportunities for indigenous communities to engage in processes of empowerment and reinvention. At the same time, it offers state and indigenous justice providers the possibility to see each other as peers, which could allow collaborative relationships to flourish. But this is far from automatic. According to Red Participacion y Justicia: 'At present, the coordination and cooperation between ordinary and indigenous justice is generally inexistent' (Red Participacion y Justicia 2010: 68). Moreover, Law 073 on Jurisdictional Delimitation, which was adopted in 2010 in order to regulate the coexistence of state and indigenous legal orders, poses far-reaching limits on the competence of indigenous disputing forums.[9] Some of the issues that are excluded from their material jurisdiction, such as agrarian and forest law, rape, homicide and assassination, and violations of the integrity of children and adolescents, have often been dealt with by indigenous communities.[10] As this chapter argues, instead of imposing these top-down limits, which in practice are rarely enforced, it is the construction of horizontal relationships of trust between state and indigenous justice providers that is needed for the protection of human rights. Collaboration between these actors, particularly at local levels, is key in the emergence of

---

[8] Arts 27, 34 and 40 UN Declaration on the Rights of Indigenous Peoples (UNDRIP), and Arts 8(2) and 9(1) the ILO Convention 169. Bolivia ratified ILO Convention 169 in 1991 by Law 1257 and incorporated the UNDRIP into national law on 7 November 2007.

[9] The following issues fall outside the scope of indigenous justice: homicide or assassination, rape, violations of the integrity of children and adolescents, crimes against humanity, the trafficking of human beings, arms or drugs, terrorism, corruption, trade and tariff law, crimes affecting the security of the state, issues related to forest and agrarian law, labour, social security, tax, information, mining, hydrocarbons, and civil law issues in which the state is a party to the conflict (Law 073 Art 10 [II]).

[10] See Barrera (2011) for a detailed discussion of Law 073.

cross-cultural ways of interpreting human rights and enhancing their implementation at the grass roots.

3. THE CASE STUDY: CURAHUARA DE CARANGAS

Curahuara de Carangas is an indigenous rural municipality at the north-west of the Oruro department, in the Bolivian highlands.[11] Its territory coincides with the Aymara territorial and sociopolitical unit of organisation, the Kurawara Marka, which groups fourteen *ayllus*.[12] There are a number of roads one may take to arrive in Curahuara, but when coming from Oruro, the nearest important city, it takes a trip of 4–6 hours (depending on the means of transport) on a zigzagging route across the seemingly desolate Andean high plateau, at about 4000 meters above sea level. But despite its remoteness, Curahuara is not isolated. Of its 6,000 inhabitants, only a minority reside in town permanently.[13] Most Curahuareños spend their life between the town and their fields, where they herd camelids and sheep, in combination with cultivating subsistence crops. The low profits generated by these activities encourage most Curahuareños to migrate temporarily to nearby regions, where they engage in seasonal work or commercial activities.[14] Lately, permanent migration to urban centres has been on the increase as a result of increasing poverty, although in many cases Curahuareños keep their communal ties and rights to land by returning temporarily to take on the role of a *cargo* and/or take part in the annual festivities (Municipal Government/Council of Indigenous Authorities 2007).[15]

---

[11] Whites and *mestizos* are rare in Curahuara de Carangas because the region was never found economically attractive by these groups since there are no *haciendas* nor mining activities in this area.

[12] Aymara is the dominating ethnolinguistic group of the Bolivian Highlands. Its sociopolitical and territorial organisation rests on various layers of authority and group formation, which are linked to the control of land. The *ayllu* groups a number of families and constitutes the basic unit of institutionalised community ties linked to a communal territory. This territory may be discontinuous and divided into different zones that are complementary in terms of ecological resources, including communal land that is allocated to a family (*sayaña*), and areas that are for the common use of a group of families (*saraqa*). A number of *ayllus* form a *marka*, which is the space of encounter at the village level. A *marka* is divided into two complementary moieties *aransaya* and *urinsaya*. In the case of the Kurawara Marka, there are seven *ayllus* in each of these moieties, totalling 14. A number of *markas* in turn form a *suyu*. The Kurawara Marka belongs to the *suyu* Jach'a Carangas, which groups 12 *markas*.

[13] About 10% of the population according to the Plan de Desarrollo Municipal Originario 2007–2011 (Municipal Government/Council of Indigenous Authorities 2007).

[14] Around 95% of the population of Curahuara live in poverty (Municipal Government and Council of Indigenous Authorities of Curahuara 2007).

[15] The term *cargo* refers to positions of leadership at the level of the *ayllu* and the *marka*. A number of interviewees reported that those community members who live in the city and return to the community for the period of one year to perform a *cargo* often have difficulties in administering indigenous justice, as they are less acquainted with the norms and practices of the community.

This inner and outer mobility enable the reproduction of Aymara institutions, while at the same time allowing for contact with state structures and the wider society.[16] The latter is also facilitated by the presence of a number of institutions representing the state at the local level. The town has three schools, a health post, the office of the mayor, a civil registry, a court of first instance, an environmental court, a police post, a military post and a local representation of the Ombudsman. In addition, there are two evangelical churches and a Catholic one. Moreover, Curahuara de Carangas has been awarded the title of 'exemplary municipality' due to the high levels of articulation between state and indigenous authorities (Municipal Government 2009).[17] As such, it constitutes an interesting site to study the relationship between different normative regimes.

The remainder of this chapter focuses on these relationships from two angles. First, it describes the procedures of indigenous disputing institutions in this locality and analyses how they relate to fair-trial standards, while reflecting on aspects of this right that raise questions of interpretation in relation to these institutions. And second, it explores how different forms of interaction between state and indigenous justice providers may open and close spaces in which tension between human rights and indigenous law may be addressed in a cross-cultural manner.

3.1. Indigenous Disputing Institutions in Curahuara de Carangas

The most common types of dispute handled by indigenous justice in Curahuara de Carangas are conflicts over the delimitation of land plots, the trespassing of animals from one plot to another causing crop damage, theft, intra-familial and marital conflicts, and fights among community members, which may include physical and domestic violence.[18] Although there is some variation in the practices followed by the different *ayllus* of the Kurawara

---

[16] According to Rodas Arano (2013: 60), such internal and external forms of mobility have been part and parcel of 'Curahuaran culture' for centuries. This is rooted in herding practices, which require and lead to mobility. However, such practices are currently under transformation with the introduction of development projects that aim at increasing the productivity of herding activities by introducing fences. This author argues that fences reduce mobility and change the perception of camelids and the territory (ibid). At another level, the capacity of the Curahuareños to reproduce elements of Aymara culture while participating in the broader society is quite visible in language: Aymara is the first language, followed by Spanish, with 80% of the population being bilingual (Municipal Government and Council of Indigenous Authorities of Curahuara 2007). Some indigenous leaders also reported that they had held positions of authority in state structures, eg as mayor, or responsible for the civil registry.

[17] Indigenous and municipal authorities meet twice a month on Sunday to explain and discuss issues affecting Curahuara de Carangas in an open forum where everybody can participate. Moreover, the office of the mayor and that of indigenous authorities are housed in the same building.

[18] Rape was also mentioned as an offence that may be solved by indigenous authorities, although many interviewees explained that these cases are often transferred to the police.

Marka, the following elements can be said to constitute a common core of the dispute process.[19]

In general, the aggrieved party presents her complaint to the authorities of the *ayllu*, although in the case of marital conflicts, the relatives and *padrinos* of the couple tend to be approached first.[20] An *ayllu* may be divided into several zones and the aggrieved party normally brings the case first to the authority of her zone, the *sullka*. However, in some cases, she may approach directly the main authority of the *ayllu*, the *awatiri*.[21] There are no strict rules concerning this and the procedures followed at both levels are basically the same, but even if the parties first tried to solve the case with the *sullka* without success, the case can still be transferred to the *awatiri*.[22]

These positions of communal leadership are characterised by a number of principles, such as *chacha warmi*, service to the community, *thaki*, rotation and consensus, which influence the way in which indigenous authorities exercise jurisdictional functions (Flores Condori 2012: 39). *Chacha warmi* refers to the man–woman complementarity that exists in a couple, and in general, it is married couples that are elected to perform a position of leadership together.[23] Appointment to such positions is considered a duty and a service to the community, which is related to the concept of *thaki* or 'movement along a path' (Canessa 2012). Every adult member of the *ayllu* is expected to follow this path, in which life experience, knowledge and maturity are accumulated, eg as *sullka*, later as *awatiri* and eventually as

---

[19] It was beyond the scope of the fieldwork to gather detailed primary data on the extent to which 'an Andean cosmology' informs different elements of these disputing practices. There is ample evidence in anthropological sources that several aspects of indigenous life in this region are underpinned by relationships of reciprocity with different forces of the cosmos. For example, Canessa explains that the relationship between *jaqis* (indigenous people in Aymara) and the surrounding environment should be understood in terms of intimacy with an animated landscape (Cansessa 2012: 162). At the level of law and justice, Fernandez Osco argues that according to Aymara normativity, human actions have repercussions beyond the human world. For example, abortion is sanctioned because it affects the agricultural cycle (Fernandez Osco 2000, 2009). Although I did not come across such statements in Curahuara de Carangas, interviewees did emphasise the importance of symbolic rituals that accompany dispute-processing practices, reflecting the interconnection among community members and the *pachamama* (earth goddess).

[20] The *padrinos* are the godparents of a couple, who are expected to give guidance and council, particularly at difficult times.

[21] The term *awatiri* can be translated as 'shepherd', and in fact, the *awatiri* is expected to perform the function of guiding the members of the *ayllu* as a shepherd would guide his sheep, or as an 'eldest brother' who takes care of the wellbeing of the community. The terms *tamani* and *jillakata* are also used to refer to this position. The terms *sullka awatiri* and *sullka tamani* could be translated as 'young brother'. In practice, the *sullka* acts as an assistant of the *awatiri* in a certain zone of the *ayllu*, but has no political authority.

[22] In general, if the *sullka* has a stake in the conflict, or if the parties simply do not consider him fit to deal with it, a case will be brought directly to the *awatiri*.

[23] Although in some circumstances, a non-married person may be chosen too. In addition, the role of men and women is not equal. The latter rarely take a leading role in public decision making (Flores Condori 2012; Gadea 2010)

mallku.[24] As a result, authority is rotational, implying high levels of downwards accountability. On their first day as authorities on 1 January, the *awatiris* and the *sullkas* are expected to visit each family and get acquainted with the 'state' of their *ayllu*, which they will lead for one year. In the case of the *awatiris*, their responsibilities entail both judicial and political functions, such as chairing *ayllu* assemblies, coordinating (and often sponsoring) the organisation of yearly rituals and festivities, the governance of land and other community resources, as well as the settlement of disputes. The decision-making processes involved in these activities are characterised by dialogue and seeking consensus. Authorities are elected democratically by the members of the *ayllu*, and are expected to capture and give expression to the common will.[25]

After receiving a complaint, the *awatiri* or the *sullka* fix a date on which both parties can attend a 'hearing'.[26] The aim of such hearings is to arrive at a decision that both sides find acceptable, even if only temporarily, so that they can continue to live side by side, avoiding the disruption of community activities. It is the responsibility of the *awatiri* or the *sullka* to understand the origins of the conflict, in order to be able to facilitate a consensual agreement. Moreover, if one or both parties are found to be 'at fault', the *sullka* or the *awatiri* need to make the person(s) understand what was wrong and why, regret it and apologise. In other words, indigenous authorities are expected to correct bad behaviour. This may extend beyond the individual who committed the fault. For example, the blame may also fall upon relatives who failed to guide a person into following the right conduct. The body of norms that influence such appraisals is oral and of general knowledge amongst community members, although these norms may be contested at some point.[27]

A typical hearing starts with a series of rituals that symbolise the interconnectedness among community members and the *pachamama* (earth goddess), such as sharing coca leaves and a drink (often alcohol), and rituals of libation called *ch'allas*. After reminding the parties that they should speak the truth since they are in front of holy symbols, the authorities listen to both sides.[28] The parties are normally accompanied by witnesses, who present

---

[24] The *mallkus* are the indigenous authorities at the level of the *marka*.

[25] Although there is a certain flexibility, typical requirements to become an authority are to be married, to work the land and make contributions to the *ayllu*, to have had fulfilled other positions of authority, to have reached a certain age (which varies depending on the function), and to reside in the community for the duration of the function.

[26] The Spanish word used by the interviewees was *audiencia*, which is the same word used by state justice to refer to a hearing. If one of the parties is not present, the hearing is postponed.

[27] For example, the relatively recent introduction of fences in the context of herding activities has led to disputes in which indigenous practices regarding communal uses of land are questioned (Rodas Arano 2013).

[28] The *awatiris* officiate their hearings in front of the the the 'Re-Patron and the Re-Maria', whereas the *mallkus* do it in front of the *Santa Wara*, a stick symbolizing ruling power.

their testimonies too. On this basis, the authority makes an analysis of the case and proposes how it should be settled. This leads to further discussions, after which an agreement may be finally negotiated. A sanction or compensation may be in order when the damage caused is considered significant, or in cases of recidivism. The authority may simply call the attention of the person in fault, should he consider that this suffices to correct the deviant behaviour. In most cases, sanctions and forms of compensation entail manual work (for the community or the aggrieved party) such as making a certain number of adobe bricks, the restitution of stolen goods and/or the payment of a fine.[29] This is negotiated case by case, based on the discretion of the authority about what is appropriate, and what is acceptable to the parties involved. Agreements are sealed by sharing a drink, which symbolises the re-establishment of normal relationships. In some cases, the agreement is written down in a document called an *acta*, although not all authorities follow this practice consistently.[30] In principle, compliance with these decisions relies on the voluntary will of the parties. But otherwise, social pressure may serve as a form of coercion, particularly when corporate interests are at stake.

If the authorities consider that the evidence presented at a hearing is not sufficient to understand the facts of a case, they undertake an investigation, for example, by visiting the disputed terrain or the place in which a robbery took place, following footsteps, interrogating other witnesses or looking for documents. When no material forms of proof are available, a *juramento* may be taken, ie swearing about one's innocence in front of a holy symbol. If the person who swears is lying, it is believed that she/he or his/her family will undergo a calamity, and even death.[31] As a result, depending on the circumstances, handling a case may involve several steps and hearings. Moreover, some cases may be transferred to a state instance, either as a form of appeal by an unsatisfied party, or as a form of referral when indigenous authorities consider that it is beyond the capacity of indigenous institutions to deal with a certain case. Nevertheless, the timeframe in which disputes are handled by indigenous justice tends to be relatively short, as it is considered important to avoid the escalation of conflicts.

[29] According to Gadea, imprisonment in the local cell for a couple of days is a common form of punishment in cases involving physical violence, including domestic violence (Gadea 2010: 72).

[30] Several interviewees reported that *actas* serve as a means of proof of what was agreed in case the conflict should resurface in the future. Contrary to the practice of state courts, these documents were not reported to function as a precedent of how certain types of case should be dealt with.

[31] None of the interviewees reported the use of supernatural forms of proof at these hearings, such as the reading of coca leaves. Legal anthropologists working in other Aymara regions found this practice to be quite frequent (Fernandez 2000). A few interviewees mentioned this practice in the context of health-related issues for which a traditional doctor is consulted in order to determine the origin of a disease, although it cannot be excluded that this may be associated to witchcraft accusations leading to disputes.

Certain conflicts may require the involvement of other levels of indigenous authority. For example, cases that involve several families or that
are considered to affect the entire community are brought for discussion
at the general assembly of the *ayllu*. This consists of a monthly meeting, in
which community members discuss the issues affecting the *ayllu*, although
in urgent situations an ad hoc assembly may be summoned too.[32] In these
meetings, the testimonies of the parties and witnesses, as well as any element
of proof that is available, are considered by the assembly, after which an
open debate is facilitated by the *awatiri*. Taken on the basis of consensus,
the decisions of the assembly are mandatory. If an assembly comes to the
conclusion that there is no way to correct someone's bad behaviour, and
hence, that the restoration of normal relationships is impossible, a person
may be sanctioned by banishment from the community. This goes hand in
hand with the loss of communal land rights. The decisions of the assembly
are enforced by means of social pressure, which may turn into physical violence in case of non-compliance. The accused may contest such decisions,
either by involving higher levels of indigenous authority, or by recourse
to state authorities. Nevertheless, in general, he/she and often also other
members of the family have no choice but to leave the *ayllu* for reasons of
personal safety. Meanwhile, they may stay at their residence in the village,
and so remain within the *marka*, the socioterritorial unit comprising the
fourteen *ayllus* of Kurawara.

Conflicts that involve more than one *ayllu* are handled by the *mallkus*, the
indigenous authorities at the level of the *marka*. The procedures followed
by the *mallkus* are basically the same as those followed by the *ayllu* authorities. The *marka* has two *mallkus*, the *mallku de marka* and the *mallku de
consejo*, representing the two moieties of the *marka*, *aransaya* and *urinsaya*,
for which they alternate yearly.[33] The *mallkus* receive cases from the *ayllus* that correspond to their moieties but occasionally, the two *mallkus*
need to handle a case together, for example when it involves *ayllus* from
the two moieties. From time to time, indigenous authorities are confronted
with more 'difficult' cases that require the involvement of both *mallkus* and
the *awatiris*, such as illegal trafficking or the appearance of a *kharisiri*.[34]
In very exceptional circumstances, the *mallkus* may call a *cabildo*,

---

[32] It is not so much the substance of a case that determines whether it needs to be treated by
the general assembly, but a balance between the stakes of the community and the interests and
bargaining power of the parties involved. For example, an offence such as adultery may or not
be treated by the general assembly depending on these factors.

[33] The former deals with the internal affairs of the *marka*, whereas the latter is responsible
for the external relationships.

[34] *Kharisiri, kharikhari, lik'ichiri* and *khariri* are the terms used in the Andean world to refer
to a person that steals the fat of another one, causing his illness and death. A *kharisiri* can be
a man or a woman. He or she will provoke an irresistible tiredness in his victim, normally a
lonely traveller. When asleep, the *kharisiri* will use a device (which can be a syringe or a 'small
machine') to extract the fat that surrounds the right kidney of his victim, which is supposed to

ie an ad hoc meeting of the members of the *marka* to treat difficult cases in an open assembly.

The next section explores the relationship between these forums' procedures and fair-trial standards. The analysis is concerned with the normativity surrounding these procedures, rather than with these forums' actual practices. Practices may of course deviate from existing norms. As explained in the introduction to this chapter, the point made by the Constitutional Court of Colombia in its judgment 523/1997 is precisely that the practices of indigenous disputing institutions should be appraised against indigenous rather than state procedural law. The discussion is based on recurrent normative discourses collected in the course of the fieldwork about which procedures should be followed by indigenous disputing forums and why. But the normativity surrounding these procedures is not necessarily explicit, let alone written. The characterisation 'indigenous procedural norms' refers to the fact that these norms are applicable in indigenous disputing forums, without entailing that there is anything intrinsically indigenous about them. Some of these procedures may have been inspired by aspects of state procedural law. Similarly, the label 'indigenous' neither implies that the discourses collected are totally homogenous, nor that everybody in this region agrees with them. The aim of the analysis is twofold: to assess the relationship between the procedural norms at play in the indigenous disputing forums of Curahuara de Carangas and international standards, and to reflect on how the latter may need to be interpreted in the context of this examination.

3.2. Exploring the Relationship between International Fair Trial Standards and Indigenous Procedural Norms

The right to a fair trial is a composite right with several dimensions, including issues of access to justice as well as requirements imposed upon decision-making bodies and their procedures.[35] These requirements guarantee that decision-making processes resulting in a binding verdict on someone's guilt

---

be of high value for magical purposes. When the victim wakes up, he cannot remember anything but feels very weak. As time passes, he gets worse, with vomits, fever, etc, until he dies. In the past, the figure of the *kharisiri* was associated with outsiders, such as priests and foreigners, but nowadays, it can be anyone, particularly persons that do not conform to communal norms and duties (Fernandez Juares 2008; Riviere 1991).

[35] In international law, the right to a fair trial is established by Arts 14 and 15 International Covenant on Civil and Political Rights (ICCPR, 1966); Arts 6 and 7 European Convention for the Protection of Human Rights and Fundamental Freedoms (ECHR, 1950); Arts 2 and 4 Protocol 7 to the European Convention for the Protection of Human Rights and Fundamental Freedoms (Protocol 7 ECHR); Arts 8 and 9 American Convention on Human Rights (ACHR, 1969); Arts 7 and 26 African Charter on Human and Peoples' Rights (Banjul Charter, 1981); and Art 40 Convention on the Rights of the Child (1989). It is also included in Arts 10 and 11 Universal Declaration of Human Rights (UDHR, 1948) and Arts 47–50 Charter of Fundamental Rights of the European Union (2000).

and punishment or on someone's duties and entitlements are made without arbitrariness or abuses of power. In order to achieve these goals, two issues are paramount: the equality of the parties and the objectivity of the decision-maker (Shah 2010; Tapia Pinto 2008). Both elements are interlinked: the fairness of the process entails that the decision-maker is a third party, who can objectively assess and balance the arguments and stakes of two parties that stand equally before him. For this purpose, certain requisites are imposed upon the decision-maker, ie he needs to be independent, impartial and competent. Independency refers to the judge or tribunal being free from external pressures, intimidation and conflicts of interest affecting its decision-making capacities. This entails clear procedures and criteria for the appointment and removal of judges, as well as respect for the principle of separation of executive, legislative and judicial powers. Impartiality means that the judge has no personal bias or interests that may interfere with his appraisal of the case at hand (subjective impartiality). The judge or tribunal must not only be impartial, but also appear so to a reasonable observer (objective impartiality). Finally, his capacity to hear a case needs to be established in advance by law (competent judge). The requirement of equality between the disputing parties means that all individuals ought to have an equal chance to pursue their rights in court (equal access), that all parties are provided with the same opportunities to challenge all the arguments put forward by the other side (equality of arms), and that there is no differential treatment of persons during court proceedings (non-discrimination). In addition, a fair hearing presupposes real and effective access to a court, that hearings are held within a reasonable time, that applicants have a real opportunity to present their case or challenge the case against them, that judgments are (made) public, except in circumstances that justify otherwise, and that courts or tribunals provide reasons for their judgments.

Furthermore, the right to a fair trial encompasses a series of guarantees of due process applicable to criminal proceedings. These include the rights to be informed promptly and in detail of the charge, to defend oneself, and to have adequate time and facilities for the preparation of the defence, to communicate with legal counsel of one's own choice, to examine witnesses and present evidence, and to be tried in person, without undue delay, and all of this in a language understood by the defendant. The accused also has the right not to be compelled to testify against himself or plead guilty, whereas any evidence obtained by coercive means is unacceptable. He also has the right to be presumed innocent, and be declared innocent in case of insufficient proof of guilt (*in dubio pro reo*). He cannot be charged twice for the same offence (*ne bis in idem*), or held guilty on account of any act or omission which did not constitute a criminal offence at the time when it was committed (*nullem crimen, nulla poena sine lege praevia*). In a similar vein, the penalties imposed cannot be heavier than what was applicable when the offence was committed, or collective. Finally, everyone convicted of a crime has the right to appeal to a higher tribunal according to law, and be compensated in certain cases of miscarriage of justice.[36]

Bolivia has ratified a number of human rights treaties that enshrine these standards, such as the American Convention on Human Rights and the International Covenant on Civil and Political Rights. In this context, a first question is whether indigenous disputing institutions constitute 'tribunals' according to international law. A positive answer to this question has two implications. First, that they satisfy the right to access to a court, and second, that international standards of fair trial apply to them. The Human Rights Committee defines a tribunal as 'a body, regardless of its denomination, that is established by law, is independent of the executive and legislative branches of government or enjoys in specific cases judicial independence in deciding legal matters in proceedings that are judicial in nature'. The Inter-American Court endorses a functional definition of a 'tribunal' based on its capacity to make decisive rulings that affect the rights of persons.[37] The indigenous disputing forums operating in Bolivia seem to meet these requirements, although the principle of separation of powers can be said to have an external and an internal dimension. The external dimension refers to whether these institutions are independent vis-à-vis the national executive and legislative branches of government, whereas the internal dimension relates to the separation of powers within indigenous structures of governance. In the case studied here, the jurisdictional functions of indigenous authorities are separated from state branches of government, but they are part of an overarching mandate to look after the collective wellbeing of the community, including the daily management of communal affairs. This comes down to no separation from (internal) executive powers. However, this does not entail a violation of the principle of independency per se. According to the Human Rights Committee, a tribunal should be independent of the executive and legislative powers, 'or enjoy in specific cases judicial independence in deciding legal matters in proceedings that are judicial in nature'.[38] In Curahuara de Carangas, indigenous norms allow the same person to embody executive and judicial tasks. It is questionable whether this constitutes an impediment to the exercise of judicial functions in a manner that is free from external pressure and conflicts of interest. As a result, some may contest whether these institutions satisfy the right to access a court according to international law.[39]

---

[36] UN Human Rights Committee, General Comment 32 on the Right to Equality before the Courts and Tribunals and to a Fair Trial, UN Doc CCPR/C/GC/32 (2007). See also Burgorgue-Larsen et al (2011: 659), Medina (2014), Shah (2010) and Tapia Pinto (2008).

[37] See Medina (2014: 191).

[38] ibid.

[39] During the fieldwork, no complaints were registered about this feature of indigenous justice institutions.

As regards the applicability of fair-trial standards to these institutions a positive answer is in order. Although the indigenous disputing forums discussed here do not always determine the outcome of a case, they have the capacity to make decisive rulings affecting the rights of persons. As explained before, indigenous authorities are in the first place tasked with facilitating an outcome that is agreed upon by the litigants. It is when no consensus is reached and/or when there is a significant communal stake that a 'ruling' is imposed by indigenous authorities or the assembly. In any case, insofar as indigenous disputing institutions make or uphold enforceable decisions about entitlements, duties and sanctions, it is pertinent to ensure that the processes in which these decisions are made are not arbitrary or allow for abuses of power. Moreover, the Human Rights Committee, in its General Comment 32, holds that Article 14 of the ICCPR (on the right to a fair trial) applies where a state recognises courts based on customary law, which are expected to meet 'basic requirements of fair trial'.[40] Finally, the right to a fair trial is guaranteed by several articles of Bolivia's Political Constitution, which are applicable to indigenous justice.[41] That said, it is necessary to consider how the context and logic in which these disputing institutions are embedded affect the interpretation of the different elements of this right.

Fair-trial standards are crafted upon an adjudicative model of justice, in which a third party determines someone's guilt and punishment, or balances the rights and obligations of two parties in a dyadic relationship. This entails similarities, but also differences, as compared to the disputing institutions discussed here. In particular, differences in the aim of the disputing process and the role of third parties therein seem to have implications in terms of the interpretation of certain elements of this right. In Curahuara de Carangas, the aim of indigenous dispute processes is to ensure the reproduction of communal life by restoring broken relationships, which entails addressing the root causes of the conflict and correcting deviant behaviour. In certain cases, this is impossible, which results in decisions to remove the (f)actor(s) that are perceived to disrupt a certain communal order. In other words, the outcome of these processes is considered to affect not only the litigants but, explicitly or implicitly, also corporate interests. Therefore, within their jurisdictional functions, indigenous authorities are expected to protect the collective wellbeing. This is also the aim of decisions made within general assemblies.

Against this backdrop, a first aspect of the right to a fair trial that needs to be reconsidered is the requirement of impartiality of the judge. In contexts of close community ties, it seems probable that third parties intervening in

---

[40] However, the Committee does not specify what these 'basic' requirements are. General Comment on the Right to Equality before the Courts and Tribunals and to a Fair Trial, UN Doc CCPR/C/GC/32 (2007).

[41] Arts 115, 116, 117, 119, 120 and 121 Political Constitution of 2009.

a case (either the indigenous authorities or the communal assembly) have prior knowledge of the litigants and the conflict. In those cases in which the role of these actors is to mediate a solution amongst the litigants, prior knowledge may facilitate this and may not necessarily mean a breach of this standard. That said, the requirement of subjective and objective impartiality seems to be part of indigenous procedural norms in the sense that indigenous authorities are expected not to let private personal stakes or opinions favour one party over the other. As a matter of fact, when an indigenous authority is too close to either party, he is not considered the right person to handle a case, which may determine whether the *sullka* or the *awatiri* should do so. However, this aspect of the right to a fair trial is not endorsed when it is the communal assembly that decides a case. Disconformities with the performance of indigenous authorities may be the subject of discussion at communal assemblies. Therefore, even if not all disputes are (made) public, the possibility of public scrutiny is a relevant means of accountability within indigenous normativity.

Regarding the competence of the judge, the requirements that the capacity of the decision-maker to hear a case is established in advance by law, and that there are clear procedures and criteria for his appointment and removal, are also part of indigenous law. This is reflected by the existence of rules stipulating the role of different layers of indigenous authority and the communal assembly. However, it is necessary to question which law is given precedence in establishing who is a competent judge in Bolivia. State and indigenous legal orders are often at odds regarding what falls within the jurisdiction of indigenous justice. Since both legal orders may be mobilised by indigenous and non-indigenous litigants as well as indigenous and state justice providers to legitimate or undermine claims to authority, this aspect of the right to a fair trial may be quite instrumental in the contestation of power relationships between dominant and subaltern groups, but also within indigenous communities. As a result, it may be problematic to take either legal order as the point of departure for assessing compliance with this standard without understanding the interests and power dynamics at play in each particular case.

Regarding standards of equality between the disputing parties, factors such as the social capital of a litigant and gender ideologies influence to a large extent whether endorsing a certain decision is perceived to serve the collective wellbeing or not. Even if all community members are entitled to resort to an indigenous authority when they have a grievance, and have the same opportunities to present arguments and challenge those of the counterparty in a hearing, equal treatment 'in court' is influenced by the position of the litigants within a web of relationships, connected to individual and collective interests. This may result in different forms of procedural discrimination. For example, cases that are similar in substance may be appraised differently, or enjoy different levels of community support for enforcement purposes. As demonstrated by anthropological research on disputing processes, mediation and negotiation require conditions of relatively equal power between the disputing parties (Nader and Todd 1978). This is not necessarily so in all cases handled by indigenous justice, which may lead to differential treatment due to power asymmetries amongst community members. Yet considering the origins of such unequal treatment, it seems unlikely that procedural standards alone constitute an efficient remedy to counter these forms of discrimination.

With regard to guarantees of due process, several standards set by international law seem to be part of the indigenous normativity examined here. For example, the accused is informed of the charge and has the opportunity to defend himself, present witnesses and evidence. He is tried in person, without undue delay and in a language that he understands. He cannot be charged twice for the same offence, or held guilty for an act or omission which was not considered an offence when it was committed. Regarding the principle *nullum poena sine lege*, the disputing institutions discussed here endorse sanctions and forms of compensation on the basis of what is negotiated as a 'solution' in each case. Although the exact scope and form of sanction or compensation may fluctuate from case to case, these institutions seem to endorse this requirement as they resort to a range of (mostly orally defined) possible measures to deal with a certain offence. In addition, these institutions seem to be concerned with the proportionality between the severity of a sanction and a certain misconduct.[42] Finally, the accused also has the possibility to appeal, which can be done by resorting to another level of indigenous authority or to state justice. Other standards of due process seem less adapted to this context. A case in point is the right to communicate with legal counsel. Since the disputing process does not involve specialised knowledge, litigants normally have the skills to defend themselves.

Furthermore, certain guarantees of due process are endorsed by indigenous law in some cases, but not always—for instance, whether an accused should be afforded time and means to prepare his defence, or be presumed innocent. This is the case when there are mutual accusations between community members, leading to an investigation about the responsibility of each party by indigenous authorities. However, in cases in which most community members are convinced of someone's misbehaviour, these guarantees do not exist. In such cases, it is considered that giving the accused time or means to prepare his defence may be counterproductive. First, since it is deemed of utmost importance to treat such cases in an assembly as soon as possible. And second, because this would allow the defendant to think of

---

[42] Admittedly, disagreements may arise as to what is proportional since the same conduct may be valued differently throughout time. Disagreements about proportionality may also exist within and across different segments of society. The reflections presented in the conclusion would apply to such situations.

excuses, which could lead to impunity. Despite these rationales, it remains a moot point whether disregard for these guarantees opens the door for arbitrary decisions. In addition, in such cases, coercive means may be justified in order to extract a confession, and it may be considered legitimate that the sanctions imposed also affect the family of the accused, particularly in cases that are sanctioned by banishment from the community. Finally, some of the decisions made by indigenous disputing forums are based on evidence that requires bridging different ontological and epistemological frameworks—for instance, the use of *juramentos* or the imposition of sanctions related to the crimes committed by *kharisiris*. From a 'Western' perspective, reliance on these forms of proof may be considered inconclusive, leading to breaches of fair trial guarantees such as *in dubio pro reo*. These may be seen as the main areas of tension between indigenous procedural norms and fair-trial standards.

On the whole, the relationship between the normative bodies examined here is multifaceted. On the one hand, certain elements of this right seem to require a flexible interpretation. On the other hand, there are areas of overlap and of tension. So how should these gaps between indigenous law and human rights be addressed? This chapter rests on the premise that such endeavours require attention to the history of oppression of indigenous peoples. This history makes it problematic to assume that these gaps can be simply declared a violation of human rights from a Western locus of enunciation. This would amount to reproducing the power asymmetries that have characterised the relationship between dominant and subaltern forms of knowledge since the colonial encounter. Therefore, in contexts of official legal pluralism, state policies, legislation and case law need to facilitate the emergence of spaces in which various normative and epistemological frameworks can be combined to inform dialogues around these issues, leading to the interpretation and protection of human rights in an inter-legal and cross-cultural manner. It is to this point that the conclusion turns.

4. CONCLUSION

This chapter started from the concern that in contexts of official legal pluralism, such as Bolivia, human rights law imposes a duty on the state to ensure that indigenous legal orders meet international standards. This entails the delicate tasks of evaluating compliance and protecting human rights in a cross-cultural manner, while taking measures for the fulfilment of human rights by different legal orders. The material presented here illustrates the complexities involved with regard to the right to a fair trial. The analysis demonstrates that different forms of social organisation and modes of dispute-processing influence how arbitrariness and abuses of power may manifest at the procedural level, and hence, which standards may be applicable to prevent this. The case study on indigenous disputing institutions in Cura-huara de Carangas shows that factors such as the aim of the disputing process and the role of third parties therein interplay with the relevance and appropriate interpretation of certain elements of this right in different disputing contexts. At the same time, the chapter identified a few areas of overlap and of tension between indigenous and human rights law. This raised the question as to how these gaps may be addressed.

Although answering this question deserves more than the few lines available for a concluding section, two issues are key. First, the actors and registers of law that are involved, and second, the power relations in which such processes are embedded. In contexts of official legal pluralism, it seems fair to expect that states take measures to enable these areas of tension to be dealt with by means of inter-legal and cross-cultural dialogues (Inksater 2010).[43] As explained in the introduction of this edited collection, legal pluralism is conducive to 'inter-legality' (Santos 1987). Exposure to various normative repertoires, disputing institutions, authority regimes and societal models in general, contributes to the mixture and interpenetration of elements from different legal orders in people's minds and actions. This precludes an essentialist understanding of the relationship between 'a legal order' and 'a people', while it directs our attention to the processes in which contact with various normative models interplays with the development of inter-legal legal subjectivities. The spaces in which these mixed subjectivities take shape may constitute privileged sites for dialogues on human rights.

However, which measures may facilitate this? Which actors should participate and in which spaces can such dialogues take place? Although not exclusively, disputing processes open considerable opportunities for this since a multiplicity of actors may contribute by bringing up different understandings of the relationship between indigenous norms and practices and human rights in concrete situations. In such cases, areas of tension between indigenous legal orders and human rights could be addressed by 'mixed tribunals' in which authorities representing different legal orders handle cases together (Yrigoyen 1999). On the one hand, this could prevent human rights being understood according to a dominant perspective, and on the other, it could facilitate dissident voices to question indigenous norms and practices in a way that neither alienates critiques from an indigenous space, nor allows for communal silencing.

In Bolivia, the 'Plurinational Constitutional Tribunal' is supposed to represent a mixed tribunal, as it is composed by seven judges of which at least two are of indigenous origin. However, constitutional judges need to have a law degree and at least eight years of specialisation in the field of constitutional law, administrative law or human rights, while having exercised the

---

[43] Inksater (2010) uses the concept 'transformative juri-cultural pluralism' to group the dimensions 'inter-legal' and 'cross-cultural' in human rights dialogue.

function of indigenous authority is only considered as an asset (Law on the Plurinational Constitutional Tribunal, Article 17). As a result, it is debatable whether this tribunal can be seen as truly inter-legal and cross-cultural. Moreover, only a few disputes may find their way up to this level. Therefore, this chapter argues that mixed disputing forums should also be foreseen at lower jurisdictional levels, and in particular at the grass roots, where more communal involvement is possible. Such collaborative spaces of joint action need not be permanent, but could be activated when there is a need for it—for example, whenever a litigant claims that indigenous justice does not respect his or her human rights, or when there is a claim that state justice is not responsive to the understanding that an indigenous community has of a certain case in which human rights are at stake. At present, Law 073 on Jurisdictional Delimitation only establishes that state and indigenous justice will coordinate and cooperate with each other, and lists a series of broadly defined mechanisms to this end, such as exchanging information and creating spaces for dialogue (Articles 13, 14, 15 and 16). Although this law does not prohibit spontaneous forms of collaboration between state and indigenous justice providers, its rhetoric seems to assume two separate spheres of dispute-processing, and it certainly does not require joint decision-making.

The proposal advanced here requires egalitarian relationships of trust between state and indigenous authorities. This is certainly a challenge that goes hand in hand with undoing histories of domination. While in some cases, these horizontal relationships have emerged spontaneously, due to daily contact, mutual knowledge and/or the perception that it is in the interest of both parties to collaborate, certain structural factors may undermine them. For example, legislation and case law that limit the jurisdiction of indigenous justice unilaterally and against the practices of indigenous communities, while rendering them vulnerable to criminalisation, are likely to form a significant constraint. It is undeniable that constitutional provisions that recognise state and indigenous law on equal footing represent powerful tools to challenge such persistent asymmetries. At the same time, they open windows of opportunity for the materialisation of intra-community and cross-cultural dialogues on human rights, both in disputing and in non-disputing situations. But despite these advances, more sustained institutional and personal efforts will be necessary in order to alter deeply rooted patterns of sub-alternisation.

Part Two

Empirical Approaches

7

Gender, Human Rights and Legal Pluralities in Southern Africa: A Matter of Context and Power

ANNE HELLUM AND ROSALIE KATSANDE

1. INTRODUCTION

T
HE UNMAKING OF gender inequalities embedded in the dual
legal systems put in place at various times during the colonial era is
a major challenge for postcolonial African states, African women's
rights organisations and international human rights agencies.[1] In southern
Africa, which is the location of this article, customary laws carried over
from the colonial era often take precedence over the equality principle in
areas of personal law concerning marriage, family affairs and inheritance.
The hierarchical relationship between the right to equality and the right to
culture and custom has to a large extent trapped women within the colonial legal constructions of unequal gender relations. Many African governments have in recent years ratified international and regional instruments
that embody the right to gender equality. Countries such as South Africa,
Kenya and Zimbabwe have enacted new constitutions that put the principle
of gender equality on an equal footing with the right to custom and culture.[2]

---

[1] A characteristic feature of the legal systems that were put in place during colonial rule in
southern Africa is their dual character. One system of law, imported European law, applied to
the settlers, while the customary laws of the different ethnic groups applied to the native population. In Africa 'customary law' was reshaped by the colonial administration and the colonial
courts (Woodman 1988). Historical studies show how 'customary law' was reinvented through
complex struggles involving Western colonisers, African tribal authorities appointed by the
colonial administration and African women, resulting in a form of law that was neither African
nor Western (Chanock 1985). Studies from Zimbabwe demonstrate how the alliance between
male elders and colonial elders resulted in patriarchal family and marriage norms (Mittlebeeler
1976: 122–35; Hellum 1999: 376–8).
[2] Constitution of South Africa 1996, Constitution of Kenya 2010, Constitution of
Zimbabwe 2013.

The increasing number of court cases challenging unequal citizenship, family and property rights show how individual women and women's organisations are using the right to equality and non-discrimination to pursue their claims through national courts.[3] The political claims of African women, often supported by women's rights activists, have in many instances yielded constitutional, legislative or judicial interventions modifying discriminatory state laws and the formal customary laws that were developed in the colonial era. While such law reform and litigation strategies mirror the growing quest for legal change, other types of interventions are also needed to ensure broad-based realisation of the right to equality at grassroots level. For the expanding equal rights framework, which is embedded in both international law and state law, is often not translated into attainable entitlements for different groups of women.

Cognisant of the apparent failure to deliver the projected human rights benefits and protections to vulnerable groups and women within them, southern African sociolegal scholarship points to the need to analyse the complex legal situations that arise from the coexistence and interaction between international law, state law, and social and religious norms. On the basis of social actors' experiences and perceptions, this body of literature explores how gender relations are shaped and reshaped in a plural, unsettled and contested terrain where human rights, state law, customary law and local norms coexist and interact in the same social field (Bentzon et al. 1998; Claasen and Cousins 2008; Corradi 2012; Derman et al 2013; Hellum 1999; Hellum et al 2007; Griffiths 1997; Ikdahl 2013; Katsande 2014; Sieder and McNeish 2013; Tsanga 2003).

Realising that formal state justice is not readily accessible for vulnerable individuals, international and national development actors operating in the Global South are today considering how informal, non-state, customary or religious justice forums can contribute to enhance access to justice (CLEP 2008; Danida 2010; ICHRP 2009; UN Women 2011; World Bank 2003). International political and economic agencies such as CLEP and the World Bank have in recent years called for liberalisation of the justice sector and

---

[3] In *Attorney-General v Dow* [1992] BLR 119 (CA) 168 a citizen of Botswana challenged the constitutionality of sections of the Botswana Citizenship Act on the basis that the sections were discriminatory and unconstitutional because they denied Batswana women married to foreign men the right to pass citizenship on to their children. *Bhe v Magistrate, Khayelitsha & Others* 2005 1 SA 580 (CC) centred on the constitutional validity of the principle of primogeniture in the context of the customary law of succession. In *Shilubana and others v Nwamitwa* 2008 (9) BCLR 914 (cc) the Constitutional Court argued that customary law, just like the common law, is adaptive by its very nature and that courts should recognise changes in customary law, especially where such changes bring the customary law in line with the values and spirit of the Constitution. In Zimbabwe the courts are leaning more towards a 50:50 division of matrimonial property: see *Nezandonyi v Nezandonyi* HH-115-14, *Mavate v Chibande* HH43/2012, *Mupudzi v Mupudzi* HH24/2011, *Simango v Simango* HH 86/2010, *Matambirwa v Matambirwa* HH 151/2010, *Usayi v Usayi* 2003 (1) ZLR 684 (S)

recommended initiatives that include non-state legal services and informal justice systems (CLEP 2008). Seeing poverty and disadvantage as a result of legal exclusion, CLEP concludes that most development initiatives fail because they 'tend to focus on the official economy, the formal legal system and the national rather than the local level' (ibid: 2).

Current attempts to use informal customary and religious norms and institutions as pathways to justice face challenges of how to best support women—and men—in struggles for basic resources such as land and water. Such initiatives may on the one hand expand the spaces for the exercise of local autonomy by different social, ethnic and religious groups, but may on the other hand reinforce existing inequalities within these groups in terms of gender, status and age. Legal pluralities, as pointed out by UN Women, often constitute an obstacle for women's rights since local customary and religious forums often disregard the rights of women within the group and rely on discriminatory norms (UN Women 2011: 69).

The aim of this chapter is to explore the options and limits of justice sector initiatives that seek to enhance access to law by marrying human rights and legal pluralism from the perspective of different African women. Our starting point is that any consideration of the gendered dynamics of human rights interventions marrying human rights and legal pluralism must be located within a broader analysis of the different forms of power that influence the relationship between the plurality of norms invoked by different actors in the family, in the local community and at the level of state law. An overarching question is under what conditions are legal pluralities a factor in producing gendered forms of exclusion? And under what conditions do they constitute a resource for women to challenge their marginalisation? To come to grips with the complex and situational relationship between gender, human rights, plural legalities and power we present two longitudinal case studies that take an actor approach—one from South Africa and one from Zimbabwe. These studies provide a window into the way in which individual women, human rights and women's rights organisations and action-oriented researchers through legal advocacy, legal literacy and legal aid seek to mediate conflicts and tensions between the international principle of equality and legal pluralities as they affect women's everyday life. By situating the interaction between international, national and local norms in a changing political and economic terrain our aim is to show how insight into long-run historical processes and changing paradigms of governance affect the bargaining power of individual women and human rights organisations seeking greater gender justice.

The chapter unfolds in five parts. Section 2 sets out the framework that is used to analyse the relationship between women's human rights and legal pluralism. With an overall focus on the complex relationship between women as individual rights holders and women as part of group claims, the South African study presented in section 3 explores how the right to equality embedded in CEDAW, the South African Constitution and the Land Restitution Act has been respected, protected and promoted by the state and non-state actors involved in different phases of the land restitution process as played out in Limpopo Province (Hellum and Derman 2013; Langford et al 2013). Addressing struggles ovefr women's rights from the 1990s up to date, the Zimbabwean case presented in section 4 focuses on the work of two organisations; the Zimbabwean branch of the Women and Law in Southern Africa Research Project (WLSA) and the action-oriented research of the Southern and Eastern Regional Centre in Women's Law (SEARCWL) at the University of Zimbabwe. Showing how women's rights organisations successfully negotiated equal inheritance rights through the customary route in the 1990s, the study explores how the breakdown of the rule of law and the politicisation of customary authorities has affected the sociolegal terrain in which rural women today negotiate their property and inheritance rights (Katsande 2014; Stewart 2013; Stewart and Tsanga 2007). By way of conclusion, section 5 emphasises the fluid and unstable terrain in which legal pluralities operates. It emphasises the need for continuous research into how the relationship between statutory and customary law changes over time and how it is affected by political changes and power relations.

2. AFRICANISATION OF WOMEN'S HUMAN RIGHTS: UNSETTLED GENDER AND POWER STRUGGLES EMBEDDED IN LEGAL PLURALITIES

In sub-Saharan Africa, as elsewhere in the world, it was the UN Convention on the Elimination of All Forms of Discrimination against Women (CEDAW), with its application in both the private and the public spheres, and the globalisation of women's rights organisations, which precipitated a major shift in the priorities of governments and human rights organisations. The World Conference on Human Rights in Vienna and the Fourth World Conference on Women in Beijing facilitated global discussions about which elements of women's rights were 'Western' and which were not. Transcending national and continental histories, these World Conferences brought about new forms of cooperation and understanding. For African women's rights NGOs these global events became stepping stones from which to claim equal access to economic resources. All sub-Saharan African states, with the exception of Mauritania, accepted without reservation to:

> Undertake legislative and administrative reforms to give women full and equal access to economic resources, including the right to inheritance and to ownership of land and other property, credit, natural resources and appropriate technologies.[4]

---

[4] The Beijing Declaration and Platform for Action was the result of the Fourth World Conference on Women in 1995.

In response to the new wave of struggles for equality and human rights in twenty-first-century Africa, the African Charter was followed by the 1999 African Charter on the Rights and Welfare of the Child. Where the African Charter was weak on women's rights, these rights were formulated and included in the 2005 Protocol to the African Charter on Human and Peoples' Rights on the Rights of Women in Africa (the AfPRW). The Protocol to the African Charter on the Rights of Women (also termed Maputo Protocol) was prompted by the growing body of African women's rights NGOs emphasising that the norms, expectations and resources deriving from membership of a family, a clan, or ethnic, religious or political group often conflict with women's rights and freedoms as individual citizens (Banda 2005). In Article 2.2 the Protocol puts an obligation on states to change gender stereotypes embedded in cultural and religious beliefs:

> 2. States Parties shall commit themselves to modify the social and cultural patterns of conduct of women and men through public education, information, education and communication strategies, with a view to achieving the elimination of harmful cultural and traditional practices and all other practices which are based on the idea of the inferiority or the superiority of either of the sexes, or on stereotyped roles for women and men.

By adding a new normative layer to existing state laws, these international and regional human rights instruments have clearly opened up spaces for individual women and women's rights organisations who have the social and economic resources to contest male privileges embedded in state law and official customary law. Throughout sub-Saharan Africa discriminatory rules embedded in statutory and official customary laws are gradually changing as a result of constitutional change, law reform and judicial review (Albertyn 2007; Banda 2005). This growing body of jurisprudence speaks to the way in which the constitutionalisation of the gender equality principle embedded in international and regional human rights instruments has paved the way for legal change.

The 'weak legal pluralism' characterised by a situation where the state legal order formally recognises a plurality of legal orders is gradually disappearing. It is, however, often replaced by a 'strong' form of legal pluralism where the same social space and the same activities, in spite of an increasingly unified body of state law, are subject to a plurality of normative orders.[5] Recognising that state law is not the sole normative body at work,

---

[5] 'Plural legal systems' is a concept that refers to a situation when the official legal order (the state legal system) recognises a plurality of legal orders. The Tanzanian legal system, for example, recognises both the customary laws of different ethnic groups within the country and Islamic law (Bentzon et al 1998: 31). Unlike the centralist notion of plural legal systems, legal pluralism refers to situations which are 'characterized by the presence in one social field of more than one legal order' (Griffiths 1986). John Griffiths uses the term 'weak legal pluralism' about situations where the state legal order recognises a plurality of normative orders, and the term 'strong legal pluralism' about situations where regulatory and normative systems other than the formal state law affect and control people's lives.

we are in the case studies from Zimbabwe and South Africa presented in this chapter turning to a framework addressing situations where the same social space and the same activities are subject to more than one body of norms: legal pluralism (Griffiths 1986, 2002; Moore 1978). This legal pluralist perspective, in our view, helps analyse whether and to what extent international human rights principles are realised, or not realised, within a scenario of rights embedded in coexisting, overlapping and conflicting international, national and local norms and practices.

To defend and promote women's right to equality in a shifty and unstable plural legal terrain where international, national and local norms interact and intersect, different UN bodies have gradually started to address both the restrictive impact of custom, culture and religion on women's human rights, as well as women's agency to assert their right to culture and freedom of religion or belief in spaces where customary and religious norms are interpreted and applied. In its concluding comments to states parties, the CEDAW Committee encourages state parties to see culture as something that can be changed (Holtmaat 2011, 2013).[6] The need for a woman-focused human rights approach that moves beyond the legal text and engages with the gendered sociocultural reality on the ground has been emphasised by the Special Rapporteur on Violence against Women. Women's human rights must, in her view, be asserted in a manner that takes cognisance of the social embeddedness of women's identity. According to the Special Rapporteur: 'Where international attention and leverage are rooted in culturally-sensitive strategies and locally supported, they can give strong underpinning to our situation-specific approaches and interventions on the ground' (Coomaraswamy 2005: xiii). Seeing culture as contested and dynamic, the UN Special Rapporteur in the field of cultural rights, Fareda Shaheed, critiques a static conception of culture that in her view 'renders invisible women's agency in both reproducing and challenging dominant cultural norms and values'.[7] In her report to the UN she stresses that 'the critical issue, from the human rights perspective, is not whether and how religion, culture and tradition prevail over women's human rights, but how to arrive at a point at which women own their culture (and religion and tradition) and their human rights'. On this background she proposes to 'shift the paradigm from one that views culture merely as an obstacle to women's

---

[6] Recent research examining the concluding observations of the CEDAW Committee to state reports from different parts of the world shows that the CEDAW Committee no longer has an old vision of culture as fixed and static, but is moving towards a more modern vision of culture as a process of continually creating new meanings and practices that are products of power relationships and open to contestation among members of the group and outsiders (Holtmaat 2013). See also Merry (2011).

[7] A/67/287 para 3.

rights to one that seeks to ensure equal enjoyment of culture rights; such an approach also constitutes a critical tool for the realization of all their human rights'.[8]

Our starting point is that any consideration of the gendered dynamics of human rights interventions marrying human rights and legal pluralism must be located within a broader analysis of regimes of governance, power relations, history and political context (Hellum 2013; Sieder et al 2013). A central question is how the power structures that inform the different norms that shape unequal gender relations in the family, in the local community and at the level of state law are handled by different actors involved in mediation of conflicts and provision of legal literacy. Interrogating power is critical because power relations affect how change is brought about. Defining and analysing different power relations enables the identification of areas for advocacy, policy and law review and reform in relation to equality and inclusion.

Andreassen and Crawford have set out a model that is highly relevant to this purpose (Crawford and Andreasson 2013). They suggest that we need to understand the multidimensional nature of power and turn our attention to the fourfold typology of power, namely power to, power with, power from within and power over (ibid: 5). Power over, in line with Lukes's theory of coercive power (Lukes 2005: 16) concerns the ability of power-holders to secure the compliance of those less powerful. It includes the visible power embedded in state law, the hidden power embedded in institutions that are not formally part of government, and the invisible power embedded in social and religious norms (Lukes 1974, 2005). Visible power pertains to public decision-making processes involving the legislative, executive and judicial branches of power. Hidden power is exercised in institutions that are not part of government, ranging from transnational economic institutions to traditional and religious institutions. Invisible power is embedded in social and religious structures that uphold prevailing perceptions, stereotypes and practices related to gender, race or class. Power to, refers to the generative and productive capacity of individuals and organisations to take action, to organise and change existing hierarchies (Crawford and Andreasson 2013: 7). With reference to Gaventa's theory on how power relations are specific of time and space (Gaventa 2006: 27), they suggest we explore successful individuals' and organisations' attempts to use law to challenge power-holders in terms of 'opening closed spaces', 'claiming new spaces' or 'creating spaces' more autonomously.

In the light of this framework the case studies from Zimbabwe and South Africa demonstrate how we can explore whether, in what ways, under

---

[8] A/67/287 para 5.

what circumstances and with what result individual women and NGOs are challenging visible, hidden and invisible power embedded in different normative structures. Under what social, political and legal conditions are the power relations underlying sociolegal inequalities and legal pluralities challenged?

The South African case study focuses on women's right to equality in the land restitution process. It illustrates how strong rights-based legislation and constitution fares in the context of a shift from a social-justice-oriented land policy towards a neoliberal economic model (Hellum et al 2013). On the basis of a longitudinal study it explores how the rights-based approach takes effect and loses out, as spaces to challenge visible, invisible and hidden power open and close in the context of changing policy trajectories, particularly when it comes down to rights that challenge traditional powers' conceptions of women's rights.

Addressing women's rights struggles from the 1990s up to date, the case study from Zimbabwe describes how spaces to carry out women's rights advocacy open and close in a situation where law has become a site of broader political and economic power struggles. It shows how women's space to renegotiate customary norms in the shadow of state law has changed in the context of nationalist political authoritarian regime that, to ensure access to power and resources, has taken control of both informal and formal justice sector institutions (Katsande 2014; Stewart et al 2007, 2013). This in turn illustrates the way in which visible, invisible and hidden power intersect and interact in different historical, economic and political contexts.

3. SOUTH AFRICA: EQUAL RIGHTS MEET NEOLIBERAL MARKET ACTORS AND TRADITIONAL AUTHORITIES

The South African Constitution and the Restitution of Land Rights Act were key elements in the fulfilment of the ANC government's promise to unmake race, class and gender injustices deriving from apartheid's land laws and policies.[9] Given the centrality of the right to equality and non-discrimination, the rights-based land reform policy adopted by the ANC government held out great promise for rural women.[10] Despite changes in the visible power structure in terms of legal recognition and political representation, women faced the challenges of invisible and hidden power. Derman and Hellum's longitudinal study following the legal claims of five dispossessed communities in Levubu in the Limpopo Province from their launch in 1997 up to

---

[9] Constitution of South Africa 1996, Restitution of Land Rights Act No 22 of 1994.

[10] Department of Land Affairs 1997, White Paper on South African Land Policy, Pretoria, DLA; Land Reform Gender Policy, Minister of Land Affairs, 1997.

2010 shows how spaces opened and closed for NGOs setting out to ensure that individual women within the claimant communities benefited on an equal basis with men. Their examination of the disjuncture between the principle of gender equality embedded in constitutional and national law and the gendered effects of the different implementation strategies associated with changes in official policy in different phases of the land restitution process demonstrates how spaces to challenge invisible and hidden power opened and closed (Hellum et al 2013; Langford et al 2013: 133, 134, 138).

With an overall focus on the complex relationship between women as individual rights-holders and as part of group claims they have explored how the right to equality embedded in CEDAW, the South African Constitution and the Land Restitution Act has been respected, protected and promoted by the state and non-state actors involved in different phases of the land restitution process as played out in Limpopo Province. With a focus on women's right to equality, this study shows how a shift from a social justice approach to a market-based governance model set up for the restitution of communal land in South Africa affected the relationship between the government, civil society, market actors and traditional authorities. Furthermore, it uncovers how the changing relationship between government and civil society has resulted in the closure of the space that civil society has to challenge the invisible and hidden power that undermines women's rights.

The Nkuzi Development Association, an NGO that primarily works for land and livelihood of rural communities, was formed in 1997 in Limpopo. Nkuzi's work to inform rural people about their rights and ways to realise them was welcomed by the Mandela government which lacked the resources to implement the new land policies and laws. In the early phase of the land-restitution process, Nkuzi, in close cooperation with the government, set out to inform rural people who had been dispossessed of their land by the apartheid government about their right to claim restitution. In this period Nkuzi provided extensive assistance to communities which wanted to lodge restitution claims. In their work with local communities Nkuzi carefully sought to balance women's rights as group rights and women's rights as equal individuals within the group. In line with the equal rights approach in the Constitution and the Land Restitution Act, efforts were made to mobilise women within the dispossessed communities. The Land Claim Lodgment Manual that was worked out gave instructions to compile lists of everyone in the local community who was dispossessed: traditional leaders, elders and family members—husbands, wives, sons and daughters. This approach was met with resistance from traditional leaders who wanted to have only male heads of household listed. Nkuzi, however, made efforts to convince the claimant communities that everyone would benefit from an approach which included women. Nkuzi referred to the new South African Constitution and the Mandela administration's policy of 'equality for all'. Crucially, Nkuzi explained how important it was for the community to ensure that the claim was as inclusive and well documented as possible. The majority of the villagers who still could remember the forced removals were elderly women. Most men were absent, working in the mines or in the cities, when the forced removals took place. As a result of the combined efforts of government policies and NGO action, the *invisible power* embedded in hierarchical customary notions of gender relations and the hidden power that was exercised by the chiefs behind the scene was addressed and women attained equal membership and ownership rights in the new common property institutions. Most importantly, the constitutions of the Common Property Associations (CPAs), which were the institutions that held the restituted land on behalf of the group, required women's participation at all levels. Through courses and workshops with the claimant communities Nkuzi encouraged local communities to elect women to the CPA committees.

In the claims' settlement and post-settlement phase, which took place more than ten years later, the ANC government introduced a new land restitution model that attempted to marry a social justice and a market model. The combination of productive land, substantial export revenues, pervasive restitution claims and past economic disappointments led the ANC government, in 2005, to embrace a new model of land restitutions aimed at economic efficiency. This model, termed the 'Strategic Partner Model', entailed the claimant communities forming a joint venture company with a private entrepreneur. In order to have the land returned, claimant communities were required to run the restituted farms in cooperation with agri-business companies (Derman et al 2010). NGOs such as Nkuzi were replaced by business actors that regarded the relationships within the claimant communities as private matters. Within this neoliberal model no measures were taken to ensure gender equal participation on the board of the new venture companies or equal distribution of the income of the new business within the community. While chiefs are provided for neither in the Communal Property Act nor in the agreements constituting the new venture companies, they are in practice playing a central role determining hiring practices and distribution of eventual profits. The new business partners are, like in the colonial days, seeking the cooperation of the chiefs in order to control the members of the claimant community. In this way the neoliberal model facilitated the exercise of hidden power. In the negotiation of power and resources within the new venture companies set up to govern the management and distribution of resources on the farms taken over by the claimant communities, it became far more difficult for weakly organised groups such as women, poor community members and farm workers to mobilise support for their claims against members of the chiefs' families, businesses and state agents. Rather than changing unequal power relations within the local community, this model left unchallenged the invisible and hidden power structures underlying unequal gender relationships. The government's attempt to marry a social justice and a market model thus curtailed the ability of both state and non-state actors to deal with power structures that uphold existing gender and class hierarchies within the local community.

All in all the South African land restitution process demonstrates how human rights organisations' spaces of operation opened and then closed in the political shift from a social-justice-based to a market-based land restitution policy. While one such organisation, Nkuzi, was invited by the government to assist the claimant communities in a process aiming at democratic and equal property relations in the claim-making phase, in the post-settlement period it was replaced by business actors that regarded the relationships within the claimant communities as private matters. The disjuncture between the principles embedded in national law and actual practice on the ground speaks to a situation where insufficient attention was devoted to the hidden power exercised by traditional authorities and the invisible power embedded in the local norms guiding access to power and resources within the communities. Thus the business model set up for the governance of restituted land in South Africa, by changing the relationships between the government, civil society, market actors and traditional authorities, closed the space for addressing rural women's rights as individuals within the group.

4. ZIMBABWE: DECREASING OPTIONS OF LEGAL PLURALITIES IN A CHANGING POLITICAL, ECONOMIC AND LEGAL TERRAIN

In 1980 the new ZANU PF-led government of Zimbabwe sought to unmake the racially skewed distribution of power and resources deriving from the white minority government's persistent violation of the civil, political, social and economic rights of the black majority. Majority status was conferred on all persons regardless of sex through the Legal Age of Majority Act (LAMA 1982). At the same time, section 23 of the Lancaster House Constitution continued to legitimise sex and gender discrimination in matters regulated by customary law, and in relation to marriage, divorce, adoption, inheritance and other matters of personal law. In 1991 Zimbabwe acceded to a number of international human rights conventions including the International Covenant on Civil and Political Rights and CEDAW without incorporating these into national law. The quest for equal inheritance rights was, however, met with considerable resistance from strong nationalist political forces that saw human rights in general, and women's human rights in particular, as a Western imposition and as such a threat to national sovereignty and African cultural values. Women's rights claims in this political context were effectively undermined by the dominant legal and political discourse that associated equal inheritance rights with an attack on African custom and culture.

4.1. Handling Invisible Power through a Legal Pluralist Discourse in an Opening Political Space

In the 1990s the dominant nationalist discourse stating that women's rights claims undermined African customary norms and values was challenged by the Women and Law in Southern Africa Research Project (WLSA). This was an action-oriented research project that set out to improve the position of women in law and society in six countries in southern and eastern Africa. In 1994 WLSA embarked on a research project that sought to describe, understand and improve women's inheritance rights under state law and customary law. Through this research a paradigmatic change took place from seeing customary law as a static patriarchal form of law that needed to be abolished, towards an outlook of customary law as a contested, dynamic and changing form of law.

In Zimbabwe, according to the case law developed by the colonial courts, widows could not inherit (Stewart et al 2007; WLSA Zimbabwe 1996). The Zimbabwean WLSA research team assumed that state court customary law, which had been turned into a static form of law by the colonial courts, was out of tune with the living customary law. The living customary law was defined by the research team as a dynamic and responsive form of law that varied with time and place. The team gathered empirical information about the norms that guided inheritance decisions made by families, local chiefs, resettlement and housing officers, and local courts among the urban and rural Shona- and Ndebele-speaking population. The living customary law was explored, not only through the upper strata of the formal state courts, but also through information about how inheritance problems were resolved both in local informal fora and most importantly in troublefree cases of everyday life (Holleman 1973: 61).

Looking at cases resolved amicably in the family, through mediation by third parties ranging from chiefs, resettlement officers and local court officers, the Zimbabwe WLSA research documented a growing preference for the appointment of the widow as an intestate heir to the deceased husband's estate (WLSA 1995). In their advocacy for legal change the WLSA team members, who also were members of the Law and Development Commission, successfully argued that the colonial version of customary law should be replaced by the living customary law evolving on the ground. On the basis of this research the ZANU PF government decided to change the legal position of widows under the Administration of Estates Act.[11]

By reconstructing the customary argument the WLSA research team created a discursive space where they effectively countered the invisible power embedded in social, cultural and political norms defining women and girls as

---

[11] Administration of Estates Act, ch 6:01.

inferior to men. This demonstrates the strength of strategies that define law not by state power but by basic moral standards that are upheld through the actions of individuals and groups. The link between living customary law and the right to equality was historically embedded in African women's struggles against colonial customary law that denied them citizenship rights. WLSA thus created a metaphorical space that contradicted ZANU PF's claim that the defenders of women's rights were acting as agents of foreign powers working to undermine African cultural values and national sovereignty.

4.2. Handling Invisible Power in a Closing Political and Legal Landscape

In 2000 ZANU PF lost a referendum over a new and democratic constitution, and since then the country has fallen into a deep political, economic and legal crisis. In response to the challenges posed by a united civil society and a strong political opposition, the ZANU PF government tightened its grip on power. NGOs involved in civic education, mobilisation and advocacy have all been affected by legislation that limits their right to freedom of speech and the right to organisation and assembly (Feltoe 2003). As ZANU PF has taken control of the legal institutions, the police and the judiciary have in many instances not been making independent decisions, but acted on the instructions from these hidden power-holders. The establishment of a government of national unity in 2008 did not, with the exception of the 2013 Constitution, make much difference (Hellum et al 2013).

Women's rights organisations have under these difficult circumstances continued to play a proactive role in lobbying for legal change through government channels, including equal land rights under the old Lancaster House Constitution. They have continued to challenge the visible power embedded in legislation that allows discrimination against women. Most importantly the new 2013 Constitution, which was passed after years of lobbying, stipulates that customary law no longer takes precedence when it comes into conflict with the principle of gender equality in the area of family and inheritance law. Katsande (2014) explores whether and to what extent women have been able to use these rights in this unstable economic and political terrain. Her doctoral work is based on an empirical study of three irrigation schemes in the Mutoko area 100 km outside Harare. Through fieldwork, Katsande observed how the power of most married women horticulture farmers to make decisions about the use, control and ownership of land was inhibited by the widespread customary notion that this was men's domain because they were the heads of households. Yet the visible power structure, in terms of state law and the irrigation communities' constitutions, put women on an equal footing with men regarding decision-making and ownership. During meetings about the irrigation scheme women were often conspicuous by their silence. Some of the women who were interviewed by Katsande said they did not contribute during the discussions because they feared being labelled as belonging to the political opposition. Such labelling had a negative effect on their horticulture business as it could lead to them confining themselves to their homes for fear of assault. Women said they were more vulnerable to assault than men because they walked long distances to the local markets and when taking sick relatives to the clinic. Women also said they were highly vulnerable to sexual assault and harassment especially during the times of political instability. They complained that the governing structure at these irrigation schemes followed the ZANU PF party structures such that once labelled as belonging to the opposition, they would be excluded.

Furthermore, dispute resolution concerning ownership in the event of divorce and death was strongly influenced by informal customary norms based on patrilineal kinship norms. In practice women horticultural farmers with very clear land rights, most importantly women who had inherited the plots from their husbands and daughters who inherited from parents, were in a variety of ways deprived of ways of exercising their rights. In terms of the Administration of Estates Act and the constitutions of the irrigation schemes, when the plot-holder dies, the plot devolves to the surviving spouse and will devolve to the children upon death of the surviving spouse. However, in practice, the woman's inheritance is dependent upon the approval of the deceased's relatives and on the condition that she not remarry. In terms of settling disputes arising from the distribution of estates or in general before a dispute reached the irrigation management committee, the expectation was that it should be settled domestically in a *family dare*.[12] Furthermore, the female complainants were denied remedy in the irrigation management committee as this impliedly surrendered such disputes to the *family dare*. Neither did women find relief from the local leaders, as these also referred such disputes to the *family dare*. In the event that women complainants were given an audience by local leaders, the case usually dragged on and on with the local leaders 'consulting' with the complainant's relatives. There was also interference in the management and functions of the irrigation management committee by both politicians and administrators. Whilst the scheme's constitution mandated the management committee to run the affairs of the cooperative, the state and other social institutions had a bearing on the management of the cooperative. The irrigation management committee would not make a decision without consulting the local leadership such as the village head and the ward councillor and the family of the parties involved.

---

[12] This is a family gathering made up mainly of family elders that is set up to discuss family issues as and when a need arises.

To strengthen women's power to take control and claim ownership, Katsande, as part of her research, informed the women farmers who were part of the irrigation scheme about their rights under the Zimbabwean Constitution, state law and the irrigation scheme constitutions. She also provided advice and assistance to those women who wanted to take legal action in order to challenge the customary norms that were applied by the local informal dispute resolution agencies. In this way she enabled women to handle the invisible power embedded in patriarchal customary norms that hindered women in making use of their formal inheritance rights. In the course of the research several widowed farmers stood up to have their inheritance claims heard in the magistrate court in the area. Through legal literacy and legal advice the researcher attempted to strengthen the women's power from within—personal power emanating from increased individual consciousness and self-confidence involving the ability to overcome internalised control or oppression (Crawford et al 2013: 7). An example of this is Martha, who inherited an irrigation plot from her husband. She defied all the odds and approached the courts when her husband's brother sought to disinherit her. In an interview with her she said that her widowhood and the sudden realisation that she had a young son to take care of and the effort she had made to develop the horticulture business gave her the willpower to fight the traditional expectation that she either be inherited by her husband's brother or pack her bags.[13] The court did not pass a judgment but facilitated a settlement whereby her husband's brother was given a quarter of the land, leaving her trapped by customary practices that see men as the rightful owners of land or the upper guardians of women. The courts in the area are hesitant to deal with land issues and thus seek family agreements or refer these matters to state agencies such as the district administrator, the village head and the ward councillor, all under ZANU PF control. The reason is that the land, which forms the greater part of the capital of the horticulture businesses, is state owned, controlled and politically significant to ZANU PF, the ruling party. In this way invisible and hidden power intersected and interacted to undermine women's rights claims embedded in state law and the irrigation scheme constitutions. This shows the power dynamics that are at work in cases where women lose out when their rights come into conflict with the interests of male family members who invoke patriarchal versions of customary norms through the local institutions that are controlled by ZANU PF politicians.

This longitudinal study shows the challenges individual women and women's rights advocates face in a terrain where the spaces to negotiate claims and hold power-holders accountable at the family, local community and state levels are opening and closing. It provides a clear illustration of

[13] Personal interview 2011.

how women's organisations in a situation with freedom of research, speech and organisation in the 1990's made space to challenge invisible power and as such successfully renegotiate customary inheritance norms. As a result of the political, economic and legal changes that followed ZANU PF's loss of the constitutional referendum in 2000, the space to hold local and national power-holders accountable has dwindled. The study of women irrigation scheme members demonstrates the multidimensional nature of power where state law regulating inheritance and irrigation scheme matters is inconsistent with prevailing social norms and administrative practices. This is affecting women's ability to challenge male power-holders' use of legal, political and administrative structures to control resources and power. It is thwarting the realisation of the rule of law, with its requirement that a clear and accessible set of rules be applied in an impersonal and non-political manner. According to Adler et al (2009), even when liberal institutional arrangements are formally adopted, as seen in this study, they often end up serving other purposes as they are transformed in practice by the coexisting norms and power relationships onto which they are transposed. As shown by this study the formal institutions are, due to the exercise of a mixture of hidden, visible and invisible power, failing to perform the functions that liberal theories of governance prescribe. This shows how invisible and hidden power intersect and interact to undermine women's access to law and justice in a situation where the space to promote women's inheritance rights has closed down as a result of the political, economic and legal power struggles following in the aftermath of the constitutional referendum in 2000.

5. CONCLUSION

In this chapter, we have looked at women's rights in South Africa and Zimbabwe from a longitudinal and plural perspective with a focus on the interaction between state law and other normative orders that regulate the distribution of power and resources in the daily activities of women and men. We have shown how the relationship between women's rights under international, national and local norms is dependent on who has the power to define, interpret, implement and enforce law at the multiple levels on which it operates. Furthermore, we have demonstrated how engagement with legal pluralities in some situations can be a resource for women to challenge their marginalisation and in other situations a factor in producing or upholding gendered forms of exclusion.

Successful human rights interventions are, as demonstrated by the South African study, partly dependent on the ability of individual women and women's rights organisations to develop situational and locally appropriate strategies of argumentation, and partly on the broader political, legal and economic power structures in which they operate. The land restitution case analyses continuity and change in gender relations in the light of shift-ing policy trajectories in terms of an attempt to marry social justice with a market model. The social justice approach to land restitution, which informed the claims-making and claims-verification period, made space for efforts to ensure that prevailing local power relations and legal pluralities undermining women's rights in the family and in the local community were addressed. In the post-settlement phase the ANC government's shift to a market- and business-oriented land restitution model resulted in a narrow equal opportunity approach which led to gendered forms of exclusion. This neoliberal economic model, which regarded the gendered hierarchies of sta-tus and power within the family and the claimant community as a private matter, closed the space for NGO initiatives addressing the gender stereo-types embedded in local customs. As a result it became far more difficult for weakly organised groups such as women, poor community members and farm workers to mobilise support for their claims against members of the chiefs' families, businesses and state agents. Rather than changing unequal power relations within the local community, the shift to this model left the invisible and hidden power exercised by chiefs and the male dominated agro-business companies unchallenged. The South African study thus reveals that legislation based on equal rights can coexist with a shift towards neoliberal economic models, while the latter in practice may trump the former, at least when it comes down to challenging 'traditional' African gender values.

The Zimbabwean studies, on the whole, lay the basis for understand-ing how legal pluralities are produced and reproduced through changing social, political and economic relations of inequality, domination and con-trol at the national and local level. The WLSA study shows how women's human rights under certain circumstances can be promoted by using living law and legal pluralism as an analytical, political and legal tool. This was possible in a political context where the ruling ZANU PF party in the 1990s opened space for civil society initiatives. WLSA was under these circum-stances able to create a discursive space where invisible power embedded in social, cultural and political norms defining women and girls as inferior to men was challenged by reinterpretation of customary law. The study of women's inheritance rights on an irrigation scheme, ten years later, shows how this reform has fared in a changing political and economic landscape. Since it lost the constitutional referendum in 2000, the ZANU PF party, to defend its access to power and resources, has limited civil rights and taken control of national and local courts. Under these circumstances the space to challenge the contested customary norms based on gender stereo-types has been closed down through the exercise of a combination of visible and hidden power. Clearly, the breakdown of independent and transparent legal institutions has created a situation of legal impunity where both state law and customary norms are reconfigured and manipulated through male-dominated political networks. The Zimbabwean study thus demonstrates how legislation based on equal rights can coexist with a patrimonial form of law and how the latter trump the former particularly when it comes to challenging patriarchal African gender values.

More generally, the longitudinal case studies from the two countries demonstrate the different effects that changing constellations of governance shaped by history, power structures and legal pluralities may have on gender relations on the ground. The two studies thus underscore the need for longitudinal approaches to gender, human rights and legal pluralities that see law as a process of constantly changing and interacting normative constellations and power relations taking place in a shifting legal, political and economic terrain.

8

Women's Rights and Transnational Aid Programmes in Niger: The Conundrums and Possibilities of Neoliberalism and Legal Pluralism

KARI B HENQUINET[1]

1. INTRODUCTION

DUE TO SEVERE food security problems and widely recognised hardships for women, the Maradi Region of Niger has become a target for humanitarian aid and gender and women's rights programmes. In particular, the transnational aid institutions CARE and UNICEF[2] have established wide-reaching programmes throughout the region with a focus on gender relations, rights for women and children, rural health and livelihoods. In addition to these programmes, however, Nigeriens in this region are affected by a host of influences on women's rights ranging from national legislation to popular religious discourses on Islam. This chapter examines aid programmes amidst these overlapping spheres of influence as they concern women's rights in the Maradi Region and in Niger more broadly, considering the spaces neoliberal governance opens up for competing and emerging rights discourses.

[1] This research was funded by a Fulbright-Hays Doctoral Dissertation Research Abroad Grant and a National Science Foundation Ethnographic Research Training Grant awarded through the Michigan State University Anthropology Department. I am grateful to CARE, UNICEF and the Madarounfa Technical Services in Niger for their cooperation on this project as well as for scholarly feedback throughout this project from Bill Derman, Anne Hellum and the editors of this book.
[2] CARE and UNICEF began their work in Niger in the mid-1970s in response to the Sahel Drought of 1968–74. Although UNICEF is a UN agency and CARE an NGO, both organisations worked closely with the Nigerien government during the 1970s and 1980s. In the 1990s, however, CARE began working more independently, using few government counterparts, while UNICEF continued to utilise civil servants to carry out its programmes. In 2004, both organisations worked in the Maradi Region on similar rural projects (eg women's savings and loans, access to seeds, health education, training health workers), carried out projects staffed by Nigerien professionals, and included a mix of public and private sector donors.

These overlapping spheres of influence are akin to Sally Falk Moore's (1973) chains of semi-autonomous social fields. Moore explains that the semi-autonomous social field

> can generate rules and customs and symbols internally, but ... is also vulnerable to rules and decisions and other forces emanating from the larger world by which it is surrounded. The semi-autonomous social field has rule-making capacities, and the means to induce or coerce compliance; but it is simultaneously set in a larger social matrix which can, and does, affect and invade it, sometimes at the invitation of persons inside it, sometimes at its own instance. (Moore 1973: 720)

In her analysis, Moore provides examples from the New York garment industry and the Chagga of Tanzania to illustrate that in semi-autonomous social fields, 'the various processes that make internally generated rules effective are often also the immediate forces that dictate the mode of compliance or noncompliance to state-made legal rules' (ibid: 721). The now foundational framework of the semi-autonomous social field in legal pluralism scholarship, which has been much tweaked and reused over the last forty years (Griffiths 1986, 2002; Merry 1988), has served as a way to expand scholarly understanding of how rules are generated and compliance is enforced in societies beyond simply state engineering and coercion. The idea of a matrix of overlapping chains of semi-autonomous social fields affecting and invading one another is useful for conceptualising women's rights in Niger.

When Moore first introduced this framework for analysis, however, she wrote in a period in which centralised states were commonly involved with much state engineering to alter societies. However, the 1980s to the present has ushered in a period of neoliberalism in which states have retreated from markets, governance and services, leaving much to the private sector. In African nations required to implement neoliberal policies to ensure World Bank and IMF loans, the state has become weak, and new opportunities have emerged for non-state actors to take increasingly critical roles in the circulation of ideas, goods and services. In the 1980s one saw widespread structural adjustment and inter/transnational aid circumventing the state in African countries, while in the 1990s one saw a push among the inter/transnational aid community for 'good governance' in downsized states (Hilgers 2012). The rising popularity of rights-based development among inter/transnational aid institutions in the 1990s should be seen as one outcome of this trend.

In his study of human rights in neoliberal Malawi, Englund finds that ideas of rights that circulate there are strongly influenced by human rights NGOs, which are entangled in transnational networks, frequently act as equal to or superior to the state, and do not necessarily approach rights from a grass roots perspective (Englund 2006: 8). This neoliberal and elitist approach to rights promotion brought a focus on political and civic rights over social and economic rights (ibid). Yet in other cases by opening a space for a wide interpretation of rights by actors outside of the state through implementing neoliberal policies that weaken the state, neoliberal market ideas may not necessarily emerge as a dominant discourse for rights. In Niger, for example, the state is weak, transnational aid institutions are quite active, and the legal system has long been plural and complex as in Malawi. Yet Nigeriens at large regularly resist the process of implementing certain UN- and equality-based notions of women's rights that circulate in transnational rights-oriented institutions by drawing on other rights discourses deeply entangled with their identities as Muslims in a secular postcolonial state but predominantly Muslim society. In such an environment, the semi-autonomous social field of informal Islamic jurisprudence on family matters is powerful in generating social rules and norms, with the state and transnational aid institutions often acquiescing to it. Considering the overlapping semi-autonomous social fields of aid organisations, informal Islamic law discourses on the family, and formal Nigerien law and governance, I examine what transpires in the Maradi Region of Niger concerning women's rights. Amidst these overlaps, this study explores in particular the ways in which two prominent transnational aid institutions, CARE and UNICEF, take on the work of promoting women's rights in Niger.

I use ethnographic data from interviews among Nigerien development professionals in CARE, UNICEF and government offices in the Maradi Region, and in Niamey, the capital city of Niger, as well as participant observation at CARE and UNICEF events that I attended in 2002 and 2004. These events were part of CARE's Gender Equity and Household Livelihood Security Project and UNICEF's Integrated Basic Services (Services de Base Intégrés, SBI). I also lived and collected ethnographic data in towns where these projects operated. UNICEF and CARE were the largest aid organisations operating in the Maradi Region, and both integrated gender and women's rights as central components of their work. Furthermore, the period of 1999–2004 was a time of considerable legislative and development programme change for women's rights issues in Niger.

In sum, my data speak to the importance of discourses on Islamic jurisprudence that circulate largely outside of formal courts and government institutions in Niger and particularly in the Maradi Region, but are also reflected in family law in the formal legal system. Aid institutions concerned about women's rights have attempted to engage with Nigeriens in a wide range of ways, including advocating for legislation, education programmes, and projects to improve women's economic status. In the end, however, those ideas about women's rights that articulate with popular discourses on Muslim family law strongly influence how women's rights are understood and which parts of globally and nationally circulating ideas get accepted and which do not in formal law and in development projects. Furthermore the relationship of CARE and UNICEF to government and human rights instruments is key in how each organisation engaged with overlapping spheres of influence concerning women's rights.

2. WOMEN UNDER LEGAL PLURALISM AND NEOLIBERAL GOVERNANCE IN NIGER

Before analysing the work of CARE and UNICEF in Niger, I first provide a brief overview of some key legal issues concerning women in Niger. By certain measures, Niger may be considered a country that is among the harshest to live in as a woman. Indicators such as a maternal mortality ratio of 590 per 100,000 live births and the highest adolescent fertility rate in the world at 193.6 births per 1,000 women aged 15–19 bear testament to this hardship (UNDP 2013: 159). A number of legislative measures to improve the status of women in Niger have been attempted over the last several decades. Some have been met with success, while others have failed. For example, representation in parliament by women soared from 1.2 per cent in 2004 to 12.4 per cent in 2006 (United Nations 2013:51). The former was the count just before the first national election following the 2000 Quota Law, which requires minimum percentages of women and men as candidates elected and in government appointments.[3] Alidou and Alidou explain these as:

(a)   A minimum of 10 per cent of candidates of one and the other sex in all electoral positions; and
(b)   A minimum of 25 per cent of appointees of one and the other sex in executive government and state positions and promotions. (Alidou and Alidou 2008: 22)

Other legal reform projects such as the Family Code and Niger's Personal Status Project (Statut personnel du Niger), seeking to bring further equality for women in family law, have failed to pass (Issa 2011). These reforms would have improved women's status under the law in matters such as divorce, child custody, marriage and inheritance (Alidou and Alidou 2008: 27; Dunbar 1991: 81–82; Issa 2011). Niger's Report to the United Nations on the Convention on the Elimination of All Forms of Discrimination against Women (CEDAW) states that if the Family Code had been enacted, it would have provided

> full recognition of women's civil capacity; recognition of women as heads of household in some situations, which derives from the legal obligation to contribute to the upkeep of the household; equality with the husband for child custody rights in the event of divorce according to the child's interests and entitlement to family allowances; prohibition against repudiation. (United Nations 2005: 64)

---

[3] République du Niger Loi 2000-008 du 07 Juin 2000.

CEDAW was ratified only with significant reservations rejecting equality in inheritance, choice of residence, marriage, divorce, family planning, choosing a family name, and modifying social patterns of conduct for men and women (United Nations 2005). These attempts to change family law have brought together a diverse collection of Nigeriens of secular and various Islamic persuasions in opposition to women's groups and political coalitions advocating for these changes (Alidou et al 2008: 27; Cooper 2010: 105–06). This mosaic of legislative efforts begs the question of why some changes have been met with success while others have not. To understand this, I turn to an overview of the legal pluralism of Niger and the powerful semi-autonomous social field of the informal circulation and application of Islamic discourses of jurisprudence.

Similar to other colonial systems of government in Africa, Nigerien law had a dual structure of civil and customary law. Customary law, which came to include many legal traditions from the Maliki school of Islamic jurisprudence,[4] was used for family matters such as inheritance, marriage, divorce and child custody. Civil law, however, was considered secular and was inspired to a large extent by French law. While customary and civil courts are no longer separate as in the colonial period (Cooper 2010: 100), the texts used for customary law are still applied in family matters, according to religion and cultural identity. My findings concur with Cooper's that '"Hausa custom"[5] in the region of Maradi has come, with a few admittedly significant modifications, to mean Maliki juridical tradition' (Cooper 2010: 100). Upon my own visit to the Maradi Justice Office, I was shown copies of two main texts used for inheritance matters. These texts largely drew from French colonial law, the 1961 Law 61–30 on customary land tenure, and a widely used tenth-century text for Maliki law in the French language (al-Qayrawani, c tenth century; Republique du Niger 1994). 'Muslim Hausa customary law is most often applied in cases of land tenure', a legal staff member explained to me.

That said, most inheritance and other family law matters are dealt with outside of the purview of the formal courts in Niger. Local village heads, religious authorities and family members play a critical role in transmitting social norms and mediating disputes about family issues. These are often done while drawing on Islamic jurisprudence in a way that articulates with wide-reaching discourses in Africa, but that does not typically connect with formal courts and selectively uses Maliki traditions. Similar to Soares' analysis of Malian use of Islamic jurisprudence (Soares 2011), Nigeriens also seek knowledge of Islamic legal traditions from prominent imams in the region who are not directly tied to any formal legal structures in Niger.

---

[4] The Maliki school is one of the four classical Sunni schools of law. It is widely used throughout West Africa (An-Na'im 2002: 284).
[5] Hausa is the largest ethnolinguistic group in Niger and northern Nigeria.

A combination of increased labour migration, Koranic schools, and mass media in Niger and neighbouring countries have further facilitated this exchange of knowledge about Islamic jurisprudence directly from person to person. While these discourses can draw from a wide variety of Islamic legal traditions, the themes of male provision and guardianship of women and children as his duty and their right, respectively, are widely shared values. To bear these rights, women are expected to be obedient. These notions of rights and duties in the family were consistently articulated to me in interviews and informal discussions with Nigeriens in the Maradi Region. Furthermore, a woman is recognised to have rights to own and inherit property both in Maliki tradition and according to many Nigerien Muslims, but in practice a woman rarely receives this inheritance until her parents' death, if at all. Her children are popularly recognised as belonging to the paternal kin group and expected to remain with them in the case of divorce, even though Maliki traditions support children staying with the mother (boys until weaned and girls until marriage) (Cooper 2010: 103–04).

An-Na'im (2002) provides context for the wider picture of how Islamic law has in much of the Muslim world come to be applied mainly in the domain of family law and become a symbol of religious identity. Divisions between religious and secular courts appeared as early as the Abbasid state, although the colonial period further bifurcated these distinctions (ibid: 8–9). An-Na'im writes:

> Whatever the reasons may have been, family law remained the primary aspect of Shari'a that successfully resisted displacement by European codes during the colonial period, and survived and outlasted various degrees or forms of secularization of the state and its institutions in a number of Islamic countries.[6] As such, IFL [Islamic family law] has become for most Muslims the symbol of their Islamic identity, the hard irreducible core of what it means to be a Muslim today. (ibid: 9)

This attachment of Islamic family law, whether formal national law or as a popular discourse, to core identities as Muslims surfaces again and again in Nigerien responses to discourses on women's rights as detailed below.

Returning to the question of why some national legislation on women's rights has been met with success while others have not, the ways in which notions of rights in legislation do or do not articulate with popular discourses on Islamic family law is critical. Similar to Tønnessen's findings in Sudan (Tønnessen 2013), portions of CEDAW that articulate with socially acceptable roles for women and that do not directly challenge male guardianship and provision in popular Nigerien understandings of Islam have made some headway. In Niger, these include girls' education, improved economic opportunities, political participation and improved health. However,

---

[6] An-Na'im uses the term Islamic countries to mean 'those countries with majority Muslim populations' (2002: 1).

globally circulating ideas about women's rights that demand equality in the family or independence of women are repeatedly rejected. While there is clear manoeuvring amongst some Nigeriens to address women's rights, this always takes place within the powerful discourses, social relations and semi-autonomous social fields of that society. Notions of women's equal rights in the family are easily labelled by opponents as un-Islamic and Western impositions, quickly gaining popular support and thereby understood as threats to core Muslim identities embodied in Islamic family law, as An-Na'im suggests above.

Saba Mahmood (2005) helps us better theorise this kind of agency and subjectivity by critiquing the ubiquitous notion in liberal feminism of a subject who desires freedom and can individually choose to resist oppression or challenge social norms. Instead she calls for an understanding of agency within social structures rather than the individual. In her study of Egyptian women in the piety movement, she explains that: 'The kind of agency I am exploring here does not belong to the women themselves, but is a product of the historically contingent discursive traditions in which they are located' (ibid: 32). Nigerien notions of rights that commonly circulate emphasise social relations and identities as central to how and when one might exercise or claim rights. Women's agency in this context is therefore a manoeuvring within particular historical and social structures, subjectivities and relations. Commonly, rather than looking to the state and formal legal apparatus to understand or claim rights, Nigeriens emphasise kin relations, religious identities, discourses of Islamic jurisprudence and informal means of conflict mediation. As detailed below, Nigerien development professionals navigating women's rights-oriented programmes and aid recipients of these programmes remind us of the strength of influences outside the state, which has weak capacity to enforce rights anyway. Both Nigerien women at large and employees of development organisations are constrained by social structures, yet in some of the examples below we can detect movements to improve women's status within these constraints.

CARE and UNICEF in Niger, as major institutions advocating for women's rights, provide examples of how women's rights advocacy is approached in the semi-autonomous social fields of the Maradi Region and in Nigerien society at large. The downsizing of the Nigerien state under neo-liberal structural adjustment policies since the 1980s has made it increasingly difficult to enforce formal law or carry out state development projects. This results from a decline in the number of civil servants and decreased budgets for state programmes. In this milieu, one sees the non-state actors and norms of other semi-autonomous social fields take on great significance. In the Maradi Region, where I conducted much of my fieldwork, the wide-reaching development programmes of CARE and UNICEF, and the informal circulation of Islamic discourses of jurisprudence through mosques, family members, radios and other media, are particularly noteworthy with regards to women's rights. Both CARE and UNICEF have elevated women's rights to a primary objective of their programmes in Niger, taking on the work of educating the public and/or advocating for legislation to ameliorate women's status. CARE and UNICEF, however, take different approaches to their women's rights work, maintaining different relationships with the state as well as human rights instruments and discourses. I examine these differences below and discuss their effects on various aspects of the CARE and UNICEF programmes.

3. CARE AND WOMEN'S RIGHTS

The ways in which CARE came to understand and integrate women's rights into its work in Niger is connected to its changing relationship to the state and to developing relations with religious leaders. CARE made the decision to pull back from tight collaboration with the Nigerien state to carry out its activities in the mid-1990s in order to maintain better control over its programmes and account to donors (Sayo 2003: 2). For the most part, it was hiring its own field agents in 2004 rather than working through government civil servants, as it used to do. While there has been some consultation with government ministries in setting priorities since the mid-1990s, CARE has worked largely independently from government programmes. Furthermore, CARE did not claim any strong commitment to international human rights instruments, although they had begun to implement a rights-based approach to development starting from 2002. CARE employees were aware of CEDAW and national legislation about women's rights, but these were not central in defining their approach to rights-based development. The CARE project I focused on in my fieldwork around Maradi incorporated women's rights into other gender and development approaches, particularly household livelihood security and women's economic empowerment. CARE's independence allowed it to approach women's rights in a way that drew heavily on informal Islamic family law discourses. It also had a robust educational programme to encourage women to take advantage of new political leadership opportunities under the new Quota Law in Niger. However, CARE had less capacity and interest than UNICEF to advocate for new legislation. Furthermore while CARE was able to articulate a discourse on women's rights that the public was open to, this strayed from a message of equal and autonomous rights to one of 'betterment' for women under male guardianship.

CARE's approach to women's rights tends to view culture and religion as resources to utilise, rather than barriers to remove, in line with many other approaches at the grassroots (Merry 2006: 15–16, 90–92; Tsanga 2007). In discussions about women's rights with CARE employees in Niger, rights were commonly spoken of as something that should be better understood by and claimed by women. These 'rights' referred to already existing rights in Niger, although not exclusively in reference to formal law. CARE employees drew from a variety of rights discourses and norms invoking 'already existing' rights in Nigerien society in the following two examples from my data: programmes to increase awareness of property and marriage rights for women and the Women's Leadership training programme. In these programmes, CARE sought to build on culturally and legally recognised rights of women. By contrast, CARE was hesitant to advocate the use of formal courts for resolving family matters, which they seemed to view as a threat to disrupt social relations and make women more vulnerable by claiming individual rights within families. The conversation below with a senior CARE administrator, who was also a Nigerien Muslim, illustrates this hesitation.

In response to a question I posed about whether or not CEDAW played a role in CARE-Niger's work, a senior CARE administrator explained to me the complications of trying to implement a set of ideas about women's rights that is so out of touch with the Nigerien reality. 'If you don't have a place you belong to, your family won't care for you. You won't have anything. Therefore it is important for a woman to have a place to belong to', he began. He went on to explain that what he meant is a woman must abide by certain norms in order to maintain these kin relationships. From numerous other conversations I have had on this topic in Niger, I understood that these include obedience to her husband in exchange for his provision. By contrast, he added, if she were to take her husband to court for violating a right, he would likely divorce her, and she would have no home to live in and belong to as a married woman. Indeed, it is common in Niger for men to end their marriage by repudiation with no reason given (Boyce et al 1991; United Nations 2007: 7). And being married is critical to a woman's good reputation and social identities in Niger.

While this CARE administrator did recognise that social change happens and culture is malleable, he did not see principles of male guardianship and provision nor patrilocal residence patterns as likely to change soon. In fact, he and a select few CARE employees, who were also Nigerien Muslims, explicitly expressed support for women's equality in principle during our conversations. However, he knew in reality that improving women's rights in the family has been repeatedly brought up and shot down in Nigerien law, most notably in the Family Code and Personal Status Project. In addition, portions of Articles 15 and 16 of CEDAW recognising a woman's rights to choose a residence and equal rights in marriage and divorce are among the reservations the Nigerien government identified when ratifying the Convention (United Nations 2005). As stated above, marital problems are typically dealt with under customary law or informal dispute resolution in one's family or community, thereby often subjecting husband and wife to unequal treatment. The principles used typically draw on commonly understood Islamic norms and discourses that circulate on Islamic jurisprudence.

Therefore as rights exist in practice in Niger, women would not do well to jump to claiming the kinds of rights that could disrupt a much-needed place to belong as a dependant, according to the CARE administrator above. This kind of rights-claiming implies a notion of the independent liberal self, rather than the communal self that is interwoven throughout Nigerien society. Rather, this administrator and many other CARE employees emphasised the importance of identifying widely recognised or 'already-existing' formal and informal rights for women among Nigeriens and encouraging women and men to know about and respect them. CARE's approach uses culture as a resource and manoeuvres explicitly within social structures and norms to avoid social isolation and exacerbating women's vulnerability under current family law. CARE's efforts to educate Nigeriens on women's rights concerning property, marriage and political leadership draw on 'already existing' rights that women could claim with less risk to social relations because they would be working with recognised rights in popular Nigerien discourses.

The Gender Equity and Household Livelihood Security Project in the Maradi Region emphasised that women have a widely recognised right to own and inherit property in Islamic legal traditions. This was communicated in particular through the Communication for Behaviour Change (CCC, Communication pour un changement de comportement) tours and the Marabout relais. The CCC tours consisted of a variety of legal and health professionals who travelled with CARE staff from rural town to town, holding information sessions for the public on topics such as women's rights, elections and HIV/AIDS. Marabout relais was a series of trainings in collaboration with some well-known Muslim clerics from the region specifically for Muslim leaders and teachers in CARE aid recipient towns. The trainings dealt with women's rights to inheritance, seclusion of women, education of women, and marital rights and duties. In 2004, CARE claimed 46 people were active in the Marabout relais programme in the Maradi Region.

The CCC and Marabout relais programmes both emphasised women's rights to inherit and own property in Islamic legal traditions, which articulate well with the still-used French colonial laws that draw heavily on Maliki law as 'custom' for family matters among Hausa people. This legal tradition apportions two-thirds to male heirs and one-third to female heirs. Men and women's rights and duties in marriage were also discussed in these CARE programs, emphasising a husband's duty to provide for his wife/wives and a wife's duty to obey her husband. Reciprocally, a wife has the right to depend on her husband for food, shelter and other basic needs; a husband has a right to command his wife. This kind of marriage relationship is not 'traditional' in the Maradi Region, where women were historically more independent economically. However, these rights and duties that were discussed in CARE forums have become more commonplace over the last several decades, as gender roles popular in northern Nigeria and other parts of the Muslim world have crept into Nigerien life. Today in Niger these can be considered widely recognised rights and duties in marriage, even if not entirely realised by all Nigeriens. CARE and the professionals with whom they collaborated in CCC tours and Marabout relais aimed to make these ideas about women's rights, which articulated well with local interpretations of Islam and informal rules about gender roles, even more widely known so that women could make rights claims, particularly among kin, that would be widely recognised as legitimate and existing in their society. In this work, CARE tended to pick up on already existing Islamic jurisprudence discourses on women's rights in the Maradi Region, further legitimising these principles. In doing so, any CARE message of equality or independence that may have challenged family law and Islamic norms in Niger was set aside in exchange for a discourse of improving women's status (Henquinet 2013).

Women's Leadership (Leadership Feminin) was another collaborative programme, in which CARE participated, to bolster already-existing women's rights in Niger.[7] This example, more than the first one, however, articulates with newer legislation on women's status in Niger. Building on the 2000 Quota Law and anticipating the 2004 elections, CARE partnered with a large number of organisations in Niger concerned about gender issues to develop the Women's Leadership training programme. The aim of this programme was to prepare citizens for the upcoming changes in government structures as part of the decentralisation process that would be implemented towards the end of 2004 and encourage women to run for office. The programme consisted largely of civics lessons for women who showed leadership qualities in rural communities throughout Niger. CARE took a lead role in conducting these trainings, and I attended one of them in April 2004. Over the course of three full days, CARE staff facilitated discussions and activities that helped the female participants understand how government worked, the characteristics of a leader, challenges for women leaders, and the responsibilities associated with newly created elected positions on local commune councils. One of the facilitators explained to the women: 'Today, only one out of 83 members of the National Assembly is a woman. But in the next elections, there must be a minimum of 10 per cent women.' After the 2004 election, the percentage was indeed 12.4 per cent. The Quota Law also applied to the newly created communes throughout the country, where some of these women in the Women's Leadership training would run for elected office. In the communes of Madarounfa Department, which contained the towns I focused on in my study, female council members were indeed elected in 2004 (République du Niger 2004).

---

[7] Participating institutions in developing the Women's Leadership training materials included: The Ministry of Social Development, Population, Promotion of Women, and Child Protection; The High Commission for Administrative Reform and Decentralisation; The United Nations Population Fund; and a broad collection of NGOs and NGO networks focused on human rights, democratisation, and/or women.

In this example, CARE capitalised on the new Quota Law and decentralisation changes to prepare more women to move into government. The idea of women representing women in Niger and women having a public voice was something that was acceptable enough for the legislature to pass and a notion also echoed in many of my conversations on gender with development professionals and civil servants in Niger. Women's rights activists report that there is a long legacy of women's leadership in Nigerien life, including in politics, storytelling and working outside the home (Kang 2013: 6). In my discussions of women's rights with CARE employees, the issue of a woman having the right to share her views with her husband and community was commonly brought up, even when certain individuals were not willing to advocate for equal leadership between men and women in Nigerien life. The acknowledgement that women have some important things to say about life that men may not understand flows from the social and physical separation of men and women in their day-to-day activities. CARE has identified this commonly accepted notion, building it into a programme for increased political participation for women based on existing rights in Nigerien formal law. Similarly they have identified other widely acknowledged rights of women in marriage and inheritance according to popular discourses on Islamic jurisprudence. In doing so, they have built rapport and found a language to talk about women's rights, although the notions of equality or independence—particularly in family law—are not part of this language. Their distance from the state and international human rights instruments, such as CEDAW, has provided a space to define rights-based work and women's rights in ways that articulate with popular discourses on the Muslim family and Islamic jurisprudence.

4. UNICEF AND WOMEN'S RIGHTS

Unlike CARE, UNICEF has continued to partner closely with the Nigerien state to carry out its work on women's and children's rights. UNICEF works directly with the Nigerien government to develop a country cooperative programme (République du Niger and Fonds des Nations Unies pour l'Enfance 2000), giving the government considerable latitude in setting priorities and defining programmes. UNICEF ensures these agreed-upon programmes are funded. At the same time, UNICEF is tightly wed to CEDAW and the Convention on the Rights of the Child (CRC) to define its overall objectives, at least at the national and international levels. At the department level, the Integrated Basic Services (Services de Base Intégré, SBI) activities—one part of the country programme—on the ground in rural Niger have been carried out through government civil servants. SBI includes work in agriculture, environment, health, animal husbandry, women's income generation and education. Civil servants running these programmes have technical training in their areas, but little knowledge of women's or children's rights legislation or international law. This has resulted in a dual nature to UNICEF's work in Niger, where notions of the rights contained in CEDAW and the CRC are strong on the national level and weak at the department level. In this section, I examine women's rights at both levels. In both levels, however, one again sees the powerful influence of popular Islamic discourses of the family, although UNICEF's distinct organisational structure provides a contrast to how this plays out in its programmes when compared to CARE.

At the national level, UNICEF has been a strong advocate for women's rights legislation. It has had some successes, but mainly concerning issues that resonated with already circulating discourses on women's rights in Niger. Those issues that challenge family law and popular discourses of Islamic jurisprudence were unsuccessful. UNICEF found work on women's rights in SBI activities to be challenging for a couple of reasons. First, there was little room to manoeuvre away from their commitment to CEDAW, yet some of the CEDAW principles were not generally accepted by Nigeriens. This left UNICEF at an impasse when it came to connecting with the public on women's rights. Second, for SBI, UNICEF works through department-level civil servants, who carry out and make recommendations for what is needed programmatically. Because of their focus on matters other than women's rights, one finds little that articulates with women's rights, in particular in SBI.

Unlike CARE-Niger that feels no formal obligation and little connection to international women's rights instruments such as CEDAW, UNICEF uses CEDAW and the CRC as the fundamental basis for its work. As one long-standing UNICEF employee, who has been involved with many gender initiatives, stated to me: '[T]he texts that are the starting point for our work are the international documents ratified by the Nigerien government.' Similarly, the cooperative agreement between UNICEF and Niger for 2000–04 started its preamble citing CEDAW and the CRC with regards to its mission to address problems of women and children (République du Niger and Fonds des Nations Unies pour l'Enfance 2000: 5). It also lists advocating for the adoption of legislation to support women's and children's rights as one of its nine main strategies for the country cooperative programme (République du Niger and Fonds des Nations Unies pour l'Enfance 2000: 10). This strategy is evidenced in UNICEF's involvement in women's rights advocacy in Niger.

While CARE has capitalised on already-enacted formal law and popular notions of rights to promote women's rights, UNICEF has played a key role in supporting the development and implementation of new legislation that bolsters women's rights in Niger, such as the Family Code (unsuccessful), CEDAW, the Quota Law, and the Personal Status project (under development in 2004, but later unsuccessful). The Family Code and Personal Status legislations aimed to address inequalities in family law between men and women in matters such as inheritance, child custody, divorce and marriage. These two attempts to reform this area of law were met with widespread resistance in Niger and neither was successful. Similarly, CEDAW was only passed with reservations that rejected sections of the convention calling for equality in these family 'customary' matters, as mentioned above. While ambitious in its aims, UNICEF has overall had success with legislation that resonates with already existing, widely shared social attitudes about women's rights, even if these attitudes are not necessarily embraced by everyone. These include notions of increasing opportunities for women to participate in politics and women's equal opportunities for education. In particular these attitudes about women in politics and education are widely shared by development professionals and other elites, but are also often palatable, if not desired, outside of elite circles. However, measures to change family law so that women have equality with men conflict with religious and cultural identities rooted in patriarchal norms.

Concerning women's participation in politics, UNICEF was involved in developing and advocating for the Quota Law, which was successful in boosting women's political participation as noted above. In terms of education, Islamic traditions in girls' education contribute to an acceptance of the idea of equality in education among many Nigeriens. Most rural towns and villages in Niger have at least one Koranic school, while many have no primary school.[8] One senior UNICEF programme officer explained that in 2004, Niger had 50,000 Koranic schools and only 7,500 primary schools in the country. He went on to say that Koranic schools in Niger were about 50 per cent girls and 50 per cent boys at the 4–6 year old level; however, overall, this ratio changes as the children get older such that boys are more likely to go to public, primary school and girls remain in Koranic school. In my experience in rural towns south of Maradi, people commonly explained that some families did not send a girl to primary school because she would marry soon. It is therefore understood by some that primary education is not needed or useful for these girls; however, the travel required for many girls to attend primary school can also be a deterrent. It is noteworthy that many girls do continue some Koranic education until marriage, which is on average 14.9 years for girls in the Maradi Region (Magagi 2002). They are typically able to do this in their hometown. Furthermore as UNICEF has implemented programmes that require equal enrolment of girls and boys for primary school support, towns have generally been responsive. UNICEF notes that in its target public schools, girls' enrolment increased from 24 per cent in 1994–95 to 42.5 per cent in 1998–99 (République du Niger and Fonds des Nations Unies pour l'Enfance 2000: 6).

UNICEF's efforts to achieve equal enrolment of boys and girls in primary school have articulated with a deep history of Islamic education in

---

[8] Koranic schools (*makaranta*) in rural Niger often consist of a teacher whose students memorise the Koran and learn basic tenets of their faith outdoors, using only wooden slates and ink. Unlike *madrasas* and government schools, there is no emphasis on literacy or mathematics in these Koranic schools.

the region. Notably, Nana Asma'u (1793–1865) established a pedagogy, voluminous written materials and the 'Yan Taru' movement for women's Islamic education in the Sokoto caliphate; this legacy of religious education has continued in parts of Hausaland (Dunbar 2000: 400; Robinson 2000: 138–39). In Niger, women also have found increased spaces to participate as leaders in Islamic education, especially since the democratisation trends of the 1990s (Alidou 2011). It seems many Nigeriens are applying the value of girls' education to public schools, indicated in increased enrolment above, particularly when given some incentive from UNICEF.

I spent a good deal of time in one department capital in Maradi Region called Madarounfa, and observed how certain aspects of improvements in women's status and rights were accepted while others were highly contentious. The civil servants in this department were the principle collaborators with UNICEF in one of the rural towns where I lived and conducted research as well as many other nearby towns. In addition to personal interviews and daily observations with civil servants in Madarounfa, I participated in UNICEF-sponsored activities, such as a four-day Integrated Community Development Training for representatives from UNICEF SBI aid recipient intervention units. Intervention units consisted of a collection of neighbouring rural towns. On average representatives included two men and one woman from each intervention unit so that the overall male to female ratio was close to two to one. While discussing women's rights and gender issues was not the main focus of the four-day training, these issues surfaced numerous times in lessons and informal discussions with participants. When the focus was on public education, child malnutrition or civic participation, there was no public debate contesting the importance of these issues for women and girls. However, when family planning and early marriage of girls came up—two issues long considered a domain of customary family law—heated debates followed.

In the Integrated Community Development Training, participants were led through exercises by civil servants or UNICEF staff about how to identify a community problem and its causes, followed by developing a plan for potential solutions. The example problems used throughout the training were: (1) lack of education; (2) lack of food; (3) child malnutrition; and (4) early marriage of girls. Concerning lack of education, there was widespread agreement in the group about the importance of education in general. While Koranic schools would certainly be valued by most people, in these trainings, the focus of discussion was on public, secular education and how to obtain or improve schools in one's town.[9] The focus of these discussions

---

[9] At least three of the approximately twenty female participants were Christians, so Koranic learning would likely not carry the same importance for them. I was unable to identify any Christian men at the training, which usually becomes clear during calls to prayer; some of the women confirmed that they also did not think any Christian men were in attendance. Christians in Niger are less than 2% of the population (US Department of State 2010).

was on lack of resources and opportunities for education, with no mention of public, secular education being an undesirable pursuit. Even when the discussion veered towards UNICEF's requirement to have half boys and half girls (totalling 60 students) in order to receive support, no objections were voiced publicly about putting girls into school. A number of comments were even made by participants about the importance of changing the attitudes of some parents in their towns to allow girls to attend and finish primary school.

However, in a later discussion on early marriage of girls, the issue of girls' education surfaced again. In that discussion, some dissenting voices did emerge—not so much in objection to educating girls per se, but rather pertaining to a critique of early marriage made by some participants and how it stands in the way of girls completing their education. Some of the male participants clearly conflated early marriage with Islamic principles. Others rejected this conflation, particularly female participants both during the session and afterwards in their comments to me. Nonetheless, it is clear that when marriage is brought into the discussion on girls' education, the tone changed to one of disagreement and a threat for some to religious identity.

Finally when the trainees were discussing the problems of lack of food and child malnutrition, heated debates surfaced again once these topics transgressed into the issue of family planning. At the start of one of these discussions, participants listed a number of ways to address the problems of lack of food and child malnutrition; some of these comments raised women's issues with no objections. These included encouraging mothers to nurse immediately after birth instead of waiting for their milk to come in (which is still common in Niger), developing capacity for and allowing mothers to bring their babies for regular baby weighing, and providing women with goats that could produce milk for their children and help the women financially. However, two additional issues were raised as causes of lack of food and child malnutrition that erupted into contentious debates. The first was the notion that there are too many people and too little space for farming. Immediately after someone said this, one of the participants turned to me—the only white person and Westerner present—in front of the whole class to ask: 'Isn't this from Allah?' Clearly he was referring to the number of people in a population or family. As I started a response about how people are able to plan the number of children they want, the facilitator erased the response from the board as a reason for lack of food. Later in the session, the facilitator in our group reported to a UNICEF administrator who visited the classroom that our group rejected too many people and too little space as a reason because this is what the Westerners want. 'This group says it is up to Allah', he continued. Diplomatically the UNICEF administrator—a Muslim Nigerien woman herself—explained that family planning is not forced on them. 'It is a choice', she explained. In fact, a woman's equal right to make family planning decisions is one of the reservations Niger has to CEDAW (Article 16(1e)), relegating family planning to much less than a right in Niger.

Later in the discussion of child malnutrition, someone brought up a practice called *rurutsa* as a cause of malnutrition. *Rurutsa* is a term to describe when a woman becomes pregnant and has another baby before her older child is weaned. Historically this practice was shunned as unacceptable since husbands and wives were expected to wait until a child was weaned to resume sexual relations (Cooper 2009: 158). While the practice of *rurutsa* still carries some stigma socially, parents today have typically not abided by the historical practice of abstinence until weaning. Rather they have adopted the Muslim practice of waiting until 40 days after birth (Cooper 2009: 159). Thus mothers who do become pregnant while still nursing are pressured to wean quickly as 'pregnancy is widely seen as spoiling the mother's milk' (ibid: 158). This presents some risk of malnutrition if the first child is still quite young and could benefit from the breast milk. The common solution proposed by development professionals and outsiders to this dilemma is family planning, suggesting a variety of birth control techniques. However, these techniques are widely resisted in Niger for reasons summarised by the training participants above—the number and spacing of children is a matter of Allah's will and not to be interfered with by use of birth control. Thus the mere mention of *rurutsa* stirred up a host of strong feelings as the discussion transgressed into further debates about family planning. The training participants debated whether or not family planning is a good idea and also whether or not *rurutsa* is a cause of child malnutrition. A couple of days later, some of the women I was chatting with from the training brought up the topic of *rurutsa* again. They were in favour of birth spacing for the health of the mother and children. One of them remarked that: 'Men don't feel any *kumya* [shame/modesty] when talking about *rurutsa*.' Clearly these women understood that they not only suffered healthwise from close birth spacing, but also bore the bulk of the social stigma associated with *rurutsa* for weaning children too quickly and putting them at risk.

When framed as an educational or nutritional issue, improving women's status did not produce contentious debates in public during this training event. Some women's ability to attend and participate in the training (including public debates with men) was also testament to the reality that women have some voice in this society, even if their rights and opportunities are not equal with men. These co-ed debates illustrate how Nigerien women can manoeuvre to challenge notions of Islamic family law in discussions at times. Furthermore while UNICEF and its government partners requested at least one woman from each intervention unit attend, this was not forced or required. In the end, most intervention units were able to find one woman who would participate in a co-ed training away from home for four days rather than reject this request. Similarly, CARE also was able to find female trainees who could travel for its Women's Leadership programme, which had only had female participants but some male teachers. This is noteworthy considering the heavy work responsibilities of women at home and the growing trend of secluding women in this region. Women of younger generations tend to be secluded in their homes, expected to come out only with their husbands' permission for special circumstances such as to visit relatives or to attend ceremonies (Henquinet 2007).

Instead of framing education, health or civic participation for girls or women as rights issues at the aid recipient level, UNICEF and its government collaborators in SBI programmes departed from a CEDAW- and CDC-based rhetoric to focus on engaging community members in identifying and planning out solutions to their most pressing problems. Yet in the example of the UNICEF SBI training, one sees how ideas about women's rights still surface in debates. Whether the ideas are widely accepted or contentious corresponds with the areas of formal law that have been accepted and rejected in Niger. The principles in CEDAW are acceptable or at least palatable at large to Nigeriens except when it comes to family law issues, which are connected by the populous to Islamic identity and discourses on Islamic jurisprudence and are also incorporated into formal legal structures. Most participants in the UNICEF training reflect these social attitudes in their discussion of women and family matters, even while not explicitly drawing on a language of 'rights'. And civil servants running the UNICEF training were comfortable framing their training as community development rather than human rights issues. This contrasts with UNICEF's national-level work on women's rights, which is strongly aligned with CEDAW and the CRC.

5. CONCLUSION

The neoliberal state, while theoretically concerned about the rule of law, has left a large opening for development institutions and discourses of informal Islamic jurisprudence to weigh in on women's rights issues in Niger. In my analysis of women's rights in two prominent transnational aid institutions, formal law and popular discourses, I conclude that other ideas about women's rights in family matters are stronger in Niger than globally circulating ideas centred around the liberal subject, exemplified in CEDAW. Formal law and development programmes have had to acquiesce to the powerful ideas of male guardianship and provision, codified in customary law and internalised through popular discourses on Islamic jurisprudence connected to Muslim identities and the family. This is demonstrated through the rejection of attempts to reform family law, the reservations to CEDAW, the legislative successes and failures of UNICEF and its allies, and the reformulations of women's rights in CARE and UNICEF programmes on the ground to often conform with popular notions of the Muslim family. Legislative successes such as the Quota Law do not challenge family law in the same way; instead, some political representation of women for other women seems acceptable in Niger. Similarly, efforts to bolster girls' education, women's rights to property and women's abilities to nourish their children adequately can be found to be compatible with Islamic discourses familiar to many Nigeriens. However, when efforts to improve women's rights overlap with family planning, early marriage of girls, divorce or other family law issues, there is considerable dissent about women's equal and individual rights.

It is not surprising in Niger that women's rights are largely conceived outside of state legislation, UN conventions or transnational aid objectives due to a complex system of legal pluralism, a weak state and vibrant religious networks. Development programmes, women's rights activists and citizens have long manoeuvred within overlapping semi-autonomous social fields to seek change. The level of commitment to the state and international human rights instruments by organisations impacts the definitions and strategies they embrace to improve women's rights. Yet they all must engage with popular ideas of the Muslim family deeply entwined with religious identities and legal histories in Niger as they seek pathways to improve women's rights.

9

Legal Borderlands: Ghanaian Human Rights Advocacy between the Layers of Law

CATHERINE BUERGER

1. INTRODUCTION

THIS CHAPTER EXPLORES the contested space of human rights advocacy in Ghana through an ethnographic description of community-level human rights mobilisation.[1] Ghana is a country with a long history of structured plurality within its legal system, and yet, this chapter does not present a classic example of 'forum shopping', where individuals choose between clearly defined legal orders to address disputes (Benda-Beckmann 1981: 117). Instead, the ethnographic examples explored in this chapter illustrate how various actors may attempt to reshape and challenge the boundaries of legal orders during the process of claims making. Although working within the same overarching framework of law, various groups may contest the meaning and appropriate implementation procedures of these laws. By mobilising outside of formal legal settings, the activists described in this chapter attempt to build flexible advocacy campaigns that borrow from various legal traditions including customary, statutory and international law. Although community activists may continue to refer to these strategies as 'human rights campaigns', their location may be contested by others who might be invested in maintaining a more narrow definition of, or approach to, claiming 'human rights'. Because of this, I have come to think of these advocacy spaces as 'legal borderlands'. Thinking about these spaces as borderlands is useful because it suggests the fluid and contested nature of the space. Whereas a *border* implies a strict and legally defined demarcation, a *borderland* connotes movement. It is a region where

[1] The ethnographic data presented in this paper were collected during fieldwork conducted in Accra, Ghana between 2008 and 2013. I am very grateful for the helpful comments provided by Dr Richard Wilson and Dr Samuel Martinez on earlier drafts of this chapter.

ideas, goods and people interact and traverse borders. Many interactions within these borderlands are unregulated, despite the best efforts of states to control and police the border. Thinking of legal mobilisation in this way allows us to see how some individual actors may interact fluidly across the borders of institutional regimes, while others may attempt to control, guard and regulate these boundaries.

The concept of a legal borderland is an extension of contemporary legal pluralism scholarship that acknowledges the mutually constitutive nature of legal orders (Ameh 2004; Clarke 2009; Hodzic 2009; Merry 2006; Santos 2002; Sierra 1995; Von Benda-Beckmann 1981; Wilson 2001). A 'legal order' is defined broadly to include centralised state legal systems but also other forms of social ordering including religious and customary norms. Whereas early scholars of legal pluralism considered legal systems to be discrete, internally ordered and autonomous (Pospisil 1971), the work of more contemporary scholars has illuminated the many ways in which various legal orders, such as customary and statutory law, are interconnected (Merry 1988; Moore 1978; Wilson 2001). Scholars of legal pluralism have also focused on the strategic relationships that legal actors build in an effort to maintain power (Hodzic 2009; Wilson 2001). These studies illustrate the fact that relationships between various legal orders are not permanent or unchanging, but are instead related to specific historical moments and the strategic needs of the associated groups. The idea of legal borderlands pushes our understanding of the dynamic nature of legal orders even further by considering how the boundaries of legal orders are created, maintained or contested by the advocacy choices of individual actors. This is related to concepts such as Santos De Sousa's explanation of 'interlegality' or the way that 'everyday life crosses, or is interpenetrated by, different and often contrasting legal orders and legal cultures' (Santos De Sousa 2002: 98). The concept of a legal borderland differs, however, in that it specifically highlights the constructed nature of legal systems. It points out not only the coexistence of multiple legal orders and the porousness of the borders between them, but also the way that individual actors may attempt to shape and redefine these boundaries for strategic purposes.

This research is also grounded within the theoretical framework of new legal realism, which emphasises the 'role of social context in shaping what law is and what it does' (Garth 2006: 941). New legal realism, which comes as a reaction to the model-driven neoclassical law-and-economics approach (Nourse et al 2009: 65), emphasises the importance of empirical research for understanding how individuals engage with law, both inside and outside of the courtroom. By examining how activists negotiate and contest meanings within the Ghanaian legal system, this research embraces new legal realism's call to undertake 'bottom-up' as well as 'top-down' empirical research with a focus on issues of power (Erlanger et al 2005: 339–40).

2. GHANAIAN LEGAL BORDERLANDS

Much has been written about customary law and legal pluralism in Ghana. The country's legal system provides a clear example of the legacy of British colonial indirect rule, and as Ulrike Schmid notes, the integration of customary law and state law in Ghana has been 'stronger than in other countries' (Schmid 2001: 10). Most of this research, however, has focused on the law surrounding inheritance or land (Blocher 2006; Crook 2004; Fallon 2003; Fenrich et al 2001; Mikell 1992; Ubink 2008). Few authors who write about Ghana have contemplated how the emerging legal order of human rights is influenced by the country's heavily managed system of legal pluralism. This chapter takes that topic as its central focus. Specifically, this chapter considers how a legally pluralistic milieu influences the implementation of human rights law. It does so by examining the ethnographic case study of a human rights campaign in Nima and Maamobi, two contiguous low-income communities in Accra, Ghana's capital city.

In 1902, when Maamobi first appeared on the Gold Coast colonial census, there were 13 residents, and the area was outside of the city limits of Accra. Nima was first settled in 1931 by Alhaji Amadu Futa, a Hausa cattle dealer (Ainuson 2009). For the first half of the twentieth century, the two communities were largely considered pastoral areas. Around 1950, however, the environment began rapidly changing. Although the 1948 Gold Coast Survey Map of Accra depicts Nima as a largely rural and sparsely populated area, the 1957 version of the same map shows Nima 'packed with an unordered mass of irregularly shaped buildings without access roads or signs of urban infrastructure' (Harvey et al 1974: 8–9). Because these areas were outside of the Accra city limits, urban planning was not regulated. As the population of Accra increased, Nima and Maamobi became popular destinations for both domestic and international migrants (Agyei-Mensah et al 2012). The rapid growth in population contributed to the still-present densely constructed, unplanned residential areas, and in 1958 Nima was officially designated as a slum (Ministry of Housing, Town and Country Planning Division 1958). This did not, however, prevent the population from continuing to grow. Both Nima and the neighbouring Maamobi saw additional increases in population during the 1960s (Harvey et al 1974). By 1964, the population in Maamobi had grown to 5,790 (Ghana Census Office, 1964: 23, 62)

The communities of Nima and Maamobi have long carried the reputation of being migrant communities. By the end of World War Two, individuals from over 20 different tribal groups were documented as living in the neighbourhoods (Pellow 2001: 64), and by 1973, Bruce Grindal estimated that 90 per cent of the community's population was 'ethnically non-indigenous, consisting of northern tribesmen and a significantly large proportion of non-Ghanaians from northern Togo and Upper Volta' (Grindal 1973: 335). High levels of local religious, ethnic and linguistic diversity continue to characterise the community. Whereas Accra as a whole is largely Christian and relatively wealthy compared to the rest of the country, there is a large Muslim population in Nima and Maamobi, and the area is substantially poorer than the surrounding neighbourhoods. These characteristics have led some community members to complain that they are viewed as outsiders by residents of Greater Accra. The abundance of diversity combined with the poverty-related challenges faced by residents has resulted in an environment where residents readily address disputes using an amalgamation of strategies that draw from customary, religious, national and international conceptions of law and justice.

Today in Nima and Maamobi, the community remains densely populated, and small twisted alleyways wind their way between cement block and wood plank homes. The neighbourhoods are also known locally for the deep drainage stream that divides them, its banks lined with homes that teeter on the slowly eroding edges of the ditch. The official name of this ditch is 'the Al-Hamdu Gutter', or simply 'the drain' to local residents. At the bottom of the gutter, stagnant water sits, blocked from flowing by piles of garbage. The drain has become a substitute dumpster, in part due to the government waste removal services' neglect of the community. When water levels rise in the ditch, the dirt banks, and the homes clinging to their edges, become vulnerable to erosion. The remaining skeletons of rooms and walls that have partially crumbled into the drain are visible from the precarious footbridges that traverse the drain. The drainage stream runs for nearly a mile within Nima and Maamobi, and it continues further on either end into the surrounding neighbourhoods. In other communities, however, the ditch has been lined with concrete. This has substantially decreased the potential erosion and has helped the water in these portions to continue to flow. The only sections that remain unlined are those in Nima and Maamobi. Residents often suggest that their unlined drain is visual evidence of the discrimination that the community faces on account of their politics, religion, ethnicity and economic status.

Another distinguishing factor of Nima and Maamobi is the fact that they are participants in an international programme called the 'Human Rights Cities' programme. This model was developed by the People's Movement for Human Rights Learning (PDHRE), an NGO based in New York City, and is coordinated locally by an NGO based in Accra that we will call the 'Ghana Human Rights Centre' (GHRC, a pseudonym). The PDHRE defines a 'human rights city' as 'a city or community where people of good will, in government, in organizations, and institutions, try and let a human rights framework guide the development of life in the community' (PDHRE 2007: 3). According to the organisation, this model specifically pushes for the achievement of social and economic rights through the implementation of democratic values and procedures. The GHRC first became active in Nima and Maamobi in 1997. Over the years, the organisation has provided human rights education events, capacity-building workshops and direct legal services. The presence of the organisation in the community added to the diversity of dispute resolution options available to local residents. Whereas previously many residents struggled with the financial burdens associated with advancing cases within the formal legal system, the organisation provided pro bono legal guidance and representation. Much of the GHRC's work in these communities, however, has focused on 'capacity building', or the strengthening of local community-based organizations that can work together to advance human rights causes in the community. These community-based organisations are then supported by the GHRC during their campaigns to address specific local issues, such as healthcare and sanitation.

Over the past six years, the Nima–Maamobi drain has been the focus of one of these community human rights campaigns. As this chapter will discuss, the campaign raises several important questions about the implementation of human rights in Ghana, including what methods are considered acceptable in the claiming of rights, what values fit under a 'human rights approach', and who has the right to decide. More generally, the campaign brings to the forefront tensions between various legal actors in Ghana and leads to questions about the stability of the boundaries that divide plural legal systems.

2.1. Culture and Rights in the Borderlands

Much of the contestation within the human rights campaign in Nima and Maamobi has been related to a decision by some community members to integrate procedures that are more commonly associated with the patriarchal systems of political patronage and customary obligation into their human rights campaign. For some local human rights lawyers, the reciprocal exchanges and uneven power dynamics implicit in the customary system are necessarily in conflict with the larger goals of human rights advocacy (personal interview, Accra, 29 June 2010). This opinion is not unique to the human rights community in Ghana. Cowan et al (2001) have noted that scholarly conversations about rights and culture are dominated by discussions that position international human rights and local culture as normative systems that are in opposition to each other. In the positioning of rights versus culture, culture is portrayed as a set of immutable beliefs and practices that impede the achievement of human rights. In her work on the practices of the Committee on the Elimination of Discrimination against Women, Sally Engle Merry explains that legal experts assigned to review human rights conditions around the world often 'concluded that the custom

162   *Catherine Buerger*

was the problem because they see 'customs' as harmful practices rooted in traditional culture' (Merry 2006: 4). Merry argues that due to time limitations placed on the committees, there is no time to examine the complex cultural and historical contexts of these practices. Thus, the presumed conflict between 'culture' and rights remains in international human rights practice.

In Ghana, discourses positioning rights versus culture have also been evident in several high-profile national debates. One of these concerned the practice of *trokosi*, or ritual servitude. Specifically, *trokosi* refers to the custom of sending young virgin girls to religious shrines to serve as slaves to atone for the crimes committed by another member of the family. The practice, which is associated with the customary religions of some ethnic groups in eastern Ghana, was, at one time, somewhat common. Recently, however, there has been a growing movement within Ghana to end the practice (Ameh 2004). Ameh (2004) notes that activist groups pushing to end the custom initially cast their campaign in the language of Christianity. Hostile responses characterising their efforts as a 'Christian attack on African traditional religion', however, quickly led the activists to recast their campaign in the language of human rights (Ameh 2004: 58, 63). For many international observers, this strategic move only reinforced their beliefs that culture is a barrier to the achievement of rights.

Although the debate about culture and rights is evident within the human rights community in Ghana, there is not a consensus that the promotion of human rights requires blocking interactions with customary institutions. When the GHRC first began its work in the community, the local Council of Muslim Chiefs played a significant role in legitimising the organization. These chiefs have continued to serve as powerful mediators between the NGO and the wider community. When asked about the role that chiefs play in community-based human rights advocacy, one lawyer stated:

> In our part of the world, you don't go into the community without letting the chief know that you are in the community. They won't be pleased with you and they won't give you their support. And they have support; they have followers. If they start bad mouthing you, you can be sure that whatever programme you have in place will not succeed. So it's important both for cultural and pragmatic reasons.[2]

During the human rights campaign advocating for the construction of a new concrete drain in Nima and Maamobi, many community residents similarly saw the integration of customary, national and human rights-based procedures as a pragmatic decision. As will be described in detail further in the chapter, when the human rights-based claims of the group met with opposition, local community advocates would shift modes and recast their claims using the procedures or language of another legal order, such as customary obligation. This challenging of the accepted human rights-based approach,

---

[2] Personal interview, Accra, 26 October 2013.

however, was controversial among some of the staff members at the GHRC. When asked about the practice of appealing to local traditional leaders during human rights campaigns, one lawyer stated: '[H]onestly, I am not a fan of the traditional system, not a fan at all. I would have to think very hard to think of any way at all that the customary system could support human rights advocacy.'[3] Other GHRC staff members disagreed. One staff member, who was not a lawyer but who worked closely with community groups, felt that engaging local elders and chiefs would help the community to be more receptive to the human rights goals of the GHRC. He stated: 'When we are talking about human rights law and these (customary) laws, it's a dicey one. But then, if we talk about respect of human rights and respect for cultural values, it is simple. You have to engage with them.'[4] As I will discuss in the following pages, these tensions concerning the relationship between customary law and human rights echo both local histories of legal pluralism and also the complex international system in which community human rights campaigns are located.

2.2. Customary Law and the State

This local debate over whether there is a conflict between customary authority figures and democratic ideals is part of a long trajectory of contestation between legal orders that began with the system of indirect rule during colonialism (Mann et al 1991). The British colonial system of indirect rule was first implemented in Nigeria by Sir Frederick Lugard, High Commissioner of the Protectorate of Northern Nigeria. It then spread throughout the colonies during the first half of the twentieth century. The system, which created a bifurcated legal structure of European and African law, was conceived of as a way to exert power over African communities through the use of local institutions (Mamdani 1996). Lugard's plan included organising colonial and African rulers in a way in which there would not be a dual system of rule, but rather, 'a single government in which Native chiefs have well-defined duties' (Lugard 1918, quoted in Roberts et al 1991: 20). This structure was seen as a way to add local legitimacy to colonial command by drawing from the influential powers that chiefs had over their people (Enwright 1985: 38).

In implementing this system, the British sought consistent sets of justiciable customary laws, easily identifiable leaders and political structures reminiscent of governments in Europe. Despite this goal, colonial administrators had to contend with local systems of fluid customary laws and variable

---

[3] Personal interview, Accra, 29 June 2010.
[4] Personal interview, Accra, 19 July 2011.

levels of political cohesiveness. In response to this, colonial administrators attempted to create uniformity amidst diversity. In Ghana, for example, certain regions, such as Ashanti, were already organised into a centralised system of authority. Other areas, such as northern Ghana and the Volta region, however, had lower levels of political centralisation (Nugent 1996). In areas lacking a clear authority figure or hierarchical structure, the British created 'warrant chiefs' in order to produce uniform systems that would facilitate trade and order (Van Rouveroy van Nieuwaal 1987: 11). There were also efforts during this time to codify customary law into a more consistent system to be used in native courts (Davies et al 2009: 306).

Although these acts to restructure systems of authority in the colonies should be viewed as strategies of British domination, it would be a mistake, as Chanock (1985) notes, to ignore the ways in which African elites attempted to manipulate the system to advance their own interests. An example of this can be seen in the codification of customary law. Many of those selected by the British to become warrant chiefs pushed forward their own self-serving interpretations of customary law to be codified and therefore found the system 'to be the most advantageous instrument for translating their values and interests into power over others' (Chanock 1985: 236). The advancement gained by chiefs through the system of indirect rule was, however, not without consequence. Apter (1972) has noted that chiefs who were able to make social and economic gains through their association with colonial officials were often viewed as being in collusion with the colonial rulers. This perceived complicity not only made the system of indirect rule less effective for the British, who relied on the legitimacy of local chiefs, but also led to tensions between customary authority figures and the African elite who assumed power at the time of independence.

Since the colonial period, Ghanaian political leaders have continued to manage the relationship between these multiple legal orders in efforts to protect their authority and pursue nation-building projects. In the years following independence, the powers of the chiefs were severely restricted by policies enacted by Kwame Nkrumah, Ghana's first president. Kwame Boafo-Arthur (2003) argues that the policies implemented by Nkrumah in the years following independence were primarily motivated by two factors. First, despite the fact that some chiefs supported the movement to independence, many were still perceived as supporters or collaborators of the colonial system from which they derived significant power. Second, there was still considerable fear that the legitimacy of the chiefs would present too large a risk to the primacy of state authority. This fear was heightened when the traditional ruler of the Ashanti region, the Asantehene, decided to support the National Liberation Movement (NLM) in what was viewed by many as a secessionist campaign against Nkrumah (Ray 1996).

One of the policies undertaken by Nkrumah was the adoption of the 1961 Chieftaincy Act, which established Regional Houses of Chiefs. These councils served as representative bodies in which chiefs could collectively advise on specific national issues, although they only dealt with matters that were referred to them by state level officials and their powers were strictly advisory in nature (Rathbone 2000). The Houses of Chiefs therefore provided a controlled space for chiefly participation, while remaining under the direct control of the state. By locating the ultimate authority over decisions concerning the system of chieftaincy within the state apparatus, Nkrumah's policies had a similar effect to the system of indirect rule (Ansere 1977; Francis 1968). The system of chieftaincy was allowed to continue, but chiefs were, at least in a formal legal sense, dependent on the state.

Although Nkrumah supported policies to constrain the individual powers of chiefs, he also attempted to advance a symbolic pan-African notion of law that was founded on customary values (Nkrumah 1962, 1963). Although this law would be adjudicated by the state judicial system, Nkrumah argued that the legal logic of state courts in Africa should be drawn from the values of customary law. Partly inspired by Nkrumah's ideas concerning law, in the 1950s and 1960s, conceptions of law began to play larger symbolic roles in many newly independent African nations, a process that Chanock has described as 'legal nationalism' (Chanock 1985: 54). In Ghana, although customary authority figures were often characterised by Nkrumah as being in opposition to the nation (Ray 1996), chiefs and customary law have remained legitimate sources of authority. As such, individual decisions regarding legal strategies have become more than just 'forum-shopping' to meet immediate self-interests (Benda-Beckmann 1981); they have become political.

As time passed, the state's negotiations with competing legal regimes also grew to include new normative orders, notably international human rights. At times, Ghanaian state officials have embraced international human rights as a justification to regulate the customary system or as a way to build legitimacy within the international community. At other times, when the human rights regime has posed a challenge to the power of the state, officials have rejected its values as being foreign impositions (Hodzic 2009). The state's use of rights language extends back to the years surrounding the country's struggle for independence when Nkrumah rejected European colonialism as a violation of the 'fundamental human right' of self-determination (Nkrumah 1958: 46). The negotiation with and strategic use of rights language became especially apparent, however, during the 10-year period under the military regime of the Provisional National Defence Council (PNDC). When Flight Lieutenant Jerry Rawlings and his military government came to power in 1981, they cited 'economic mismanagement' as a primary justification of their coup (Adedeji 2001). In an attempt to build support in the international community, during the period in which the PNDC ruled, Rawlings and other government officials loudly promoted collective 'economic rights' while simultaneously violating the civil and political rights of citizens (Haynes 1991; Oquaye 1995).

Under the PNDC, government actions and new laws placed serious limits on the rights of citizens. One such law was the Habeas Corpus Amendment Law (PNDC Law 91). This law prevented courts from making inquiries into discretionary detentions made by the military regime under the Protective Custody Law (PNDC Law 4). Another law, the Public Tribunal Law, (PNDCL 78) 'imposed the death penalty by firing squad for political offences' and prevented the Superior Courts of Judicature from overseeing or reviewing these decisions (Oquaye 1995: 564). In addition to these laws, associates of the military regime also perpetrated extrajudicial killings, arbitrary arrests and detentions, disappearances, and other acts of violence against suspected political opponents (Haynes 1991; Anyidoho 2011).

During the same time that supporters of the PNDC were committing acts of violence against their suspected opponents, the international community was placing more pressure on developing countries to support policies of democratic rule. As Mike Oquaye (1995) notes, in the late 1980s and early 1990s, 'good governance' became a requirement to continue receiving aid from international agencies. These persistent domestic and international pressures led the Rawlings regime to prompt a transition to democracy in 1992. During the 1992 elections, Rawlings won the presidency. He and his regime were therefore able to exert significant control over the character of Ghana's new constitution.

In many ways, the 1992 Constitution stands as the clearest example of the attempt by the Ghanaian elite to maintain 'conscious coordination between legal orders' (Schmid 2001: 10). The 1992 Constitution also provides several examples of how political elites may attempt to shore up and police the borders of different legal orders in an effort to preserve their authority and prevent laws from being used against them. First, the 1992 Constitution of Ghana blends aspects of various competing legal orders in the country, including customary law and human rights, while continuing to maintain the state's primacy of law. Chapter 22(1)–(2) of the 1992 Constitution states: 'The institution of chieftaincy, together with its traditional councils as established by customary law and usage, is hereby guaranteed.' The power of the House of Chiefs is also maintained through a provision that gives the House advisory power over any issues relating to chieftaincy as well as the duty to oversee, collect and review customary laws (1992 Constitution of Ghana, Article 272(c)). Despite these provisions, however, the Constitution draws a clear boundary between the state authority system and the customary system. Chiefs may advise on customary issues through the regional and national Houses of Chiefs, but they also are restricted by Article 276, which states: 'A chief shall not take part in active party politics; and any chief wishing to do so and seeking election to Parliament shall abdicate his stool or skin.'[5] Individuals may attempt to traverse the border established by the Constitution between the state and chieftaincy, but these actions are contentious. One example of this is when chiefs are perceived as too openly supporting one political candidate or another. The press, as well as elite members of both the government and the chieftaincy, tend to treat actions such as these with suspicion[6] because they see them as threats to the Ghanaian system of 'divided sovereignty' that offers both government officials and chiefs protected spaces to rule and adjudicate disputes (Ray 1996).

In addition to outlining a clear divide between the state and chieftaincy systems, the 1992 Constitution also clearly delineates the boundaries of the human rights system in Ghana. The Constitution enumerates many of the specific rights contained in international human rights treaties such as the International Covenant on Civil and Political Rights (ICCPR) and the International Covenant on Economic, Social and Cultural Rights (ICESCR). It also, however, places limits on how these rights may be interpreted and claimed. The most specific limitations on the use of human rights law by citizens are contained in the Constitution's 'Transitional Provisions' section. In this section, the Constitution states that members of the PNDC cannot be held liable either jointly or severally, for any act or omission during their administration of the PNC (Article 34). Therefore, although there are procedures for claiming remedies for human rights violations that may occur in the future, the violations committed by the PNDC do not fall within this category. The version of human rights that is presented is therefore narrow enough to protect the self-interests of past PNDC members while still catering to the demands of the international community and the desires of those Ghanaian citizens who were attempting to push forward a burgeoning 'culture of human rights' (Daniels 1996: 190; Ameh 2006; Akosa-Sarpong 2006).

3. LEGAL MOBILISATION IN THE BORDERLANDS

The previous section describes a system of law that is plural, and yet clearly defined with each normative system being allocated a space for relative autonomy. However, by following the methodological principles of the New

---

[5] 'Stools' and 'skins' are the ceremonial symbols of chieftaincy in Ghana. In northern Ghana, chiefs sit on ceremonial animal skins during ceremonies, whereas chiefs in southern Ghana sit on ceremonial stools.

[6] For recent examples, see Kwame Okoampa-Ahoofe, 'Is this Another Peace Council Gimmickry?', *The Daily Graphic*, 13 February 2013; Michael JK Bokor, 'Is the NPP Really Asante, and Asante truly NPP?', *GhanaWeb*, 23 December 2012.

Legal Realist mode of thought and placing a focus on 'law as it is practiced in everyday life' (Merry 2006: 975), a far more convoluted reality emerges. Individuals, guided by differing priorities, employ various informal strategies to navigate the organised formal legal system. Individuals who are closely tied to the individual legal institutions, be they statutory, customary or human rights, are often invested in maintaining clearly defined borders, even if, as Wilson (2001) has shown, these borders may change over time. Individuals who are less closely associated with specific legal institutions, however, may find that their interests are best served by operating in the borderlands where they may more easily challenge and move across legal boundaries. This is especially true when legal mobilisation occurs outside of the courtroom. Broadly defined, legal mobilisation can refer to a variety of practices including lobbying legislators, participating in legal education programmes, using legal discourse, and building coalitions between legal actors and activists (Goedde 2010). When operating away from formal legal structures, individuals may find more possibilities for innovative and flexible advocacy strategies.

Although there is a specific court in Accra devoted to hearing human rights cases brought under Chapter 5 of the Ghanaian Constitution, most human rights legal mobilisation efforts in Nima and Maamobi take place outside of the courtroom.[7] According to local activists and human rights lawyers, this is largely due to the fact that bringing court cases related to large social and economic rights issues is very costly, both in terms of time and money. Ghanaian courts are afflicted with a heavy backlog of cases, and this often makes alternative methods of dispute resolution more popular among claimants (Appiagyei-Atua 2013). Because most advocacy in Nima and Maamobi occurs outside of the courtroom, community activists are less tied to one set of laws and procedures. Instead, in the mobilisation effort focused on the building of a new drain, community activists often combine the discourses and procedures of multiple normative systems over the course of a campaign. This process is clearly illustrated by looking at the events that took place over the summer of 2008. During this summer, the community scheduled a large protest to raise awareness of the conditions in the community and the government's failure to act. The demonstration quickly became the centre point of conflict for the human rights campaign. A local youth club that was supported by the GHRC scheduled the protest to take place on Republic Day, a Ghanaian national holiday. The celebration of Republic Day in Ghana marks the ending of British colonial administration, and the day is generally reserved for honouring elders and politicians. As it is a holiday to honour political officials, the decision to stage a protest in

[7] Chapter 5, titled 'Fundamental Human Rights and Freedoms', outlines many of the same rights contained in international human rights documents such as the ICCPR and the ICESCR and makes them justiciable in Ghana's court system.

direct criticism of the nation's president was seen as highly contentious. The leader of the youth club stated that this choice was intentional. The group's hope was to use the controversy to gain national attention. The youth club assumed that the government would want to prevent the protest and therefore would likely grant a meeting with a high ranking official in order to dissuade them from proceeding.[8]

After several months of holding community advocacy meetings and writing opinion articles in the local newspapers, the group's strategy began to produce results. The group was invited to attend a meeting with the Regional Minister, a man they were told had the power to effectively lobby for funds to build the drain. I was invited to accompany the group to this meeting along with two other Americans interning with the GHRC. The meeting was held on a weekday afternoon, in a conference room at the Regional Minister's office. In attendance were 16 men dressed in military and police uniforms. When the group's turn came, we were ushered to a row of chairs facing conference tables and curtly told to introduce ourselves. Upon hearing that some of us were Americans, the Minister initially accused the youth club of bringing along 'the press'. It was evident from these first moments of the meeting that it was not called with the intention of expressing solidarity or reaching a compromise. As the meeting proceeded, members of the youth club explained how they had brought a petition to the Regional Minister six months prior to that day's meeting. The petition stated that the human and constitutional rights of the community members had been violated. It continued by stating that if the youth club was not granted a meeting concerning the building of the drain within one month, the community would hold a protest. Over the six months, the group had attempted to meet with the Minister several times, and at least once was kept in a waiting room at the Minister's office for hours and then told that there would not be a meeting. As the Minister had, until that day, refused to meet with them, plans for the protest had commenced. At this explanation, the Regional Minister became visibly angry and the following exchange occurred:

> Minister: 'I want to make sure we are all understanding each other—especially the Americans in the back that you came with. You never came to me where I refused to meet you. Did you ever try to meet with me?'

> Youth club members (at once): 'Yes.' 'We did!' 'You did.'

> Minister: 'No. You never came and knocked on my door and were told to go away. Why are you planning to protest on Republic Day? You are expected to be at Independence Square and you choose to do something so contrary.'[9]

In this last statement, the Minister is attempting to limit the ways in which the youth club may claim their human rights. Contemporary Ghanaian

---

[8] Personal interview, Accra, 12 June 2008.
[9] Personal observation, Accra, 24 June 2008

governmental officials generally discuss justice, human rights and the rule of law as being closely aligned with national purpose. Although the Minister said nothing that broke with this stance, during the meeting he made a point to note that claiming these rights through a *protest* on a *national holiday* would be unacceptable.

The meeting continued after the above exchange for several more minutes, but little progress was made. The Minister made it known that the protest was not to go forward. He stated that he would do what he could to lobby for the drain. A member of the youth club mentioned that the community would likely only be convinced not to protest if they believed that progress had actually been made at the meeting. If there were no proof of some progress toward the drain, residents would assume that the youth club had been 'bought off'. To prevent this rumour from starting within the community, the youth club requested a signed document stating that the Minister was in support of the drain being built. At this request, the Minister yelled that the meeting was finished, and we were immediately dismissed. As we were leaving the room, the Police Commander, who had been sitting next to the Regional Minister during the meeting, added his own comments. He stated:

> They will protest on July 1st over my dead body. He says he is going to lobby. If you have any other issues, speak to me directly.[10]

After the meeting, it appeared that the conflict over the protest had stalled negotiations. But a meeting the following day between the Police Commander (the man who uttered the harsh parting words just the day before) and three members of the youth club revealed a different story. In this meeting, which I was also able to attend, the mood was completely different. During this meeting, the discourse reflected notions of community obligation more than the language of international human rights. The leader of the youth club began by reiterating that the community's rights had been violated. He proceeded by asking for help to secure a letter from the Minister to prove that they had not been 'paid to call the protest off'. After making this request, the group's leader stated: 'We see you as a father and a leader. You are from the same community as we are. We are prepared to write an apology if our conduct was inappropriate.' The Police Commander responded that it would be 'professionally odd' for him to try to convince the Minister to make a written statement. Instead, he suggested another strategy. He stated:

> Let me be the father and you be the boys. We do not want to do anything political. Demonstrating cannot solve these problems. We need diplomacy and dialogue. I know he [the Minister] is a father, and he will lobby with whatever he has. I cannot pressure him, but if some of you would go to his home and apologise for your

---

[10] Personal observation, Accra, 24 June 2008.

behaviour, I believe he would be happier. (*pause*) But if there is a protest, certainly I will allow my men to confront them [protesters], and confront them bitterly.[11]

The emphasis on themes such as apology and patriarchy by the youth club members signals a switch away from the strategies commonly associated with human rights advocacy. By telling the Police Commander that they are from the same community and that they see him as a father, the youth club is both making a statement of conciliatory respect and also attempting to appeal to the Commander's sense of community obligation. In this case, alluding to a patriarchal relationship is not simply a passive acceptance of hierarchy; it is part of the advocacy strategy. In her study of access to justice among women in Botswana, Anne Griffiths has noted that individuals are constrained in their ability to engage with law by 'their non-legal power networks' (Griffiths 1997: 93). When an individual can pull support from a large social network, they also often increase their access to institutional knowledge and economic capital, two factors that Griffiths found to be related to success in legal action. By combining the discourses of human rights and customary obligation during the course of advocacy, members of the youth club are attempting to increase the number of social networks of which they may make claims. When community members frame their claims in terms of community obligation, they may be able to gain support from other powerful community members, even if those individuals are opposed to the idea of human rights. When community activists refer to their campaign as a 'human rights campaign', the group may appeal to a much larger transnational community that is interested in promoting social and economic rights. Additionally, community groups can gain support from local NGOs that may have access to international funding circles to help support human rights legal mobilisation.

If pushed too far, however, the decision to combine legal strategies may also have negative consequences for community activists. At the conclusion of the meeting with the Police Commander, the leaders of the youth club made the decision to comply with the Commander's requests and issue a formal apology. They also made the decision to cancel the protest, although there was not a consensus within the club in regards to this decision.[12] Some members argued that the primary purpose of scheduling the protest was to get the attention of the government, and they had succeeded. Others felt that the protest should go forward, even if it led to violence or causalities among the participants. Never during this time did the youth club stop referring to their campaign as a 'human rights campaign'. Despite this (or perhaps, because of it), the decision of the youth club to cooperate with

[11] Personal observation, Accra, 25 June 2008.
[12] Today, some members of the youth club argue that the club never had any intention of following through with the protest, but was simply using the 'threat of protest' to motivate action.

the suggestions of the Police Commander was controversial among human rights NGO workers associated with the larger campaign. Several members of the youth club explained to me that they did not see their decision as being inconsistent with a human rights model.[13] For some of the lawyers at the NGO who were invested in upholding a specific human rights-approach, however, the borderland advocacy employed by the youth club was problematic. For these lawyers, patriarchal requests, such as those made by the Police Commander, and a human rights approach were inherently incompatible. For these lawyers, the youth club was not only accepting a violation of their right to protest; they were also introducing new potential constraints on their future advocacy by bending to patriarchal practices more commonly associated with customary law and partisan politics in Ghana. In response, during the weeks following the meetings with the Regional Minister and the Police Commander, one lawyer even attempted to temporarily shift the focus of the campaign away from the drain construction and onto a more clearly defined human rights topic: the right of peaceful assembly.[14]

There are several possible explanations for the NGO's concern over the combination of human rights and customary discourses. As I have discussed previously, individual actors who are closely connected to legal institutions may be particularly invested in maintaining clearly defined legal procedures and parameters. Staff at the GHRC are intensely committed to a specific set of human rights values that are generally seen to be in conflict with patriarchal systems. It is through the policing of these boundaries that legal forums maintain their jurisdiction. The reaction of the GHRC may also reveal constraints placed on local NGOs by the international community. As Merry and others have noted, the actions of local human rights NGO workers, acting as translators between the local and the global, are often influenced by their funding sources. Kamari Clarke (2009: 65) also notes that organisations that are more closely connected to the community are not necessarily as tied to one mandate, but do have to balance the desires of the community as well as those of larger NGOs, which provide access to institutions and donor circles. For local NGOs to continue to exist they must 'speak the language of international human rights preferred by international donors' (Merry 2006: 42). The international human rights community often views 'culture' as a barrier to the fulfilment of human rights (Merry 2006). Therefore, if local NGOs such as the GHRC are to continue receiving the funding that enables them to support community human rights campaigns, they are limited in the kinds of advocacy that they can publicly endorse.

---

[13] Personal interview, Accra, 2 August 2008.
[14] Personal interview, Accra, 4 August 2008.

4. CONCLUSION

Debates such as these illustrate the complexity of negotiations that occur within legal borderlands as activists engage with law outside of the courtroom. Although discussions of law may occur in multiple locations, the strictly regulated spaces of courtrooms do not generally allow for the same innovation that can occur during a meeting with government officials or an interview with the media. Although many actors in these spaces attempt to regulate the confines of various legal orders, these borders are also contested by individuals operating across boundaries. When operating in the unregulated spaces of the borderland, members of the youth club are able to blend aspects of international, national and customary discourses during their human rights advocacy campaigns. And by refusing to relinquish the category of 'human rights' while doing so, community activists contest the more narrow definition of a human rights approach that is extolled by many human rights NGOs.

At this point, however, it is also important to note that although the youth club may challenge legal borders, it would be inaccurate to describe them as being entirely free from restrictions. Activists will still have to meet the procedural expectations of individual legal forums that they choose to include in their campaigns. If the strategy employs the use of customary law, an adherence to specific procedures will be expected. The same goes for the use of human rights. Community activists may attempt to balance these expectations, but conflicts can still arise between the procedures of various legal regimes (as was the case in the situation described above). In these instances activists may risk a loss of support from one or more of the associated legal institutions. Although these constraints do not preclude the flexible assemblage of legal strategies, they do potentially complicate the process.

On 18 July 2011, over three years after the controversy over the protest, the Ghanaian Parliament passed a supplementary budget, including 6,608,697 GH₵ (about $3,486,823) for the completion of the Nima drains. This action came after many years of continued negotiation between local advocacy groups, human rights organisations and government officials. When I asked the leader of one of the local organisations what changes had brought on the budget allocation, he explained that the change had primarily been political. In the end of 2008, several months after our meetings with the Regional Minister and the Police Commander, the drain became a talking point for then presidential candidate, Dr John Atta Mills. During the final days of the presidential campaign, Mills even held a press conference on the banks of the drain.[15] When Mills and the new Members of

---

[15] Personal interview, Accra, 26 July 2011.

Parliament took office in 2009, local advocates noticed a marked improvement in the willingness of the government to work with the community. One likely reason for this is that Nima and Maamobi have long been considered strongholds of Mills's party, the National Democratic Congress. As the social and political environment of their advocacy campaign changed, the legal mobilisation strategies also shifted for those involved in the project. Community activists continued to use the languages of human rights and customary obligation in their campaigns, but also highlighted the political connections between the community and the ruling political party. Despite the incorporation of these multiple discourses, however, the youth club has continued to portray this as a human rights project.

The example of the Nima drain human rights campaign brings to the forefront the contested nature of human rights and the relationship between normative orders in contexts of legal pluralism. It also reveals that the answer to the question of whether the human rights legal system is broad and flexible or narrow and specific is one of perspective. How one chooses to answer this question largely depends on self-interest. Whereas community activists may be best served through a flexible definition of rights, NGOs may depend on preserving a fairly restrictive set of human rights rules and procedures that support their ideological commitments and allow them to continue receiving funding. Likewise, government officials are often invested in promoting a version of human rights that is broad enough to appease international critics, but narrow enough as not to surrender too much power to their citizens. In an attempt to defend their jurisdiction, institutional actors attempt to portray legal borders as clearly defined and stable. The actions of community activists in Nima and Maamobi, as they apply law to their everyday challenges, however, reveal that these borders are anything but. Instead, legal boundaries are dynamic, strategically negotiated, and challenged by individuals navigating the borderlands.

10

Insiders' Perspectives on Muslim Divorce in Belgium: A Women's Rights Analysis

KIM LECOYER[1]

1. INTRODUCTION

LEGAL PLURALISM 'AT home' (Merry 1988: 874), in the sense of a plurality of legal orders endorsed officially by states in the Global North, is often considered to be at odds with human rights and therefore contested, if not wholly rejected, in public debates.[2] However, regardless of whether a state's legal system 'recognises' plural legal systems, all human societies are in fact subject to the coexistence of various normative orders in 'semi-autonomous social fields' (Moore 1973), which may come under particular public scrutiny in situations of increased cultural and religious diversity. In this context, legal pluralism and especially 'sharia-based' dispute resolution or so-called 'sharia courts', are frequently seen as a threat to state sovereignty and human rights and problematised in particular in terms of gender equality.

Nonetheless, little is known about the actual legal practices of ethnic and religious minorities in Western Europe and more generally in the Global North. Some authors have denounced that, in such debates, led in the name of the protection of Muslim women in need of saving, these women's voices have largely been silenced (Korteweg 2012; Zine 2012). In a few cases, researchers have attempted to study empirically non-state dispute resolution and/or arbitration processes under the auspices of Muslim religious

[1] This research was supported by the Belgian Science Policy Office (Belspo). The author wishes to thank all the interviewees who participated in the interviews and focus groups and Victoria Vandersteen for her assistance in conducting the fieldwork. The author is especially grateful to Eva Brems and Giselle Corradi, her supervisors, for their guidance, stimulating discussions and constructive feedback that greatly improved this contribution. Finally, thanks are also due to Saïla Ouald Chaib for the inspiring exchanges and her comments on an earlier draft of this work.
[2] But see Eva Brems' chapter in this volume.

norms (see Bakker et al 2010; Bano 2007, 2012, 2013; Cutting 2012, 2013; Keshavjee 2007, 2013; Macfarlane 2012a,b). These studies tend to show that on-the-ground realities are far more complex than what has commonly been assumed in many debates. Bano's (2007, 2012, 2013) research on women in Britain turning to sharia councils has, for instance, shown that these councils are rendering services at the demands of women and that the perceived marginality of Muslim women in this process needs to be questioned. Cutting (2012, 2013) observed similar findings in Ontario. However, the normative conceptions and practices of Muslim families have been seldom studied outside North America and the United Kingdom.[3] Belgium, with its fairly large presence of Muslims, and a policy and migration context quite different from these countries (see for instance Favell and Martiniello 1998), constitutes an interesting study field.

With this chapter, I intend to contribute to the knowledge on human rights and legal pluralism in Western societies by analysing the women's rights implications of empirical findings concerning the experiences of Muslim women with divorce in Belgium.[4] I explore how the interaction between (global and local) Islamic normative discourses available to Belgian Muslim families on the one hand, and lived realities of disputing of Belgian Muslim families on the other hand, shapes Muslim women's legal consciousness and agency regarding access to (religious) divorce.[5] The chapter is structured in

---

[3] Exceptions are, for instance, the study of Bakker and his colleagues in the Netherlands (Bakker et al 2010), or Liversage's work in Denmark (Liversage and Jensen 2011). Research on non-state dispute resolution in Muslim communities is ongoing in the Netherlands (Leiden University) and in Germany (FAU).

[4] The empirical research in Belgium is based on fieldwork conducted between April 2012 and June 2014 which aimed at gathering qualitative data about non-state family dispute resolution practices among families of migrant origin in Belgium. It included: visits to and discussions with various civil society associations and community organisations; exploratory as well as in-depth interviews with various field actors playing a facilitating role in dispute-resolution processes (called 'justice providers'); and also focus groups and in-depth interviews with individual members of families of mainly Moroccan and Turkish origin and a few of Pakistani origin, who (had) experienced marital conflict and/or divorce or other family dispute(s) (called 'disputants', or simply 'interviewees'). About 50 field actors or (non-state) 'justice providers' were interviewed: lawyers and mediators, social workers, psychologists and therapists as well as religious actors and informal mediators working with families with a migrant background—and frequently having the same ethnic and/or religious background. The interviews with the Muslim religious actors among them will be examined in the first section of this chapter. About 100 members of families with a (partly) Muslim background, mainly of Moroccan origin, but also of Turkish origin and a few of Pakistani origin, living in Brussels or other Belgian cities, took part in an in-depth interview and/or a focus group. Most of them where women involved in a marital conflict. A majority of the interviewees self-identified as Sunni Muslims. In total, 72 interviews and 15 focus groups were conducted. This fieldwork was part of a broader research project financed by the Belgian Science Policy Office (Belspo) aimed at studying pathways to family justice in families with a migrant background in Belgium.

[5] Legal consciousness refers to 'the ways people understand and use the law' (Merry 1990) and will encompass in this chapter understandings and uses of both state law and non-state normative repertoires. Agency may be defined as 'the socio-culturally mediated capacity to act' (Ahearn 2001). Both concepts are crucial in understanding how human rights are practised and exercised as will be developed further in the fourth and fifth sections of this chapter.

six sections. After providing the background of Muslim presence in Belgium, section 3 provides a description of Islamic normative discourses concerning marriage dissolution addressed to and/or available to Muslims in Belgium. This is done through a combined analysis of Islamic discourses available in European and Belgian Islamic juristic opinions found (mainly) in online publications, and interview data collected by means of field research with local imams and other community actors in Belgium. The fourth section examines the narratives of Belgian Muslims about their practices and experiences concerning divorce, with particular attention for women's access to religious divorce. The fifth section develops an analysis of the implications of these empirical findings in terms of gender differentiated consequences and gender equality. Based on this, the sixth and concluding part formulates an empirically grounded understanding of how the human rights of women may be best protected and promoted in this context.

2. MUSLIMS IN BELGIUM

Although the presence of Muslims in Belgium can be traced back to the 1910s, it is mostly later, in the 1960s, that the inflow of Muslims in Belgium became more important, with the arrival of workers originating from Muslim countries—mainly Morocco and Turkey—with which Belgium concluded bilateral labour agreements. Contemporary Muslim presence is to a large extent still shaped by this history, as the largest Muslim communities in Belgium are the Moroccan and Turkish communities. There are some much smaller communities of more recent immigration, from South Asia for instance, as well as Muslim populations from the Balkans and sub-Saharan African countries, as well as native Belgians who converted to Islam. Estimates of Muslim populations in Belgium are hard to obtain, since no statistics about religious affiliation are available and establishing estimates necessarily implies the use of demographic information about Muslim-majority countries of origin. No reliable demographic information about Belgian-born Muslims is therefore available. Nevertheless, the total number of Muslims in Belgium is estimated at a minimum of 416,000 people (Manço and Kanmaz 2004) up to 450,000 (Fadil 2011) or 500,000 (Bousetta and Bernes 2007), which represents about 4–5% of the total Belgian population.[6]

---

[6] More or less recent estimates of the population with a Moroccan background range from 220,000 people (according to statistics based on nationality and number of acquisitions of Belgian nationality, in which Belgian-born descendants of migrants are thus not taken into account) (Ouali 2004) to almost 300,000 based on figures from Moroccan consulates in Belgium (Ministère Chargé des Marocains Résidant à l'Etranger 2012). Estimations of the population of Belgian Turks (including different Turkish ethnicities, also non-Muslim minorities), range from 140,000 people (Manço 2004: 157), up to 200,000 people (Kaya, Kentel, and Zemni 2008: 27).

Most Muslims live in urbanised areas, although distributed very unevenly. Moreover, they mostly live in geographically circumscribed areas within the major cities and show on average a low level of socioeconomic and educational achievement. In the capital, Brussels, it is estimated that there are 200,000–300,000 Muslims (Dassetto 2011), about half the Muslim population of Belgium and approximately 20% of the population of Brussels. Muslim elites are slowly emerging, but Muslim leadership and intellectual development constitute a major challenge for Belgian Muslim communities (see for instance, Allievi and Dassetto 1997; Pedziwiatr 2008; beyond Belgium see also Cesari 2004).

Within the Belgian legal framework, religiously inspired legal rules that form part of a foreign national legal system could find application through private international law, but any purely religious rules or norms will be disregarded by the Belgian (family) judge who shall only apply Belgian law to family-related or other domestic legal cases. Contracts, as well as mediation agreements, could theoretically be concluded between parties based on Islamic norms, but these will only be considered legally valid and binding provided they respect all legal requirements of Belgian law. The practice of concluding Islamic contracts or mediation agreements is not common though, and probably nearly non-existent among Belgian Muslims. This does not mean that Islamic normativity is irrelevant in the lives of these families. Especially in family matters such as marriage dissolution, it does frequently play an important role, but it does so 'in the shadow of the law'.[7]

3. ISLAMIC NORMATIVE DISCOURSES

In many Muslim families, whether living in Western secular democracies or in Muslim-majority countries, family-law-related practices, such as marriage and divorce, are influenced, though not exclusively, by normative religious considerations at different levels (see, for instance, Fournier 2012; Macfarlane 2012a). In Belgium too, besides religion, traditional or cultural practices as well as other factors, such as financial interests, play a major role (Lecoyer 2017). Nevertheless, many interviewees mentioned that Islamic knowledge, and the 'right' way to do things were important to them.[8] Therefore, it is interesting to look at the Islamic discourses about

[7] This refers to 'private orderings' not regulated by state law, but wherein parties may still draw bargaining power from state law (see Galanter 1981).

[8] In the field of family law, questions formulated in terms of Islamic normativity are, for instance: what is the Islamic validity and status of a civil marriage concluded according to Belgian law? What is the Islamic validity and status of a Belgian civil divorce? Is there a difference whether the husband consents to the civil divorce or not? What Islamic options for the conclusion and dissolution of marriage are available to Belgian Muslims? How do these differ for women as compared to men and why?

family law available to Muslims in a minority setting, and how these in turn relate to the way in which they handle their family life and disputes.

3.1. Islamic Principles for Muslim Minorities

From an Islamic law perspective, the first question, before anything else, pertains to the legitimacy of non-Islamic legal orders for Muslims.[9] As is often the case in Islamic jurisprudence or *fiqh*,[10] a plurality of legal opinions exists on the matter. A key concept in this regard is the classical dichotomy between *dar al-islam*, land of Islam, and *dar al-harb*, land of war.[11] Definitions of Europe in Muslim legal thought range from one side of this dichotomy to the opposite side of it, through various intermediary classifications:

> From being *dar al-harb*, land of conflict, and *dar al-kufr*, land of unbelief, Europe has become *dar al-hijra*, land of migration, then *dar al-'ahd*, land of the covenant, then *dar al-da'wa*, land of the mission, then *dar al-shahada*, land of the witnessing, and finally simply *dar al-islam* in a full and proper sense. (Allievi 2011: 35–36)

Those rejecting the legitimacy of non-Muslim legal orders tend to be those considering European and other Western countries as *dar al-harb* or *dar al-kufr*, mainly because of the absence of an Islamic legal system, generally seeing the legal system of Western liberal democracies as placing man-made laws above God's law. As to the applicability of Islamic law to Muslim minorities, classical as well as contemporary jurisprudence argues that Muslims should always live according to the principles of sharia.[12] Nevertheless, from early on, Islamic jurists considered that the obligations of Muslims outside *dar-al-islam* could be reduced, depending upon the liberty they enjoyed there to practice their religion and live according to its principles (Ali 2007: 70).

Therefore, the dual obligations European Muslims fall under as Muslim citizens of a European country, being required to obey the laws of the land

---

[9] In contemporary Western countries, this legitimacy question mainly concerns normative debates between scholars. Very little is known about how these debates influence the broader Muslim public living in the West.

[10] The Arabic term *fiqh* is commonly translated as 'Islamic law'. The term 'sharia' being often translated in the same way, it seems useful to conceptually distinguish both terms here. Sharia can be broadly understood as 'the right way of religion', or 'a set of values that are essential to Islam and the best manner of their protection' (Kamali 2010: 2), which provides the term with a divine character, whereas *fiqh* refers to 'human understandings and knowledge of Islamic law' (ibid: 40).

[11] It is to be noted that these categories of *dar-al-islam* and its counterparts are not Quranic, but rather emerged in the writings of Muslim jurists, evolving with the territories and relationships of Muslims and non-Muslims. For a historical perspective, see the works of El Fadl (1994a,b).

[12] Among contemporary scholars, T Oubrou likewise recalls this principle (Oubrou 2000; see also Qaradawi 2003).

they live in and feeling morally bound by religious principles and rulings stemming from divine law, gave rise to a variety of Islamic legal opinions. It is worthwhile noting that a large number of legal opinions regarding Muslim minorities in the West, such as those that can be found on the Internet, are produced by scholars who are not themselves living in these circumstances, but live in Muslim-majority countries. Even the European Council for Fatwa and Research (ECFR)—a private collegial *fatwa*[13] body of Islamic jurists created in 1997 to 'guide Muslims in Europe', promote 'a unified *fatwa*' and 'become a reference' for Muslim and non-Muslim institutions, including state authorities—is composed of a large number of scholars from Muslim-majority countries, with different backgrounds and opinions.[14] Perhaps as a consequence of this, many of their collective legal opinions are highly theoretical in their approach and offer little concrete guidance as to how Muslim families living in the West should deal with these dual obligations.

3.2. Islamic Normative Discourses on Marriage Dissolution on the Internet

For many young Muslims the search for answers to religious questions often starts with 'Sheikh Google'.[15] It is therefore interesting to explore Islamic information available on the Internet. With regard to the situation of Muslim minorities, traditional Islamic law may lack relevance or put forward solutions that are unpractical at best, or worse, inappropriate under contemporary Western state legal systems. The ECFR has formulated rulings in various areas of *fiqh*, including family law, but not all their rulings are available online or in print. At the time of writing, only the Arabic version of the website was operational, whereas the English version was not accessible.[16]

---

[13] A *fatwa* (Arabic pl *fatawa*, anglicized pl *fatwas*) is an answer from a qualified Islamic scholar, called *mufti*, to an individual petitioner, called the *mustafti*. It is a non-binding, but generally authoritative, religious opinion or advice. A *fatwa* may be issued orally or in writing, face-to-face or over the phone, on the radio or television, or via the Internet, such as the many *fatwas* that can be found on Islamic websites and online discussion forums, posted by the *muftis* themselves or community members disseminating *fatwas* published elsewhere. One can find a broad range of different approaches online, 'from democratization ... to authoritarianism ...', with intermediate spaces' (Caeiro 2003).

[14] The ECFR is chaired by the notorious and controversial Islamic scholar, Sheikh Yusuf al-Qaradawi. On the ECFR, see eg Karman (2011). Caeiro also published extensively on the topic of the ECFR (eg Caeiro, 2011a,b). For a description of their ambitious goals, see the introduction to (the translated version of) their first and second collection of *fatwas* (European Council for Fatwa and Research 2002: 1–2).

[15] The expression is borrowed from de Koning (2009) and refers to the search for Islamic normative answers on the Internet; *sheikh* being a term commonly used for an Islamic scholar.

[16] During my research, the website was renewed and the English pages eventually simply disappeared.

There is a clear—but not so easily accessible—*fatwa* concerning divorce from the ECFR declaring that a divorce issued by a non-Muslim judge in a European country is valid for Muslim couples (European Council for Fatwa and Research 2009a).[17]

Despite this 'equivalency *fatwa*',[18] the ECFR has issued other *fatwas* that concern modalities of religious divorce. With regard to unilateral divorce initiated by the wife, which is the way many divorces are initiated, for Muslim couples like for any other couple,[19] the ECFR (European Council for Fatwa and Research 2009b)[20] states that a woman may unconditionally initiate a divorce if a provision for such an action was written into her marriage contract. But otherwise, it underlines the exclusive right of men to initiate divorce, and makes the initiation of divorce by women dependent on judicial authorities or on the husband's agreement. According to this *fatwa*, which highlights several times the importance of reconciliation, divorce possibilities for women are:

— by mutual agreement;
— through a delegated right to unilateral divorce, expressly stipulated in the marriage contract;
— before a judge and by returning the *mahr* or bride gift (this type of divorce is called *khul'*);
— before a judge, due to harm being inflicted upon her (judicial divorce).[21]

Consequently, according to this opinion, except when there is an explicit stipulation in the (Islamic) marriage contract, a woman can only divorce by obtaining her husband's consent, or through a judicial authority—leaving unclear whether this refers to religious or secular instances. It appears that no Islamic authorities entitled to 'perform'[22] religious divorce currently

---

[17] An English translation was found on Islamopedia (Islamopedia Online, 2010a).

[18] This is how Macfarlane refers to the above-mentioned ECFR *fatwa* (Macfarlane 2012a: 235).

[19] Statistics from the USA indicate that throughout most of the nineteenth century about 60% of divorces were filed by women and that the proportion today remains slightly above two-thirds (Brinig and Allen 2000). French and Belgian statistics display the same trend of women initiating the majority of non-consensual divorces (Chaussebourg et al 2009; Institut national de statistique (Belgium) 2006). Even in a country such as Morocco, where women were only recently given equal access to divorce rights, women file the majority of (non-consensual) divorce cases (Mdidech 2013).

[20] An English version was found on Islamopedia (2010b).

[21] It is to be noted that differences in viewpoints exist concerning divorce rights for women under Islamic law and that this *fatwa* does not reflect the more equitable viewpoint that *khul'* divorce only requires the returning of the *mahr* and not necessarily judicial intervention and/or the husband's consent, as is sometimes held in other Muslim juristic opinions (see eg Khir, 2006).

[22] This term is used by John Bowen to signify the dual act of announcing and changing (status) implied in divorce by sharia councils. He developed an interesting analysis of the 'performative ambiguity' of UK Sharia Councils in dissolving Muslim marriages in a forthcoming work that was presented at a seminar at Leiden University on 18 September 2014.

exist in Belgium. Does this mean that, from an Islamic viewpoint, Muslim women can or even should resort to Belgian state justice for their divorce? The answer is not univocal in the examined Islamic discourses. In fact, it is unclear how exactly the 'equivalency *fatwa*' and the *fatwa* concerning Islamic divorce for women are to be understood together.

Belgian law does not recognise religious divorce, hence the only way to dissolve a legally valid marriage is through a Belgian divorce, or in some cases a foreign one. However, it is noteworthy that very little information can be found on Islamic divorce proceedings in a Western context. Many Islamic scholars who write and lecture extensively about various topics in Islamic law refrain from engaging clearly in this subject. Lectures and articles about divorce in Islam mainly touch aspects such as reconciliation and ways to prevent divorce and do not articulate how actually to settle it.

Members of Muslim families, when interviewed, frequently mentioned searching for Islamic knowledge about family matters on the Internet. Some explicitly said they appreciated Belgian Islamic scholars because they are seen as being more aware of the situation in Belgium. Upon searching for online opinions from a number of Belgian '*muftis*'[23] who seem to be appreciated by young Belgian Muslims, I found very similar (general) guidelines with regard to divorce.[24] These Belgian 'cyber-*fatwas*' do not, however, provide practical directives as to how a woman in Belgium should proceed with her unilateral divorce (through *khul'*). One such *fatwa* states that a woman can ask the judge—does this mean a judge in a Belgian civil state court?— for divorce in case of mistreatment or harm or absence of her husband. If she wants to divorce because she 'doesn't love her husband', then she separates from him through *khul'* by returning her *mahr* to him.

From the formulation of this *fatwa* one could deduce that the 'right' way to divorce for a Muslim woman is to resort to the Belgian judge for a civil divorce and, if she left her husband because of a lack of affection, to make sure that she moreover returns her *mahr* to him. This is all but explicit from the *fatwa* itself:

> The woman requests for divorce before the judge in case of neglect, mistreatment, long absences, on the ground of harm or moral or material damages. In case of a

---

[23] See n 13.

[24] Below, two Belgian Islamic website, fatawas.be and sajidine.com, are examined; both were mentioned by study interviewees. Fatawas.be is a website proposing religious teachings, such as real-life and online Islamic courses, and *fatwas*, by Hassan Amdouni, a Tunisian-born scholar who studied in Medina, Tunis and Paris and writes and lectures extensively for French-speaking Muslim audiences with whom he is quite popular. The team of internauts behind Sajidine.com highlight, on the 'about' section of the website, that they are not religious scholars, but simply aim at disseminating religious knowledge. They claim not to belong to any particular tendency or school of jurisprudence, although *salafi* influences can be noticed. Both websites are in French. It seems no similar Dutch-language Belgian websites exist, and that 'Sheikh Google' will therefore orient Dutch-speaking Belgian Muslims towards Netherlands-based websites.

request based on a lack of love: this means the wife saying: that she feels no affection anymore for her husband, she can separate from him through Khul'. She frees herself from the marital bond by returning the received bride gift to her husband (Amdouni 2011: question 2).[25]

The author further specifies that this type of divorce 'needs to be proclaimed in the civil and religious way and announced before witnesses' (Amdouni 2011: question 3). It is, however, not specified what that actually entails.

Another popular Belgian Islamic website, Sajidine.com,[26] provides a very detailed legalistic discourse based on classical Islamic jurisprudence, though without any link to concrete legal practices. This can be an appealing source to gain Islamic knowledge about the topic of marriage and divorce in classical Islamic *fiqh*, because of the detailed approach and many references; however, with regard to the integration of Islamic legal practices within the Belgian state legal system, no concrete solutions are proposed, or even discussed. This is not so surprising though, given that this is clearly not the aim of the webmasters, who are much engaged with purposes of purely religious nature.

It should be noted that when Muslims search for answers on the Internet, they may equally likely come across transnational 'cyber-*muftis*',[27] such as Shaykh Ibn'Uthaymeen,[28] who provide much clearer and more concrete—though sometimes highly constraining—answers to these types of concrete problems, simply prohibiting Muslims from resorting to any non-Muslim judge.[29]

---

[25] Translated by the author.

[26] See above, n 24.

[27] The Internet is a supranational virtual space transcending national boundaries. Interestingly, the counter showing the number of online visitors on fatawa.be displays visitors from various West-European countries and generally even more from France than from Belgium. Likewise, it is therefore to be expected that Belgian Muslims consult Islamic cyber resources beyond national boundaries as well. As to Belgian Dutch-speaking Muslims searching for Islamic answers online, they will most likely be attracted by the numerous Netherlands-based Islamic websites such as vragenenislam.nl, or the more *salafi*-oriented al-yaqeen.com or islamkennis.com.

[28] Ibn Uthaymeen is a Saudi *ulama*, often quoted in *salafi*-oriented internet forums in several languages. He wrote, together with Ibn Baz, another Saudi *mufti*, a collection of *fatwas* for British Muslims (Ibn Baz and Ibn Uthaymeen 1998).

[29] Concerning divorce procedures in non-Muslim countries, his *fatwa* reads: 'It is not permissible for a Muslim to follow, either in his worship or in his dealings with others, other than what is laid down in Islaamic law. Divorce is one of those issues which is dealt with by Islaamic law in the most complete manner. It is, therefore not permitted for anyone to go beyond or transgress the limits set by Allaah (Subhaanahu wa Ta'aala) concerning divorce. ... Such are the limits set by Allaah and whoever transgresses Allaah's limits has wronged his own soul. [Soorah at-Talaaq, Aayah 1]. It is, therefore not permitted for a Muslim to transgress those limits set by Allaah and he should divorce according to the stipulations of Islaamic law' (Ibn'Uthaymeen, n.d.).

3.3. Islamic Normative Discourses in Interviews with Belgian Muslim Religious Actors

The interviews with Muslim religious actors in Belgium show that compliance with Belgian state law is strongly encouraged and, very much in line with ECFR's standpoint, civil divorce of Belgian Muslims is generally considered as religiously valid. Nevertheless, despite the broad or even unanimous acceptance of this general principle of validity of civil divorce, in discussing modalities of religious divorce, the viewpoint that in Islam divorce is a male prerogative is quasi-unanimous. This inevitably leads to ambiguity in explanations about how a Belgian Muslim woman should handle her divorce 'correctly'. It is probably this same tension that explains the vagueness in the Belgian 'cyber *fatwas*' above. Amdouni's description of *khul'* could be interpreted as providing women with religious agency to exit their marriage autonomously. He does not mention, contrary to ECFR, the need for an (Islamic) judge in this case, nor does he mention the need for the husband's consent. The fieldwork in Belgium nevertheless tends to show that women's options may be more restricted in the viewpoint of a number of religious actors, some stating that religious authorities would be required for *khul'* but are non-existent; others stating that the husband needs to consent in case of *khul'*. One religious actor even claimed that the husband could ask his wife for any amount of money, even beyond returning the amount of the *mahr* or bride gift she received.

By contrast, a few interviewed religious scholars considered that, based on the ECFR *fatwa*, civil marriage implies some sort of implicit delegation of the right to divorce (*tafwid*) to the civil judge. One of them said: '[T]herefore, in fact it is the position of the European Council of Fatwa, who says that any person who basically marries before a civil court, automatically knows that the judge will be able to divorce him, so indirectly he is basically giving that permission.'[30]

This may sound surprising at first, but rereading the *fatwa*, this is precisely what it says.[31] This would therefore mean that as soon as there is a

---

[30] Interview on 24 February 2014 in Liege with a local Islamic preacher and lecturer, imam in a mosque in the area of Liege.

[31] Islamopedia Online (2010b) provides the following English translation: 'The principle is that a Muslim only resorts to a Muslim Judge or any suitable deputy in the event of a conflict. However, and due to the absence of an Islamic judicial system in non-Muslim countries, it is imperative that a Muslim who conducted his marriage by virtue of those countries' respective laws, to comply with the rulings of a non-Muslim judge in the event of a divorce. Since, the laws were accepted as governing the marriage contract, then it is as though one has implicitly accepted all consequences, including that the marriage may not be terminated without the consent of a judge. This case is similar to that in which the husband gives authority to the judge to do so, even if he did so implicitly, and which is considered acceptable by the vast majority of scholars.'

civil marriage, the parties not only understand that this entails that their marriage dissolution will be subject to civil divorce proceedings but also that this is a type of delegated right to divorce considered valid according to Islamic law, suppressing any need for further religious formalities. Moreover, these and other (pragmatic) understandings of the ECFR's *fatwa*, reaching the same normative conclusion that additional formalities are not necessary, often insist on the practical aim of divorce, which is to end a marriage, and therefore argue in favour of a close interrelatedness between civil and Islamic marriage dissolution.

One interviewed religious actor, who also subscribes to the equivalency principle, highlighted that Islamic divorce may nevertheless sometimes occur before the civil divorce proceedings are finalised. Such proceedings may take a long time, he explained, and it would be absurd to ask people to consider they are still religiously married in this case (preventing them from remarrying and consequently barring the road to any religiously licit intimate relationship). Islamic divorce proceedings in that view would then apply to exceptional situations, in the absence of a (completed) civil divorce. This explanation was not widely held among religious scholars though. Moreover, some indicated that the ECFR's equivalency *fatwa* is not 'ideal' from an Islamic standpoint, but that it is a pragmatic response to a particular situation, weakening in a way the *fatwa*'s legitimacy.

From the Islamic normative discourses examined, the following options thus emerge. First, some religious actors consider there is complete equivalence between civil and religious divorce, suppressing any need for religious divorce proceedings (with some exceptions). Second, other religious actors seem to hold the view that there would be imperfect equivalence between civil and religious divorce, recognising civil divorce as valid, but still encouraging Muslims to complete some additional religious 'formalities', which may be more or less constraining and are different for men and women. Husbands are encouraged to pronounce a *talaq*, a unilateral Islamic divorce uttered by the man, (and pay any *mahr* not yet paid), whereas wives who initiate divorce unilaterally without the husband's consent for reasons of 'lack of love' (*khul'* divorce) are encouraged to return the received *mahr* to the husband. In addition, wives may also be told that they need to obtain their husband's consent for this, and/or that they need to turn to a religious authority, or even that they will have to pay any amount requested by the husband in exchange of his 'acceptance' of the divorce. Third, the possibility of a contractual delegation of the right to divorce is generally admitted, thereby establishing equal access to divorce for the wife, but this option is not encouraged by local actors. Finally, some online transnational Islamic normative discourses reject the legitimacy of the civil judge or at least consider Muslims who would resort to non-Muslim state justice as sinful. This stance was not found among the religious actors interviewed in Belgium.

As a result, besides the option of complete equivalency, equal access of women to divorce is dependent on a contractual agreement. Importantly, not all interviewed religious actors and scholars were aware of the possibility of including an equal right to divorce for the wife in the marriage contract and those who were aware of this possibility generally rather advised against it, 'to avoid divorce as much as possible' and remain 'in the joyful atmosphere' of marriage.[32]

In the interviews, some explain why in Islam—as they understand it—divorce is a right given to men rather than to women, such as in the following example, based on strong gender stereotypes:

> First of all, it is the man who bears the financial responsibility, let's imagine that this man has invested his money, to build, this construction, this family, and the wife she says, now I divorce, she will break everything, he will be the first who loses ... the second thing, that the man is more rational and the woman she is more sentimental, that also plays, if Islam would grant the divorce to the wife, with a simple phrase, a formulation 'voilà, I am divorced', it's a catastrophe, if she's upset she will say that word, even with men we find [these types of] problems.[33]

Hence, from all the above, the importance of civil marriage and divorce appears as crucial for women's (equal) access to marriage dissolution. The question is how these different types of normative discourses influence the divorce practices of Muslim families in Belgium.

4. ISLAMIC NORMATIVITY IN ACTION: MUSLIM DIVORCE PRACTICES IN BELGIUM

The research in Belgium confirms that when Muslims are referring to 'sharia'[34]—interviewees almost never used this word themselves—or Islamic law, in their legal practices, they are not referring to it in terms of an Islamic state, or implementing a sharia-based legal system, they rather mean religious rules or simply ethical norms, a moral code of conduct. Some simply think of it as (religious) values. In the interviews many mention they want to live and act *halal*[35] or refer to something they see as a kind of moral code that they would want to respect in their family engagements for instance. Hence, the role and meaning of this normative framework appears as very

---

[32] Interview on 9 December 2013 in Liege with a local religious leader and imam of a mosque in the area of Liege.

[33] See previous note.

[34] For a definition see n 10. Only one interviewed 'disputant' in the research spontaneously used the term, in contrast to several interviewed 'justice providers'.

[35] *Halal* means permissible according to Islamic norms and constitutes a quite popular term among Western European Muslims, including the interviewees in this research, together with the opposite term *haram* (see eg Arslan, 2014).

important to many Muslims. Nevertheless, this does not necessarily imply that state laws are being disregarded. In most cases, Islamic prescriptions are being implemented on top of legal and administrative imperatives stemming from the state legal framework.

Secondly, it appears that with regard to non-state family dispute resolution, the religious normative framework—in this case the reference to Islamic principles—can be both a risk factor and a potential facilitator for women's agency in (equally) exercising their right to divorce. Some interviewed (religious and other) 'justice providers' have, for instance, mentioned that shared religious principles and values can be extremely helpful in finding a mutually accepted solution between disputants. Conversely, certain interpretations of religious rights and duties can very strongly restrict individual rights and freedom, especially women's range of morally legitimate or socially accepted options, as was seen with regard to the right to divorce, for instance. At the same time, knowledge of religious rights and duties may not only broaden one's options, but also offer powerful arguments, both to women and men, providing power in bargaining for solutions.

Thirdly, it is known that transnationalism plays a major role in the lives of many families with a migrant background. This is also the case for Turkish and Moroccan families in Belgium, as well as for other communities such as the Pakistani. Besides cultural transnationalism and economic transnationalism, religious transnationalism tends to create a global community in which Islamic law operates in a de-territorialised virtual space. Of course, the Internet plays an important role in this. However, the importance and actual impact of what have been called 'cyber-*muftis*' in this chapter should not be overestimated. Research on sharia councils in the UK has indicated that very often the immediate network of disputants has a major influence on the types of disputing forums people turn to.[36] It is most likely that local forums, and especially social and family networks, have a stronger influence on legal practices than such virtual forums.

Finally, whether it is in the field of Islamic legal solutions and reasoning or in matters of customary, traditional and cultural practices, there is an enormous diversity within and among families.[37] In our research, the importance given to religion varied strongly between different interviewees. However, attachment to religious marriage and divorce was not necessarily linked to

---

[36] Bano (2007: 19) found that it is often family members who act as the initial point of contact with the council and that, viewed this way, 'Shariah Councils are a continuation of the process of dispute management by the family'. Likewise, research in the Netherlands highlights the primordial role of family and friends, confirming also that virtual spaces may play a role in the search for religious knowledge or (anonymous) advice-seeking, but are comparatively of much less importance to dispute resolution processes (Bakker et al 2010).

[37] Sociological research in Belgium indicates, for instance, that only about 10% of Muslims in Belgium are 'practising Muslims' (Torrekens 2005).

the level of religiosity and belief, supporting the view that '[r]eligiosity and use of law is therefore a complex negotiation' (Cesari 2012: 7).

4.1. Divorce Practices of Belgian Muslim Women

Not all Muslim couples in Belgium, probably not even a majority of them, feel Islamic divorce is imperative.[38] As an illustration of this, one inter-viewee, a young Muslim woman of Moroccan origin, stated very clearly that she never assumed that she needed an Islamic divorce. She simply went to the Belgian civil court to obtain a divorce and never asked herself the question of the Islamic validity of it. 'You're divorced, it's over.'[39] From many collected narratives about divorce, it becomes clear that many inter-viewees have very little knowledge about the topic of Islamic divorce before they face a divorce situation and decide, at least some of them, to gain infor-mation about it. Even when interviewees were informed about prescriptions concerning Islamic divorce, they nevertheless relied on civil divorce, espe-cially if an Islamic divorce was (particularly) difficult to obtain.

A few women mentioned that they were told that they needed a religious authority for their religious divorce. However, the research found no reli-gious bodies based in Belgium that dissolved marriages. Some Shia commu-nities, and a number of Pakistani families, rely on religious bodies abroad for this. But apart from these situations, women wanting a religious divorce mainly negotiated a *talaq*, ie a religious divorce uttered by the husband.

Women negotiating a *talaq* from their husband need not be seen as pas-sive victims of male 'repudiation'. Many of them pressured their husbands to grant them the religious divorce *they* wanted, sometimes with the help of family members or a religious figure. Several female interviewees mentioned asking their husband to 'give them a *talaq*' in order to obtain the Islamic divorce they wanted irrespective of who initiated the separation/divorce. A few interviewees did this without seeking a civil divorce, considered 'less

---

[38] The very notion of 'Islamic divorce' seems to be new or even surprising to several Mus-lims encountered during the study, as divorce is commonly seen as a prerogative of the state. Moreover, it seems that especially Belgian Muslims with Turkish roots are largely socialised with the idea that divorce (as well as marriage to a certain extent) are matters of civil status and hence operated by the state, possibly because of the long-standing tradition of secular state laws regulating family law in Turkey. A female lawyer of Turkish origin from Antwerp indicated that although the practice of superposed civil and religious marriage is quite similar among both Moroccan and Turkish origin families, practices related to Islamic divorce are much less common in Turkish families as compared to Moroccan families. The religious impor-tance of prior reconciliation is, however, of utmost importance to many Turkish families, she said (interview, 21 June 2012).

[39] Interview on 2 May 2012 in Brussels with a female social worker of Moroccan origin.

important', and had only a separation enacted by the judge, but remained officially married.[40] One interviewee declared:

> [S]o he said to me 'I divorce you' and so during several months we have to stay together in the house to see whether there is a possibility to return together again and after three menstrual periods[41] we are divorced.[42]

Other women have also asked their husband for *talaq* in order to get an Islamic divorce. For example, in a case where the husband had a relationship with another woman abroad, the husband decided to divorce when his wife found out. She then asked him to give her a *talaq*, while the civil divorce procedures were still running:

> [Y]es, I put him under pressure really, to give it ... please just give a talaq in Islam and he just gave it to me ... over the phone.[43]

Another of the interviewees declared:

> I contented myself with his decision to divorce and I asked him to pronounce it clearly, so not just say I want to divorce or we need to divorce, to say 'I divorce you' 'you are not my wife anymore'.[44]

Civil marriage and civil divorce are frequently considered very important to safeguard one's rights. Some women, especially among the younger generations, explicitly stated that it is—in their own words—'unsafe' not to have a civil marriage, mainly because of the perspective of marital abandonment and 'marital captivity'.[45] The importance of civil marriage emerged strongly in one of the focus groups, in a discussion about divorce. A young practising Muslim woman declared that she would first conclude an Islamic marriage

[40] Some women in this case seemed to be unaware or at least not fully aware of the legal (and financial) consequences of remaining legally married. For some, it was the perspective of 'returning before the judge' that discouraged them, but one, elder, woman, considered it was her religious duty to continue to take care of her husband instead of 'abandoning' him.

[41] The interviewee refers to the *'idda*, or waiting period to be observed after the uttering of divorce, before the divorce is definitive and during which remarriage is not allowed. It is generally considered that this period is intended to determine possible paternity and to allow for reconciliation between the spouses.

[42] Interview on 26 July 2012 in Brussels with a Belgian female interviewee (Muslim convert), age 35, married to a husband of Moroccan origin. They had a religious divorce and were legally separated but not divorced at the time of the interview.

[43] Interview on 2 August 2012 in Antwerp with a Dutch–Moroccan female interviewee (second generation), age 31, married to a Dutch–Moroccan man. At the time of the interview they had not yet started civil divorce procedures (in the Netherlands).

[44] Interview on 17 August 2012 in Brussels with a 36 year old Belgian female interviewee (Muslim convert) married to a man of Moroccan origin (second generation). She wanted him to 'clarify' their situation, so that she would know what to expect. They were not yet divorced under civil law, she made an appointment with a lawyer planned for a few days after the interview.

[45] Marital captivity refers to situations where a person, generally a woman, is unable to terminate his/her religious marriage (van Waesberghe et al 2014).

to be able to spend time alone with her husband/fiancé, but would not live with him or have intercourse before they concluded a civil marriage:

> So that he can communicate with me, so that if we need to go get something [for the wedding], we can do it, so that we are 'halal' in our contact with each other but he should not, you understand, I will not have intercourse, I will stay with my parents until, it's all good and well, but I say it, one, we don't live in an Islamic country and, two, we don't live anymore in the time of the Prophet.[46]

The same woman explained how she considered civil divorce of utmost importance, right before she said that she would certainly conclude a civil marriage:

> If you live in an Islamic country, then ['informal' religious marriage] it is not a problem ... because if you go to the judge and say 'here are my two witnesses', ok. But here, if you go to the judge and you say 'here are my two witnesses', the judge is going to laugh at you and say 'now you may bring what's on paper'. I just think it's unsafe. ... and I feel like, why should you take the unsafe while we have something that gives us, you understand, that man can say, and it happens so often, in France mainly, I have heard that it really happens a lot, that the man says, 'yeah', um, 'bye'. He doesn't pronounce the talaq. Because it is only the man who can say the talaq. The wife has to go to the judge. She cannot say 'enta talaq' [I divorce you]. Thus he leaves her behind, he goes and remarries and what is the woman going to do? She cannot remarry because then she simply is 'in zina' ['adultery', sex outside of a (religiously valid) marriage]. Whatever she does, whatever she says.[47]

This young woman demonstrates her awareness of rights in several normative repertoires and the practical limitations of these rights in the legal and the Islamic framework. In her own words, 'it's just a matter of playing it smart'. In so doing, she demonstrates her quite strong agency in playing strategically, while at the same time taking for granted a certain gender-discriminating religious norm concerning access to divorce. Her viewpoint is also an illustration of the 'equivalency principle'[48] and its importance for women, the need for a woman 'to go to the judge', being understood as going to the civil judge in the context of Belgium.

On the other hand, several interviews confirmed that, practically speaking, it was often difficult for women to find out how to proceed with their Islamic divorce if they didn't have a *talaq* from their husband. Women frequently indicated that they searched for Islamic information, on the Internet, in books, and by talking with friends and/or by asking one or several imam(s).

Not so surprisingly, given the attitudes of most religious scholars in this regard, none of the interviewed women had included the right to divorce

---

[46] Female participant in a focus group held on 29 May 2014 in Mechelen, age 20, of Moroccan origin (third generation).

[47] Female participant in focus group of 29 May 2014, see previous note.

[48] See above, n 18, referring to ECFR's *fatwa* considering civil divorce religiously valid.

in an Islamic marriage contract,[49] and it seems none of them was in fact (made) aware of this possibility. The ECFR and its *fatwas* were simply never mentioned by the interviewees, male or female. But, as explained, that does absolutely not mean that all Muslims consider that Islamic divorce is a necessity to dissolve a marriage, nor that they care about it.

Among those who did care about Islamic divorce, several women considered they could self-enact their religious divorce and did so, based on different ways of reasoning, frequently quite disconnected from the previously examined normative discourses. A female interviewee who had been married several times and had her previous marriages dissolved by her successive husbands through *talaq* interestingly enough considered she could pronounce a *talaq* herself:

> I do my duty what I have to do, halal is halal, haram is haram and I'm allowed to divorce if it's irreparable, and it wasn't possible anymore ... and I have been so strong myself [to say] now enough is enough, I stop with this ... also with these other men [her previous husbands who pronounced the talaq] I had learned as well if you say three times divorce, divorce, divorce, then you are divorced ... I take the law into my hands'.[50]

A few interviewees mentioned they had studied Islam or Islamic theology, mostly in local community institutions, and that they had also learned about marriage and divorce in their classes. One woman, for instance, reported that she remembered from her lessons that Islamic divorce occurs after a separation of 4 months and 10 days. Therefore, she explained that while the civil divorce proceedings were running, 'after those 4 month and 10 days, I already considered myself divorced'.[51]

Women's agency in this context clearly appears as a 'socio-culturally mediated capacity to act' (Ahearn 2001), within structural constraints of an Islamic normative repertoire and its interplay with other legal repertoires, such as the national legal system and possibly also the system of the country of origin. Some women take the freedom to consciously define their (own) religious understandings, especially when they have built a certain confidence in their knowledge of Islamic normativity. But even otherwise, women frequently were able to navigate more or less skilfully within the

---

[49] In most Islamic sources Islamic marriage is considered to be a contract, which may be made in writing and include a number of specific clauses. However, in practice it is often limited to an oral agreement that only includes a stipulation of the *mahr* or bride gift.

[50] Interview on 1 October 2012 in Antwerp with a Belgian female interviewee, age 42 (Muslim convert), who was religiously married to a Moroccan-born man (first-generation migrant). They did not have a civil marriage. She had been married (religiously) several times before. She remarried, also through a religious marriage only, and her current husband (a first-generation migrant from Morocco) with whom she has established a legal cohabitation, obtained his residency status through this relationship. Despite her insistence, he refuses civil marriage.

[51] Interview on 9 October 2012 in Brussels with a divorced female interviewee, age 41, with Moroccan roots (second generation) who was married to a man from Morocco through a consulate marriage arranged by her parents.

boundaries of Islamic normativity as defined by (locally) dominant normative discourses. Some turned to religious actors such as local imams, whereas
others were able to forum shop strategically by making sure *not* to go an
imam; one woman for instance said she wouldn't go to an imam because
she 'didn't feel like receiving advice that would not go in [her] direction'.[52]

Other structural constraints frequently seem to play an even more important role than Islamic normativity in women's access to marriage dissolution,
such as social pressure produced by dominant sociocultural understandings or expectations and a very powerful stigma associated with divorced
women.

4.2. Agency and Legal Consciousness in Muslim Women's Access to (Islamic) Divorce

All women are in principle guaranteed equal legal rights and protection
by the Belgian state. However, in the private ordering of their lives, Muslim families, men and particularly women, may sometimes experience constraints in the enjoyment of certain rights because of a number of (religious
and cultural) normative considerations. Women's difficulties and inequality in exercising their right to divorce are thus best understood through
empirically grounded knowledge of the 'options and limits for women as
subjects of legal pluralism' (Hellum 2000). This implies a need to examine
obstacles and potentialities in Islamic normative discourses as well as the
consequences thereof on the lives of women. Therefore, this gender analysis
focuses on women's legal consciousness, ie women's understandings of their
rights and legal entitlements as well as when and why they use or do not
use certain (state and/or non-state) disputing mechanisms. In this analysis,
agency is conceptualised in a way that allows for various forms and nuances
of it, accepting Mahmood's critic of the articulation of agency as solely
'resistance to power' (Charrad 2010; Mahmood 2001) and accepting the
idea that agency can be embedded in religion, opening a conceptual space
where women's capacity to act can be informed by religiosity (Burke 2012;
Korteweg 2008, 2012; Mack 2005; Mahmood 2001).

Agency and legal consciousness are closely interrelated. Ewick and Silbey
(1998) conceptualised legal consciousness as a social practice that integrates
human action and structural constraint in a process of ongoing mutual cau-
sation. 'Although a product, in part, of desire and will', it is 'not entirely
individual or subjective', as it is 'always a collective construction that simultaneously expresses, uses and creates publicly exchanged understandings' or
schemas (Ewick and Silbey 1998: 46). Therefore, to look at the legal consciousness of the women who participated in this research means to study

---

[52] Interview on 26 July 2012, see n 42.

their participation in the ongoing mutual process of constructing the legality that is at play in many Belgian Muslim families. Legal consciousness varies individually within a given socially defined context and depends on the available repertoires of action and interpretation as well as on the ensembles of resources these women have at their disposal.

As explained above, there are a range of different understandings of what Islamic normativity may imply for family matters such as marriage dissolution in the context of Belgian Muslim communities. There is a clear tendency towards the superposition of normative repertoires. Recognition that Belgian state laws regarding marriage and divorce need to be respected is widespread, while it is generally understood that additional steps may be required to conform with Islamic normativity. Apart from the prior civil marriage requirement,[53] however, there seems to be very little engagement with the substance of state law. Integrated legal solutions incorporating both repertoires beyond simple coexistence alongside each other have apparently yet to be elaborated.[54]

As was also seen above, different normative understandings and social realities comprise more or less constraining elements and options for women's access to divorce. These are operating as 'available repertoires of action' and 'cultural codes for interpretation' (Ewick and Silbey 1998). Potentialities clearly exist within Islamic normative discourses to provide gender-equal access to marriage dissolution, either through a contractual agreement between spouses delegating an unconditional right to divorce to the wife, or through the viewpoint that civil marriage entails an implicit delegation of the right to divorce to the civil judge, thereby suppressing the need for any religious divorce modalities. Both options are, however, currently rarely encountered in practice. In the first case, such contractual agreements are unknown by some community leaders, looked upon with suspicion by others, or at least not encouraged by most. Consequently, Muslim families generally do not seem aware of this possibility and of its advantages. As to the second option, it was only upheld by a tiny minority of interviewed religious leaders, although this is what the ECFR's *fatwa* about divorce for Muslims in Western Europe entails.

There seems to be room for the development of a third way, based on the understanding that women may self-enact their religious divorce, provided they return their *mahr* or bride gift, or waive whatever they were promised

---

[53] The Belgian Constitution (Art 21) and Belgian criminal law (Art 267) requires civil marriage to occur prior to religious marriage celebration and prohibits religious clergy from marrying couples who are not married in civil law. Contrary to France, no convictions have been pronounced in Belgium.

[54] This contrasts with initiatives developed in North America and the UK by legal scholars who are well versed in both secular law of the land and Islamic law such as solicitors Aina Khan in the UK and Abed Awad in the USA. Academics are contributing to the elaboration of an integrated framework as well (see eg Quraishi and Syeed-Miller 2012).

as a *mahr* but did not receive.[55] This option is perhaps more likely to find ground in Belgian and other European Muslim communities, provided women themselves are aware of this possibility granted by Islamic legal theory.[56] Several religious actors, however, resisted this possibility, based on the understanding that women need their husband's consent and/or that they should resort to a religious authority for such a proceeding. The need for the intervention of religious authorities is not deemed necessary for male self-enacted divorce or *talaq*, despite the fact that in many, if not most, Muslim-majority legal systems *talaq* is now equally subject to judicial control. This is probably best understood in the light of the surrounding social realities women generally face and that were often encountered in this field research and mentioned by interviewees, namely the fact that social control and pressure on women tends to be (much) stronger as compared to the control of male behaviour. Underlying reasons for this are to be found in the strong gender stereotypes and irrational fears of social and family disruptions conveyed by normative discourses in which these views are mistakenly and sometimes misleadingly presented as religiously inspired.

The religious normative framework thus clearly contains both enabling elements, such as the permissibility of divorce, and at the same time constraining elements, such as the limited divorce options for women in dominant understandings of Islamic divorce regulations. Nevertheless, other, more enabling options exist within this framework, such as *khul'*, viewed as women's self-enacted unilateral divorce or the implicit or contractual delegation of equal divorce rights to women, but these are insufficiently known by women, who tend to rely on (local or transnational, real or virtual) religious scholars' viewpoints, which unfortunately often resist or obscure these understandings.

Women's legal consciousness is shaped by experiences with different types of justice mechanisms and the (experience with the) Belgian legal system also

---

[55] *Mahr* amounts are not very high in most Belgo-Moroccan families, generally between a few hundreds euros to at most a few thousands. Belgo-Turks tend to more often follow a tradition of offering gold jewels, where amounts might be higher. A trend of symbolic gifts associated with romantic love is currently developing across ethnic divides. In cases of an agreed sum as *mahr*, several women mentioned they had only received part of it, or sometimes nothing.

[56] It could be objected from a strict equality perspective that this option would still be unfair to women, because they have to return their *mahr*. This is, however, contradicted by insiders' perspectives. On the one hand, women are in principle completely free to decide themselves whatever they would like to receive as *mahr* and field findings confirm that this freedom was indeed usually theirs, and on the other hand, women in the research didn't consider it unfair to return *mahr* in case of *khul'*. *Mahr* is seen as overall beneficial to women, and keeping it in a wife-initiated non fault divorce is viewed as a sort of unjust enrichment. Nevertheless, disputes around *mahr* were quite rare in the research; therefore additional research on this topic would be beneficial. Yet in this research, Muslim women appear to be having difficulties with having access to *khul'* and not with its consequences in terms of *mahr*.

comprises both enabling and constraining elements. Several young women advocating in favour of civil marriage were, for instance, contradicted in focus group discussions by elder divorced women who remarried Islamically without civil marriage, or intended to do so, in order not to have to go through civil divorce proceedings again in case the marriage breaks down.[57] The empirical findings demonstrate that many Muslims lack (in-depth) knowledge of Islamic regulation of marriage and divorce proceedings and that they therefore tend to assign imams or other religious actors a central role in defining these.[58] Yet, Muslim women and men are not naïve passive consumers of religious discourses, since they are at the same time aware that different religious actors may say different things and many were critical in denouncing that some religious actors may be not so well versed in the knowledge of modern realities of Western Muslims. Although there is some awareness about the inherent plurality of Islamic normativity itself, expectations that Islamic legality entails one correct answer to each question (but not always knowing where to find it) are not exceptional.[59] Moreover, in several instances there seems to be a gap between Islamic scholarly discourses and the understandings 'ordinary' Muslims may have of these. This emerged, for instance, in frequent mentions of 'triple *talaq*', ie the triple uttering of *talaq*, despite this practice being heavily criticised in most Islamic legal discourses and even being declared invalid or 'un-Islamic' (Ahmad 2009). There is no indication that knowledge of Islamic norms in Belgium would differ according to gender.

In this sense, it seems noteworthy that most religious leaders and imams interviewed adopted a very legal(istic) type of normative discourse concerning Islamic norms, whereas most (Muslim) lawyers interviewed were only trained in Belgian law and tended to disregard matters of Islamic normativity as 'non-legal'. Furthermore, it seems as if Islamic normative understandings of marriage and divorce developed in Muslim majority countries are simply transplanted to Muslim diasporas living in Western legal systems with minimal transformation, although the interface between these understandings and the broader society and legal framework remains imprecise. One religious scholar, who studied both in Muslim-majority and in Belgian universities, is a clear exception in questioning this approach and advocating an ethical understanding of Islamic normativity. 'Religious leaders are

---

[57] Disempowering experiences with state family justice were also observed with regard to matters of child residency in a co-authored contribution elsewhere (Lecoyer and Simon 2015).
[58] Research with Dutch Muslims shows similar findings (Berger 2006; referring to Dessing 2002).
[59] This is similar to the findings of a legal consciousness survey in Malaysia (Moustafa 2013).

misleading Muslim families in thinking that they need a religious marriage', he claims. To which he adds:

> [W]e shouldn't make people think that the religious can interfere in the normative, it merely orients, the gaze is ethical. I can have an almost moral view, but I shall not say 'here the contract isn't valid or so' if it is legally permitted.[60]

This type of discourse or mode of talking about Islamic norms—highly exceptional among the religious actors interviewed—could qualify as what Merry (1990: 112–14) called a 'moral discourse' of relationships and ethics, as opposed to 'legal discourses' of rights and legal validity, and 'therapeutic discourses' of helping professions. It is especially interesting, in terms of gender, to note that many Muslim helping professionals encountered in the field research, such as psychologists and social workers, seem to have more or less all three types of discourses in their repertoire, but are generally hesitant to engage in Islamic 'legal discourse', which they leave to religious actors. This shapes a fragmented and strongly gendered landscape where legal and moral discourses about Islamic normativity are in the hands of religious scholars, mainly—if not exclusively—men, who remain largely insensitive to the need to adjust such discourses to the realities of contemporary Muslim families and women, living in Western European liberal democracies such as Belgium, or are insufficiently equipped to do so. Apart from some notable exceptions, (Muslim) helping professionals who are quite well aware of these social realities do not or very seldom engage with matters of Islamic normativity.

Likewise, at the level of lived realities, although most interviewed Muslim family members were women, it seems significant that female narratives of Muslim family life are largely descriptive, whereas the few collected male narratives tend to comprise more normative elements.[61] This is best understood if discursive practices in Muslim families and communities are viewed as gendered practices or 'floors', where women tend to be marginalised in normative discourses that mainly take place among men, about women. Women's (and men's) narratives can be seen in a sense as 'speech strategies', best viewed 'as practices actively constructed by speakers in response to cultural and structural constraints' (Gal 1989: 8). Indeed, 'gender relations are constructed, in part, through different possibilities of expression for men and women' (ibid) and women in this research consequently often referred to 'the' Islamic normative framework, of which they seek to gain knowledge through various ways, rather than situating themselves as actors on the discursive floor of this normative framework.

---

[60] Interview of 6 June 2013 in Liege with an Islamic scholar who formerly was active as an imam and preacher in the area of Liege.

[61] For instance, in the following statement one of the male interviewees issued about marriage: 'I align myself a little with what the scholars say, that means that in fact in order for a marriage to really exist, one has to go to the municipality' (interview of 10 January 2013 in Brussels with a male interviewee of Moroccan origin (second generation), 39 years old.

Women's legal consciousness appears in various shades and shapes and this variety of understandings and experiences influences women's attitudes and actions. Besides the options and limits offered by normative discourses and the—more or less—concrete understandings women have of these, other factors act as powerful contextual structures for women's agency. Within this highly diverse landscape of plural normativities, 'forum shopping' appears as an important enabling factor, since having access to several options for marriage dissolution enhances women's opportunities and ability to act in their own (and sometimes also others') best interests. Support of the social and family networks is yet another powerful enabling factor for women while social pressure often appeared as the most difficult obstacle to overcome. The following quote illustrates how dominant conceptions are being resisted and contested by Muslim women, 'from within', and may use Islamic normativity as a resource:

> I had the courage, because my parents have precisely educated me in that sense, to say, no I don't accept and I take the lead, I divorce, yes it is shame to divorce maybe, in the eyes of people maybe, yes it is shame he took another wife, but I don't feel responsible, and I will remarry even if I have children, yes it is possible to remarry with other children, I am 36 and I take up my studies again, it doesn't matter, we start all over from zero … I really think it is necessary to change mentalities and especially … when I restarted my studies that is when I have heard the most things 'and the children ?', it was 'you are the woman', 'you are the mother' and that is what I hear from everyone, 'how could you have left the children?'. Well no, the man is as responsible as the mother, from an Islamic viewpoint it is the man who is in charge of the children.[62]

5. IMPLICATIONS FOR THE PROTECTION AND PROMOTION OF THE HUMAN RIGHTS OF WOMEN

Of particular importance for the protection of the human rights of women, including in situations of de facto legal pluralism, is the fact that under international human rights law, states have 'a positive duty to protect all citizens and other inhabitants from violations of their human rights by other persons or private organisations' and 'to do their utmost best to ensure that no human rights violations by non-state actors take place' (Holtmaat and Naber 2011: 16). The UN Convention on the Elimination of all forms of Discrimination Against Women (CEDAW), the most detailed human rights convention concerning women's rights, entails a particular obligation on

---

[62] Interview on 3 July 2013 in Brussels with a female interviewee of Moroccan origin (second generation), age 37. She divorced and remarried and studied law in addition to her professional activity, as a mother of four children.

states parties to combat systemic or structural gender discrimination and to address the persistence of gender-based stereotypes.[63]

Culture—and religion—are frequently seen as an obstacle in human rights discussions, rather than as a resource (Merry 2003; Preis 1996) and in many of its Concluding Observations, the CEDAW committee considers that principles of women's equality and non-discrimination clearly prevail over culture-based claims (Holtmaat and Naber 2011: 42–43). Nevertheless, it is increasingly acknowledged that both human rights and culture are neither static nor monolithic (see eg Cowan et al 2001; Phillips 2010) and that it is crucial to the effective realisation of human rights that global ideals of human rights become 'localised' (De Feyter 2006) or 'vernacularised' (Merry 2006; Levitt and Merry 2011) in local cultures. CEDAW, in its Article 5(a), explicitly calls for social and cultural changes in gender roles. The aim of this chapter therefore is to bring an empirically grounded insiders' perspective to the question of the protection of the human rights of women, and in particular gender equality, in a situation of 'privately ordered' legal pluralism.

Tensions in the field of human rights and religious and/or cultural practice are frequently framed as conflicting human rights, in particular as a conflict between the right to culture of minority groups and the individual rights of vulnerable group members (Shachar 1998, 2006; Amien 2008, 2010; Meerschaut and Gutwirth 2008). Negative attitudes towards legal pluralism, and particularly towards the accommodation of Muslim family law in Western countries, have largely been the result of a number of assumptions present in public, as well as—to a lesser extent—academic, debates in this regard. Many of these assumptions have been shaped by the particular focus in these debates on one particular type of accommodation of cultural and/or religious diversity, namely community-based alternative dispute resolution, resulting in 'multicultural jurisdictions' (Shachar 2006) and the question of its regulation by the state. Faith-based—and especially Islamic—alternative dispute resolution has been seen as necessarily enhancing group autonomy at the expense of individual autonomy, 'possibly because of the belief that women and other vulnerable people are often coerced into [it]' (Ahmed 2013: 34) and the concern that the norms used in it disadvantage women. Islamic norms or 'sharia' in this view have been largely considered to be monolithic, unchanging and inherently incompatible with human rights.[64] Religious norms, and especially Islamic ones, are seen as necessarily

---

[63] See especially Art 5(a) which implies a modification of social and cultural patterns of conduct, requiring states parties to 'take all appropriate measures to modify the social and cultural patterns of conduct of men and women, with a view to achieving the elimination of prejudices and customary and all other practices which are based on the idea of the inferiority or the superiority of either of the sexes or on stereotyped roles for men and women'.

[64] eg *Refah Partisi v Turkey*, ECtHR (Grand Chamber), applications no 41340/98 41342/98 41343/98 41344/98 (13 February 2003) para 123.

oppressive to women (Razack 2007; Bakht 2007) and as posing a threat to secular law (Selby 2012) and state monopoly.[65] Another underlying assumption is that state monopoly is a necessary—and sufficient—requirement for the protection of human rights.[66]

Among the Belgian Muslim families studied in this chapter, protecting the human rights of women seems to be a matter of marrying women's human rights to equality and non-discrimination, with the right to participate in all areas of life, including their culture and their religion. Moreover, the private orderings at stake here operate *regardless* of state recognition and regulation of non-state normative orders. It becomes nevertheless quite clear from the previous sections that the assumptions underlying a general stance that Islamic normativity as such, as well as legal pluralism more generally, would necessarily contravene human rights standards does not hold true. This does not mean, however, that no human rights tensions are present in the empirical findings presented above. Yet these tensions need to be appropriately framed. Two main issues are at stake. First, important stereotypical views of women and gender relations are persistent in Belgian Muslim communities, both at the level of Islamic normative discourses and at the level of social practice. Under CEDAW's Article 5, this is worthy of being framed as a human rights issue. Second, whereas all women are in principle guaranteed access to the dissolution of their marriage by law, in a number of situations, women are pressured into staying married because of social norms and a powerful stigma associated with divorced women or even de facto remain captives of their religious marriage because of (a particular understanding of) their rights under religious norms. These situations involve a number of human rights standards, such as the right to gender equality and non-discrimination (in access to divorce), and the right to personal autonomy, as well as the right to religious freedom.

Therefore, the empirical findings presented here call for policies in support of greater gender equality to take Muslim women's right to autonomy and freedom of religion into account, and warn against forcing believing women (into thinking they have) to choose between religion or equality. Consequently, an appropriate and truly inclusive human rights framework to deal with the 'privatised oppression of Muslim women' (Amien 2008: 386) is needed, one that fully acknowledges the complexity at play. Proposed solutions in the literature have mainly focused on legislation, either through the rejection of legal pluralism, such as the prohibition of religious arbitration following the 'sharia controversy' in Ontario, or through integrationist approaches. The latter are based on the idea that state recognition opens the door to state regulation of non-state normative frameworks,

---

[65] As was argued by the ECtHR (*Refah v Turkey*, ibid, para 119). See also Meerschaut and Gutwirth's analysis of this case (Meerschaut and Gutwirth 2008).

[66] See Brems' chapter in this volume for a critical evaluation of the state monopoly argument.

allowing the state to articulate conditions for multicultural accommodation, with the aim of protecting women and other vulnerable people.

A 'gender-nuanced integrationist approach' (Amien 2008: 383–88), for instance, proposes to solve the conflict between freedom of religion and gender equality by respecting 'freedom of religion only as long as it does not undermine women's right to equality' (ibid: 387). Nevertheless, such an approach is unlikely to be successful in changing social practice if it fails to take into account social realities. Moreover, it presents a number of conceptual weaknesses. First of all, it analyses the problem of the privatised oppression of Muslim women as a conflict between the right to equality and freedom of religion, completely disregarding the dimension of religious women's autonomy. Secondly, it considers the conflict between the right to equality and freedom of religion as unavoidable and prioritises one right over the other, rather than seeking to maximise the protection of both rights at stake.[67] On the other hand, Christopher Cutting has argued that rejection of legal pluralism does not offer a solution to women's privatised oppression either.[68]

In fact, legislation is probably simply not the most appropriate tool to promote the human rights of women in many cases where existing legislation already offers sufficient protection of the human rights of *all* women. In the particular case of Muslim communities, the 'globalized phenomenon of imposing extraordinary measures of surveillance and control on Muslim communities in the name of gender equality' (Bakht 2006: 4) may further contribute to the stigmatisation and marginalisation of Muslim women. 'Privatised oppression' of women often results from the fact that human rights may be insufficiently or inadequately promoted to find ground in local social practices, regardless of legislation. This empirical research found that *some* women will refrain from challenging discriminatory practices for various reasons, such as a lack of awareness of their legal rights, for instance, or because of stigmatising stereotypes they do not want to reinforce by making their disputes public in civil courts, or even because they do not consider practices, that could be labelled as discriminatory by outsiders, to be discriminatory and/or harmful.

Consequently, approaches promoting the human rights of women that are based on the empowerment of Muslim women through enhanced awareness

---

[67] Eva Brems (2013) has developed a model for dealing with conflicting human rights. In this model the first step requires an examination of 'whether it is possible to *avoid* the conflict between these two rights' (Brems 2013: 210, emphasis original). If it is not possible 'to fully protect both rights', preference has to be given to a solution that finds a compromise for the purpose of guaranteeing maximum protection of both rights, rather than giving priority to one right over the other (ibid: 211).

[68] Cutting (2012) contends that 'limping religious divorce' (also called marital captivity, see n 455) is the most pervasive form of religious oppression within Muslim communities in Ontario and that the vast majority of private ordering of civil matters in Muslim communities remained untouched by the legislative change.

of their rights under several normative frameworks offer much greater potential. Such approaches offer maximum protection of women's rights to autonomy, freedom of religion and equality, based on a human rights framework that views these rights as intersecting rather than necessarily at conflict with each other.

6. CONCLUSION

The Belgian case demonstrates that there is no univocal homogeneous Islamic normative discourse regarding divorce for Belgian and European Muslims. There seems to be a strong tendency towards the superposition of normative layers, encouraging Muslims to respect both national legal requirements and religious ones, leaving relatively unclear how this should concretely be done, especially in the case of women seeking to divorce. Discourses about Islamic normativity are generally produced by male actors and tend to lack sensitivity for and knowledge of women's lived experiences. The examined Islamic normative discourses on marriage and divorce frequently refer to the need to offer protection to women (through civil marriage, for instance), while at the same time they are not gender-neutral and frequently advantage men while discriminating against women. Potentialities for gender equality are, however, also present. The ECFR's standpoints seem to exert significant influence on Belgian religious actors, but despite their 'equivalency *fatwa*' declaring civil divorce religiously valid, women's access to divorce is mildly to strongly restricted in most local Islamic normative discourses. This shows that a gender discriminatory framework for access to marriage dissolution is at play, in which divorce is a right that remains largely, if not exclusively, in the hands of husbands. The existence of sharia councils in the UK, and the announcement of Islamic arbitration which gave rise to the 'sharia-debate' in Ontario are to be understood in similar contexts, as these aimed at providing a solution to those Muslim women who were confronted with the lack of possibilities to dissolve their marriage according to the (dominant understanding of the) rules of their faith whenever their husband did not grant them a *talaq*. In the Belgian context, however, no such religious bodies dissolving marriage seem to exist.

Additionally, a strong stereotypical view on women and men and their relationship in marriage emerges from the examined data. Fear of widespread dissolution of Muslim marriages is very present in the background. In most Islamic discourses that were examined, views about the inherent nature of women and the preservation of harmony and 'public order' largely outweigh sensitivity for women's lived realities and interests, even when there seems to be a sincere concern for women's well-being. In fact, these mainly legal and moral discourses pay very little attention to the social realities of women because they tend to focus mainly or exclusively on providing 'correct' Islamic answer(s).

The findings concerning divorce practices of Belgian Muslim women exemplify how 'a woman's use and non-use of her legal [and religious] rights and freedoms must be considered in the light of the wider socio-cultural structure(s) she operates within' (Hellum 1995). 'Action theory, which does not assume consensus over norms and expectations, emphasises the active participation of individuals and groups in creating norms and ideals during interaction' (ibid). Muslim women in this research are indeed not passive in the process of generating norms, which they actively shape by their questions and demands for solutions, or by simply disregarding certain norms and using others. Some women actively resist or even contest dominant under- standings of Islamic normativity by shaping new understandings, taking the 'floor' in the mainly male universe of normative discourses. Despite the struc- tural constraints examined in this chapter, several women engaged in the pro- duction of a counter-hegemonic discourse with the aim of inducing a change in mentality within Muslim communities. Women's agency in this research appeared as a multifaceted concept that basically refers to one's capacity to manoeuvre for one's own interests (Charrad 2010; Korteweg 2012), but unfolds in various nuances (Villalón 2010). This was visible in instances of female-empowering understandings of legal and religious entitlements or as resistance against certain social structures oppressive to women, but also as strategic self-interested action that leaves unchallenged gender-unequal nor- mative discourses, or even in instances of women's compliance with religious and/or social norms. Approaches to gender equality that view agency solely as resistance to gendered religious practices are not only at odds with the empirical findings of embedded agency that show more nuanced images of Muslim women as both agentic and religious subjects. They also narrow possible policy responses, coming dangerously close to racialising Muslims, and ultimately, impeding Muslim women's capacity to act (Korteweg 2008: 2012). It is therefore crucial, in order to enable Muslim women to exercise fully and effectively their human rights, that state policies take into account these complex processes, as well as internal diversity, change and contesta- tion and engage in a 'fruitful dialogue' (Holtmaat and Naber 2011) with local leaders and actors, including Muslim women themselves.

Although in many debates culture and religion are presented as opposite to women's rights, the findings presented here call for a different approach, at the intersection of women's rights to autonomy, gender equality and religious freedom. In fact, the empirical findings presented in this chapter underscore that there is room for combining Muslim women's right to equal- ity with *the same* women's right to autonomy and religious freedom. The viewpoint that religious normativity in itself constrains women's capacity to act and endangers their equal treatment was challenged by a more nuanced image of both enabling and constraining elements contained within religious normative understandings and social realities. If we are to support women's equality and autonomy, this complexity needs to be acknowledged.

11

Through the Looking Glass of Diversity: The Right to Family Life from the Perspectives of Transnational Families in Belgium

BARBARA TRUFFIN AND OLIVIER STRUELENS

1. INTRODUCTION

T HIS CHAPTER PROPOSES a bottom-up approach to the right to family life, empirically grounded in daily experiences and representations of the family. Taking diversity as a general and empirical characteristic of family life in contemporary societies, we focus on transnational families—in our case families with a Congolese background in Belgium—whose experiences are particularly relevant to the analysis of diversity in family regulation. In doing so, our general objective is to reflect on a renewed articulation between the normative and empirical aspects of legal pluralism, and human rights.

The chapter is divided into five parts. Following the introduction, section 2 delineates the scope, as well as the conceptual and the theoretical underpinnings of our undertaking. In section 3, we rely on the concept 'internormativity' in order to get to grips with the tension between competing normative frames or family models that are identifiable within the narratives we have collected during the fieldwork conducted for this study.[1] While our material

---

[1] This research is part of a broader project called BEPLULEX aimed at describing the different trajectories of families with a migrant background, confronted with family conflicts. This project is promoted by Professor Eva Brems and financed by the Belgian Federal Public Planning Service Science Policy (Belspo). Interested in the narratives of conflicts inside families with a Congolese background in Belgium, the two of us were part of one of the team of this broader project. We have conducted interviews about family conflicts with fourteen informants about their personal experiences of family conflicts and with seven other informants in regard with the roles they have played in the conflicts of their relatives. Other researchers contributed to the data collection, among them Valentina Marziali and Laura Aubert. This material has also been compared to the data obtained from the observations of judicial settings in which spouses and parents with a Congolese background also appeared.

contains a recurrent opposition between an egalitarian or horizontal model of family relationships and a hierarchical one, none of them can be strictly assigned to a specific normative order. On the contrary, these competing normative references unfold in a continuum across different levels or legal orders, blurring the lines between public and private spheres.

In the fourth part of our analysis, we move from the perspective of inter-normativity towards that of legal pluralism, and focus more narrowly on diversity in family regulation in the public sphere. The pathways and the representations of conflict of many families with a Congolese background shed a powerful light on the internal plurality of state law as these families frequently face and suffer from the contradictions that arise between state family law and foreign law. We discuss this second manifestation of diversity as an instance of legal pluralism, which is more or less voluntarily ignored by state agents.

Acknowledging the continuum between private and public spheres regarding family life and the peculiar nature of legal pluralism attached to it, in the fifth and concluding section we discuss how human rights standards—here the right to family life—should address these empirical realities. Based on the analysis of our case studies, we conclude that any such normative move should be integrated into public policy, especially regarding the formation of state agents.

2. THE RIGHT TO FAMILY LIFE AND LEGAL PLURALISM

The general objective of our research is to reflect on the protection of family life—the right to family life—from an alternative human rights perspective, empirically and normatively grounded (Goodale 2006). This objective requires further clarifications.

2.1. Descriptive and Normative Standpoints

The descriptive reality and extent of the plurality of family norms is not easily translated into policy-making and normative categories, especially legal ones.[2] Aiming at a bottom-up formulation of the right to family life and the public protections this entails, our normative standpoint is resolutely not a classical legal one. Far from it, we shift away from a positive-law approach and seek to integrate a more empirically grounded understanding of the plurality of family norms into a normative conception of the right to family

---

[2] On the difficulty of giving a place to cultural pluralism in legal and judicial reasoning, see generally Gershon (2011).

life. We thereby take the position that to rely on empirical methods—mainly through interviews about family conflicts with youths, parents and elders with a Congolese background in Brussels—does not preclude the necessity to address the normative challenges of human rights. On the contrary, we use legal pluralism both at a normative and at an empirical level.

The point of departure of our reflection is precisely to take at face value the normative commitment toward legal pluralism contained in the right to respect for family life.[3] Granting a right to respect for family life logically presupposes that families are producing some type of normative orders and values, even though this recognition contains within itself the affirmation of the superiority of state orders to control and limit its scope when properly justified. This procedure of delegation or recognition is a classical one in the studies of legal pluralism as policy, from Griffiths (1986) to Hoekema (1999) and Tamanaha (2010). Here, state or officially recognised forms of legal pluralism fuel the tensions at play between public and private spheres in family relationships.[4] Indeed, the plurality of family norms and standards is not only tangible in the historical changes undergone by family state law and policies (Commaille and Martin 1998), but is also at play in the vast majority of families in their private spheres.[5] The hypothesis of Giddens of an overall democratisation of the private sphere (Giddens 1992), according to which the organisation of the private sphere, especially the family, would be increasingly infused by the egalitarian values of the democratic repertoire used in the public sphere, is generally not accomplished at the level of the reality of many individuals for whom social and/or gender status and equal access to resources are factors impeding their participation in a truly egalitarian model of relationships (Comaille and Martin 2001).

Studies on legal pluralism and sociological or anthropological studies on contemporary families rely on different, rarely intersecting, theoretical and methodological frameworks.[6] Legal pluralism scholars in the field of gender and family relationships explicitly address diversity in cultural terms (see eg Griffith 1998), whereas sociological and anthropological scholars studying contemporary family configurations tend to use other approaches to diversity or plurality, as they frequently use these concepts to characterise forms of kinship linked with new reproductive technologies (eg Cadoret 2006, Porqueres i Gené 2014) or to take into account the diversity of socioeconomic

---

[3] eg Art 8 European Convention of Human Rights which states: '1. Everyone has the right to respect for his private and family life, his home and his correspondence. 2. There shall be no interference by a public authority with the exercise of this right except such as in accordance with the law and if necessary in a democratic society in the interests of national security, public safety or economic well-being of the country, for the prevention of disorder or crime, for the protection of health or morals, or for the protection of the rights and freedoms of others.'

[4] On the supposed democratisation of the private sphere, see Giddens (1992).

[5] As illustrated in Belgium by d'Ursel (2010) or earlier in France by Kaufman (1992).

[6] But see eg Grillo (2008) and d'Ursel (2010) at the intersection of these fields.

conditions affecting family life (Commaille 2006). More comprehensive studies combining the different aspects of diversity should be conducted in order to give a better understanding of the complexity of contemporary families. Nevertheless, at this stage, we can at least draw from this vast and heterogeneous literature the common observation that plurality of normative references is a prominent feature of family life in contemporary societies, a feature which is far from being limited to transnational families.

Therefore, at the basis of our research lies the normative commitment of (positive law) human rights to recognise and accommodate family normative orders to a limited extent, but regardless of the diversity of their forms. Taking this normative challenge seriously, our contribution proposes another way to approach family rights by positing internormativity (ie diversity of references and norms) as an inherent descriptive feature of family life, which should be fully acknowledged before engaging in any normative reflection.

2.2. Internormativity and legal pluralism

Legal pluralism is a concept that has undergone a wide range of developments during the last decades in diverse academic fields seeking to grasp the dynamics of law. Increasingly used by different scholars from diverse academic backgrounds, this concept has received many definitions and has also been questioned many times regarding the theoretical and analytical value it could bring to the social sciences as well as to legal theory (eg von Benda-Beckmann 2002, Dupret 2007, Tamanaha 2010, Twining 2010).

In our research, we follow the direction taken by Baudouin Dupret and his invitation for scholars to engage in a sociology of normative plurality (Dupret 1999: 36). Although the classical definition of legal pluralism elaborated by Merry as 'a situation in which two or more legal systems coexist in the same social field' (Merry, 1988: 870) has proven to be highly valuable for the comprehension of complex situations where multiple legal orders are intertwined, the plurality of norms we want to address requires another analytical stance. The dominant approach of legal pluralism allows tackling law from a standpoint that decentralises the focus from the ideology of state law, thus bringing to light the multiple ways in which official and unofficial forms of law interact (Merry, 1988). This implies a need to look at the intersections of different normative orders and to concentrate on the type of interactions they maintain, whether they are contesting, competing or strengthening state law. It follows that assuming the mutually constitutive relations between state law and unofficial normative orders is a crucial analytical moment of such approach. Concretely, in order to put this approach in motion, one might consider looking for separated orders— even though mutually constituted—in the narratives and representations empirically gathered and encountered. However, as we shall demonstrate below, such analytical angle constitutes a poor choice for the comprehension of the material at stake here. Indeed, from the actors' perspectives, the plurality of family norms—in this case, egalitarian and hierarchical models—are at play both at the family level and at the state law level. Subsequently, there is an important conceptual difficulty to consider state and family orders along a set of specific and truly differentiated values and norms. In other words, taking a stance that assumes internormativity a priori prevents us from falling into the temptation of presupposing normative categories, fields or communities. The very first moment of the description and the analysis takes internormativity for granted, as expressed by the subjects in context, without postulating the existence of 'semi-autonomous fields' (Moore 1973), which implicitly refer to a particular normative order originally ascribed to a field.

Authors such as Tamanaha and Dupret have meticulously addressed the analytical problems encompassed in legal pluralism studies (Dupret 2007; Tamanaha 2008). Both shift away from an essentialist definition of law and urge that law be analysed in concrete situations, always embraced in particular sets of legal orders and in singular historical contexts. Such a shift implies that a social scientific definition of law is not necessary to study legal pluralism (Tamanaha 2008: 396). Indeed, as shown by Tamahana, the struggle over the social scientific definition of law has been more a harmful bickering to the discipline than a helping hand, regardless of the fact that it is impossible to construct it as a scientific category (Tamahana 2000). Instead, the meaning of law should arise, in particular situations, from 'what people in social group have come to see and label as "law"' (Tamanaha 2008: 396). In this sense legal pluralism exists 'whenever social actors identify more than one source of "law" within a social arena' (ibid) and this statement inverts the relations between law and social control.

The resolution of this analytical problem through the assumption of a methodological nominalism is not easy to put in practice. How and when can one grasp what the label of 'law' stands for, during interviews and real-time interactions?[7] This methodological difficulty prompted us to limit the analytical scope of our research and to rely on the concept of (inter)normativity, instead of embracing legal pluralism and (inter)legality as seen and labelled by the actors. Indeed, even if Tamanaha's proposition is satisfying on many grounds, it causes too many distortions and a process of endless interpretations when applied to interviews in which the bias introduced by the interviewer regarding his or her own conceptions of law and legality

---

[7] Dupret resolves this difficulty at a methodological level through a strong praxeological commitment (Dupret 2007). The setting of his observation and the conversational (micro) analysis on which his research rely are indeed highly consistent with such a nominalism stand. However, it is much more difficult to assume this position when dealing with interviews and the setting it creates.

are too high to be dismissed. By not using or defining law, we are simply looking at the expressions of the plurality of family norms which along Dupret 'can be perceived as "assumptions", "meanings" or as "instruments of evaluation"' (Dupret 1999: 31). In other words, we do not elevate law to the rank of an analytical instrument (Dupret 2007: 16), but we look at the different conceptions of norms and family models as perceived by the actors in the private and public realms. In doing so, we pay particular attention to the porosity between the different models of family norms and posit it as a situation of internormativity.[8] Taking a step outside the arena of the analytical debate about distinct normative orders and considering the literature about contemporary family features referred above, we therefore assign internormativity a purely descriptive function from which any normative effort of standardising family rights should depart. Thereby, our aim is not to promote the normative recognition of plurality of norms and models as culturally defined—a typical shortfall of neoliberal multiculturalism—but to take seriously its scope and reality into account, when determining the objectives assigned to the protection of an institution—family—profoundly marked by normative diversity.

2.3. Transnational Families in Belgium

For the purposes of this study, we chose to focus on the experiences and representations of conflicts of members of transnational families (Beck and Beck-Gernsheim 2010; Grillo 1998) with a Congolese background and therefore assume a methodological position drawn from a sociology of conflict. Among families with a migrant background, Congolese families or families of Congolese descent are both relatively new and diverse in Belgium. Since the 1990s, Belgium has seen increasing numbers of immigrants, predominantly European but also a significant number from Africa (18% of the total immigration) (DEMO, 2013). Nevertheless, Congolese immigration represents only 1.7% of the total immigration into Belgium, even though it is the most represented sub-Saharan nationality. Furthermore, different waves of migration, from the 1970s onwards, have given Belgium a great diversity of Congolese migration trajectories—from the student loans offered by the Belgian State during the 1970s to the actual restricted politics of family reunification or refugee status.

The Congolese and Belgian of Congolese descent maintain nonetheless a special historical relationship to Belgium, knowing that the latter was long involved in the colonisation of the Congo over the last two centuries. The number of Congolese migrants who possess a higher-education diploma is

---

[8] On porosity and hybridity in norms and law, see De Sousa Santos (1987, 1995, 2002).

much higher than any other migrant group in Belgium, but their unemployment rate is overrepresented compared to any other migrant group (SPF, 2013). On top of that, migration is often a source of debt (morally and economically) towards the family left in the Congo. In this sense, we could say that migration is placing a certain 'weight' on migrants. We can point out directly that this weight, stemming from the migratory trajectory, can be a source of frustration and is a factor that puts greater pressure on families with a migration background than on families without a migration history. These two waves are framed by different migration policies that have an important effect on the experience of the migration and the families' strength and fragility. From the 'migration-mobility' of the 1970s to the 'migration-exile'[9] of recent years, the migration experience of Congolese families in Belgium can indeed present very distinctive stories and the latter mobility is more likely to endanger family cohesion (Mazzocchetti, 2011).

Drawing on fieldwork involving families with a Congolese background, our analysis focuses on two typical conflictual situations that individuals may face in their adolescence and adulthood. The first concerns the intergenerational tensions between young people and their parents and the remedies sought to address them. The second relates to the contradictory model of conjugal relationships produced by the diverse fields of state law affecting the life of couples. Both types of conflict comprise tensions between self and groups in reproducing family relationships and bring into question the limits of private life and state interventions. In the stories we have been told, the tensions between self and groups draw complex correspondences and ruptures between an egalitarian normative frame and a hierarchical one. Our analysis establishes how the activation of private and public actors as remedies for conflicts influences the nature of tensions between those normative models—egalitarian and hierarchical—and the impacts they have on the promotion of the right to family life.

---

[9] Until the late 1950s, only a few members of the Congolese elites migrated to Belgium in the framework of agreements between some Belgian and Congolese universities. The arrival of significant numbers of Congolese starts rather in the 1960s, after the independence of Congo. However, if the flow in that period reached an average of 1,000–1,500 people per year, until the deceleration of legal immigration in 1974, it has never been a labour migration (Demart 2008; Kagné 2001; Schoonvaere 2010). It is only in the late 1980s that the second wave of migrations started and the strategies of Congolese migrants began to correspond more to an idea of installation (Schoonvaere 2010). From 1984 onwards, Congolese migrations to Belgium have accelerated to reach in the course of the 2000s 80,000 new arrivals per year. This evolution took place despite the partial closure of European borders, due to the economic crisis that affected all industrialised European countries from the mid-1970s (Schoonvaere 2010). Indeed, Congolese, like other foreigners, tried to obviate this closure, using the legal instruments available, such as family reunification, asylum or the historic canal of scholarships (Schoonvaere 2010). But the literature also reports arrivals in Belgium through organised illegal channels, implying payment of large amounts of money or sham marriages (Mazzocchetti 2011).

3. AMANI AND MAKA: THE MEANINGS OF FAMILY BETWEEN EGALITARIAN AND HIERARCHICAL REFERENCES

We will follow the stories of two youths with different migratory backgrounds to show the crucial role that internormativity plays in the emergence of family conflicts. The stories of Amani and Maka that we are about to depict here represent a recurrent type of familial conflict arising from our fieldwork: the intergenerational conflict between children and parents. These two narratives will allow us to gauge the pressure that the migration trajectory can put on a father–child relationship, leading rapidly to an intergenerational conflict. Furthermore, the analysis of these reconstructed stories will show that the frames of reference, used by the fathers and children to make sense of the conflict, are different, sometimes even paradoxical, presenting little or no common interface allowing closure. Far from granting a special normative order or 'cultural values' associated to a type of community, this section will also underpin how an essentialist vision of the 'Congolese' or 'African' community, and its associated culture, is mobilised by the family members, giving these notions a social reality. This use of essentialist concepts will blur even more the perception from the state agents, strengthening a culturalist approach, defining traits linked to a community.

Before we develop the narratives we would like to stress that in many ways families with migratory backgrounds do not differ from non-migrant families. In that sense, the frames of references that constitute resources for understanding family and conflict situation are a blend of two family models, respectively the 'traditional' and 'modern' models of family (d'Ursel 2010: 29–33). The former represents a hierarchical model of family in which specific members of the family occupy places of authority, and which is based on inequality and complementarity of parental roles (eg d'Ursel 2010: 31). The latter is based on an egalitarian vision of family, in which the conflicts are to be treated by negotiation and dialogue (ibid). These two visions, as we shall demonstrate, do not belong to a specific community or culture and are not limited to the private sphere. The temptation would be great indeed to attribute to 'Congolese families' a traditional model of family relationships in the private sphere and to state actors and institutions a modern public one.[10] Yet, as we shall see, the private and public spheres are intertwined in a blend of these two models in tension, leading to paradoxical frames of reference for family members.

---

[10] Interestingly, this vision coincides with the representation and explanations of many judges or state agents in Belgium (D'hondt 2009; Wyvekens 2012). It might be reinforced by a culturalist ideology that ascribes a type of culture to a 'community'.

3.1. Amani: Ruptures and Authorities

We shall now delve into the stories of Amani and Maka. Amani was born in the Congo but moved to Brussels with his father, his stepmother and his brothers. He arrived in Belgium at the age of eight with his father who was joining his new wife, a Belgian woman, leaving Amani's mother behind. Amani's father was the eldest child of the household and a source of success for the whole family as he brought his brothers to Belgium. He is seen as a successful member of the family and enjoys a privileged status. For a time everything was going fine for Amani but at the beginning of high school he started to encounter difficulties with his father and frequent disputes arose about educational matters, ending most of the time in violent behaviour from Amani's father. Amani was getting bad grades at school, thwarting his father's dream for his son.[11] One day, after a particularly violent conflict, in distress, Amani decided on the spur of the moment to call for help to the nearest police station. He just couldn't go back home and he then stayed several days in a youth refuge. After a few days, his uncle came to him, begging him to come back home, for he was bringing dishonour upon his entire family.

This event represents Amani's first encounter with the state administration in the domain of child protection and family justice. Based on this experience, Amani became convinced that the solutions provided by the state's agents on family matters were 'absolutely inappropriate', that they 'didn't represent him', that 'they didn't go along with his conception of things', for the only solution to the conflict they presented would result in a social fracture between Amani and his family. As he says: '[T]hey [the state's institutions] withdraw you from your family but don't solve the root of the conflict.' For Amani, separation is not the 'appropriate method', but it is also the interlocutor who doesn't fit. To resolve his conflict, Amani argues that the person talking to his father is more important than the content of what is expressed, it must be 'someone that his father would esteem'.

Here is an important point: the status of the person dealing with the conflict is absolutely crucial to the outcome of the resolution. That is why a public agent, eg a judge or social worker, is generally seen as an incapable

---

[11] The urge to successfully accomplish school constitutes a second kind of 'debt' on the children's shoulders. Indeed, their success represent one of the main goals of the migration. As explained by Mazzochetti, the obligation passed along to the new generation is generally seen as a way to accomplish the obligation of success of the parents who moved to Europe with the material and moral support of the family back in Congo (Mazzochetti 2011).

figure who doesn't understand the 'Congolese' vision of family.[12] As Amani says:

> [W]e [the family] don't like that people outside from the family come to meddle into our problems. The social services and the police are people that don't understand the 'African' conception of family.

Nonetheless, a solution started to emerge when Amani's godfather came to play the role of intermediator. It has to be stressed straight off that the meaning of family is seen by the interviewees as different from a presumed 'Belgian' conception of family. First of all, and most importantly, its extent stretches outside the nuclear family, encompassing uncles and aunts, nieces, nephews and cousins, who are seen as important as the 'biological parents'. This is what the interviewees refer to as 'family as a community'. Moreover, the relationship with a paternal uncle is often of utmost importance for a child during his education because he is a person whom can be a successful intermediator and a source of knowledge on taboo topics such as sexual education. However, this task of intermediator and educator can be assumed by another member of the family according to his status, prestige and honour. The appropriate person to take on this role varies according to the familial context, itself being conditioned by the migratory trajectory of the family. But it is nonetheless a member of the 'family as community' who must carry out this task. The growing discord between Amani and his father precluded direct discussion, and required a permanent process of mediation.[13]

So in this sense, mediation from within the family, outside of state justice, is the only acceptable option, or at least the one that is seen as the best way to resolve an intergenerational conflict. As Amani stresses, 'the goal of mediation is to protect the family unity', not to tear it apart as in his view the state mode of resolution does. Indeed, the mode of conflict resolution coming from the public agents represents a sort of 'unselective' rupture, where the baby is thrown out with the bath water. Amani states clearly that: '[I]t is not because I have a problem with my father that we are going to withdraw me from my aunts, my grandmother, my cousins, my uncle. ... That is how I experienced it, this representation of the "help" that they wanted to offer me.' After his stay in the youth refuge, it became even harder than before to

---

[12] This statement is well illustrated through an anecdote brought up by Amani when his father was dealing with a social worker. Amani's father concluded a stormy exchange with a social worker by shouting at him: 'Who the hell are you anyway!? Tomorrow you'll forget us! Who the hell are you? Huh?' Nevertheless, we do not project a vision of family that would be typically Congolese, we simply use the categories that make sense and structure the perception of the situation for the concerned actors.

[13] Nonetheless, internal intermediation should not be seen as a smooth and flawless mode of conflict resolution. Indeed, the intermediation can also be a source of new discords between other members of the family or can contribute to fuelling the conflict.

establish a dialogue between Amani and his father. It became very clear for Amani that the lack of dialogue constituted the source of the conflict with his father. Furthermore, the absence of dialogue is, maybe more than the physical violence, the hardest aspect to handle because the punishment is perceived as profoundly unfair. As Amani states:

> My father, he has a bad methodology. He gets angry, he hits and he doesn't explain. ... You, you stand there, you see your father coming, he yells at you, he hits you and then goes away. ... You tell yourself: 'OK, why did he hit me?' That is what breeds frustration, that is what I found unfair, really unfair, when I was little. Really! It is unbelievable, just an explanation! We are not animals! All I ask is a little explanation that could justify the act! That I can tell myself 'he hit me because there was something important I didn't do'. That is what I think is unfair.

He adds that 'with my father there is no dialogue. He talks, we have to follow. And if you talk, if you don't agree. ...You don't have anything to say.' According to Amani's view, it is partly because his father is the eldest of his brothers and the source of the successful migration of the family towards Europe that makes it so hard to reason with him on educational matters. Amani's uncles tried multiple times to discuss the matter but 'they weren't in a position to lecture him [his father] about his own children', especially because 'they wouldn't be here [in Belgium] if it wasn't for him'. The status of the father has to be taken into account to be able to understand the logic of the conflict at stake here and the specific ways in which the references to incompatible normative frames (egalitarian v hierarchical) are constructed.

Another aspect of education that greatly deceived Amani is that 'his father gave up really easily and rapidly on his [ie Amani's] education'. Indeed, since the age of fourteen, Amani has had to manage without his father, relying on his own resourcefulness by doing 'little jobs'. The source of this abandonment, according to Amani, is to be found in the interaction with the police and the social workers, coming to judge his father and lecture him about his way of educating his children. This state intrusion into the private matters of family education led his father to a state of frustration, until he decided one day that 'if I can't educate you, go then, go and do what you want'. Here again, the issue from the conflicting normative frameworks is the rupture of the relationship (unsatisfactory and frustrating according to Amani's view).

Nonetheless, Amani saw a change in the type of education provided by his father concerning his younger brothers. Indeed, Amani's two half-brothers maintain a good relationship with his father, communicating and rarely having conflicts. As he says, his father 'has undergone a certain adaptation'. It is then confusing for Amani to see the 'African' way of educating transforming into something different, and it seems to him even more unjust that he had to endure the 'traditional' way.

Finally, at the age of twenty, after a really long and difficult time of struggle with his father, Amani found himself in a tough situation, without a diploma, without a job and with little ties left to his family. When a close friend of him died, he went through a critical moment in his life. 'I lost the meaning of life', he says, 'I couldn't see what I was living for. I was going through existential questions.' He then heard of Islam from a close friend and as a non-practising Catholic he began to get highly interested in Islam. He did intensive research for a month and 'found what he was looking for'. That is, in his own words, 'what saved him'. His conversion to Islam did not help him to repair his relationship with his father but it started to give meaning to his life, helped him to begin to study again and somehow re-establish links and relationships with others again. He is now achieving his degree in industrial engineering.

3.2. Maka: continuities and histories

Let us keep in mind Amani's difficulties in coping with incompatible normative frameworks impinging on his adolescence and switch to Maka's story, which presents some common ground with Amani's experience. Maka is twenty-five years old and, unlike Amani, he was born in Belgium. Nonetheless, he also had difficulties with the schooling system, the violent behaviour of his father and a lack of explanation for that violence. He suffered from the same 'gap' between his vision of life and education and the one imposed on him by his father. He did have the same trouble that Amani encountered in establishing a dialogue with his father. As he states: '[T]he elder is always right, you cannot argue with him.' Maka didn't lose the relationship with his father and family as Amani did; he has always avoided a direct confrontation with his father. Instead, he directed his anger and rebellion towards his school. After a relatively tumultuous adolescence, Maka is now working in an association as an educator.

From these two stories three first points can be drawn. First, for Amani and Maka, the origin of the conflict is found in the impossibility of dialogue with their respective fathers. Second, the status of the father, stemming from his *position in the family* and the *role played in the migration* history, is partly what prevents this dialogue. Third, the best way of resolving the conflict is conceived as a process of mediation coming from within the 'family as community'. But as we look deeper, we can appreciate that both 'egalitarian' and 'hierarchical' models of family are entangled in the public and the private spheres, resulting in situations of internormativity, which are actually the *main source* of the impossibility of dialogue and the fuelling of the conflict. As stated above, these two models should not be conceived as in a mutually exclusive opposition but more as two ends of a continuum, as family, state justice institutions or schools are always simultaneously egalitarian and hierarchical.

First, let's take the family. On the one hand, this realm is sometimes presented by Amani and Maka as a hierarchical structure in which the father's status is hardly negotiable and his authority goes unexplained (well represented by what one of the interviewees calls the 'law of respect'). On the other hand, the privileged mode of resolution of family conflict is based on a mediation from within the family that attempts to challenge the rigid status of hierarchy, 'flattening' the relations between members of the family by means of negotiations and dialogue. But even in this 'flattening' process of mediation, both negotiation and authority are present, for the advice and help provided by the intermediary is exhortative in nature and therefore difficult to discuss even if not applied.

We clearly see the two types of normativity entangled in the family sphere. This internormativity is a source of tensions between these adolescents and their respective fathers, for they both clumsily 'craft' a model between the two poles but fail to meet in a meaningful confrontation. Their mutual expectations are not fulfilled, leading to a frustration and a disappointment for both of them. It is not only the migratory history and the hierarchical model of family that prevents dialogue but rather the difficulty of finding one's place in the intertwined and blurry mix of normative references from which they both draw their understanding of the situation. They simply do not meet on a common understandable ground.

But the picture gets even more complex when we add the state's treatment of family conflict. On the state's side we can see this internormativity of egalitarian and hierarchical ingredients in the way in which family conflicts are handled. From the standpoint of the interviewees, the action of social workers, associated with and supported by the framework of children's rights, is basically seen as an authoritative power that does not seem interested in negotiation or dialogue, but rather in the resolution of conflict by radical actions resulting in the rupture of family relationships. The 'protection of family life' supposedly granted by human rights is here absolutely deceived in the youths' views and this leads to a situation in which they again have unfulfilled expectations of resolution by a supposedly egalitarian institution.[14] The youths therefore find themselves in a situation in which they cannot make sense of the violent behaviour of their father, as it goes unexplained, and struggle to call for help outside because the solutions provided misunderstand the youths' vision of family.

An excerpt from the interview with Amani shows quite clearly the confused frame of reference between two normative models of family—between

---

[14] Nonetheless, this negative perception of the state mode of resolution results from Amani's concrete experience with the state. He is originally tempted to go to a public institution to call for help, as he does when going to the police station, obviously looking for dialogue but ending up in a youth refuge and with a feeling of frustration.

children's rights and hierarchical relationship ('law of respect')—when dealing with his father:

> We [Amani and his brothers] didn't feel very affected by everything linked to children's rights and all that stuff ... for us this is really just blabbering ... they are useless! My father used to say sometimes 'So what, you're going to make a complaint again? Invoke children rights? What do you think? That you are in Belgium, so you have rights?' ... Actually, it is the environment that breeds these kinds of ideas in your head, notions like children's rights. 'I have rights! I'm going to say no this time, I have to say no!' Then it goes through your brain, you say 'yeah! I'm saying "no!"'. Then you see that 'everything breaks' and you flee. It's all those ideas that you have in your head. ... That's why I say: 'the children's rights? stop fucking around, yeah. ... Your father gives you a slap and you're going to sue your own father? No!'

Amani is caught in a situation of internormativity that makes any move doubtful and highly confuses him. On the one hand, he is calling for help, hoping that he could both be protected from his father and have a good relationship with him. On the other hand, he does not believe in a solution coming from the public sphere and is under direct threat from his father. Indeed, according to his representation, the solution provided by state agents reproduces in an inverted fashion an authoritative relationship.

In this context we can understand the trajectory taken by these two youths as a *need for meaning* that could not be fulfilled in the familial sphere and, if the ties to the family are weak, a *substitute of family*. In this sense we can suggest that Amani's conversion to Islam can be interpreted as a way of making sense of his father's behaviour as well as a potential tie to a collectivity to fulfil a lack of family resources. In Maka's case, we can understand his work in the association as a way to make sense of his father's behaviour. If the meaning cannot emanate from the direct confrontation, he is trying, by looking back into history, to grasp something meaningful at the 'source' of his father's way of life, above the arbitrariness of his situation, in the 'Congolese culture'.

It should also be taken into account that migration has an important role to play in both the emergence of the conflicts and the possibility to resolve them. The weight of the debt often associated with an experience of migration and the drop in the social scale put pressure and frustration on the parents, leading rapidly to conflict. The lack of family members likely to epitomise a resourceful person in a process of mediation is often a result of migration, for Belgian laws and regulations on migration impose a narrow vision of family, excluding from the family reunification rights the uncles, aunts and the 'family as community'. These persons play an important role both in the emergence and in the resolution of family conflicts, granting education on taboo subjects and bearing a status that makes them more likely to handle mediation. Obviously, migratory law has a role to play in this topic, but it can lead to situations where its effects on family relationship and conflict resolutions are even deeper and more noxious. We are going to delve into this dimension in the next section.

4. CHRISTINE AND ERIC: THE STAKES OF PUBLIC LOVE

In conducting our fieldwork, we have identified other typical situations in which the articulation of private and public spheres fuel and transform family conflicts. It is especially the case for young couples in which residency rights derive from civil marriage. For these couples, migratory regulations are painfully lived as intimate constraints or resources in negotiating reciprocal rights.

While Belgian civil and procedural state law have granted family state justice the power to separate or divorce spouses according to an egalitarian concept of marriage on 'incompatibility' grounds, migratory law disrupts this egalitarian economy of relationships by linking residency rights to the permanence of the marriage for at least three years. During this period of three years, and in the absence of the birth of any children, foreign law promotes dependency-type relationships, whereas the publicly proclaimed model of an egalitarian couple serves as the normative basis for civil state law.

Belgian state law is therefore more plural than it appears at first sight, at least when it is inserted in the pathways of couples with a migrant background—here a Congolese background (on plurality inside state law, see: Goodman 1998; Von Benda-Beckmann 2002). The specific consequences attached to separation in the first three years of civil marriage serve as powerful and sometimes coercive instruments for one spouse against the other, seriously preventing the possibility for an egalitarian model of conjugal relationships to unfold.

The instrumental and disintegrative character of processes involved in producing the papers and the suspicions they arouse are specifically marked in one case we observed in a family state justice hearing in Brussels, the story of Eric and Christine. In this case, permit dependency and socioeconomic constraints frustrate a young husband, Eric, upon whom large transnational family projects of success relied. He did not succeed in realising them, or in being involved in the relationship with his young wife. Christine and Eric are both of Congolese origin and have been married for one and a half years. They are almost thirty years old and hold university degrees. She is a lawyer and he just began a new business. He is the son of a specialist doctor currently living in South Africa and holds a commercial degree. He really wants to gain economic independence from his father and wants to start his own company. Both Eric and Christine encounter difficulties starting in the job market, but his are greater.

Christine has initiated the action demanding separation—a non-mandatory step prior to divorce—to Eric's evident surprise. They speak for over an hour without being much interrupted by the judge. She does not want a definitive dissolution of their marriage, but only a provisional separation, maybe in order to shake her husband who, according to her, neglects their conjugal life. Eric stays for long periods of time in his former flat to work on his business project. She does not accept his having a 'retreat' space and wants him to be involved in all aspects of their life. But she doesn't trust that he really wants that. Eric explains to the judge that it is more important to him to first seek a stable professional situation by starting his own company, which is of course difficult in a time of crisis, and that it is only with a stable situation that he will be able to face his conjugal life.

During the exchanges, Christine remains firm. She really wants a change. Otherwise it is going to be a separation, she warns. She tries to 'reason' with him, to show him every single element that went bad. He repeats, in a rigid manner, that he does not see what has changed in their situation and asks for patience. He does not understand the demands of his wife and considers that he has been clear about his projects since the beginning. But their life together does appear to be quite difficult and the economic problems do not help.

Judge to the husband: Do you have an incomes for the moment?

Christine: No.

Eric: Me, personally, no.

Christine: And besides that, I hadn't finished yet, Mr [speaking of her husband] is very aggressive. He is impulsive.

Eric: Verbal violence is violence too. ... She always pushes where it hurts to get me understand that I don't comply with my male status. Then what does she do in return? She has stopped performing a wife's role: she doesn't want to cook, and I have left aside our intimate life.

On top of this tension surrounding the gendered perceptions of themselves, the question of the papers pops up. Eric has lived in Belgium for twenty years. However, his residence permit is currently intrinsically linked to the 'persistence' of his legal marriage. Because they have been married for only one and a half years, a legal separation pronounced by the judge might be identified by the 'Foreigners Office Administration' and ultimately lead to the termination of his right of residence. This insecurity, accompanied with the double dependency toward his wife, saps him. The tensions then increase. Eric is obsessed with his papers and proposes some 'little financial arrangements' for Christine in order to stabilise his administrative situation. She is shocked and distrusts him. However, both agree in front of the judge and during our interviews that when they married everything was fine. They had known each other for a long time and at the beginning the problem with the papers was only an accessory issue 'because they loved each other'. Now, it is impossible to untangle the motives of the one and the other among the disappointments, manipulations and threats.

By his own admission, the judge is puzzled and feels generally power-less regarding this 'papers situation'. He explained in an interview after the hearing that it makes no sense for him to leave people in an uncertain status for so long (the three-year period after obtaining the permit through mar-riage). But he cannot do anything regarding the 'papers infection', as he insisted during the interview. At the most, he observes the complex process between state strategies concerning foreign marriages and family tactics. According to him, it is not his job as a family court judge to evaluate these or to rule on the validity of the marriages, but he is nonetheless struck by the displacement of migratory elements and concerns into his 'family' office. He is perfectly aware that important threats linked to the termination of the residence permit underlie the recourse to his office by one of the spouses. He knows that some sort of inequality is at play when one party decides to terminate the conjugal union, and consequently perhaps also the resi-dence right of the other. However, according to him, he cannot do anything. Feeling 'constrained' by the family law frame he is supposed to act within, but which has nothing to do with 'bargaining' over the papers, his job is ultimately to evaluate if the 'harmony in the couple is seriously disrupted', and if so, he is compelled to pronounce a separation—whatever the conse-quences might be. Therefore, he routinely ignores and overlooks the disrup-tion of the normative egalitarian model by another quite effective part of state law.

Here, the normative diversity between conjugal models is to be found in the incoherence of state law. The consequences of family migration poli-cies, especially the measures against marriages of convenience, are a huge presence in explanations for the failure of marriages and the difficulties in coping with conjugal lives (Maskens 2013; Truffin and Laperche 2010). The consequences attached to this definition of public love cannot properly be addressed by civil judges and will remain invisible if we do not adapt the standards of the public protection of marriages through human rights.

5. CONCLUSIONS

Our analysis of the narratives of family conflicts aims at contributing to a critical theory of human rights (Goodale 2006), which addresses the normative level of human rights standards through empirically documented reality. Drawing conclusions from the representations of conflicts in our interviews and observations, we have underlined the importance taken by internormativity and legal pluralism into family lives. According to the interviews we have conducted with persons with a Congolese background, family matters are to be resolved inside the family, in a private sphere. As they outlined, 'we don't like that people who are strangers to the family meddle in our problems'. While this doesn't seem to be specific to members of the Congolese 'community', it is also a highly difficult aim to achieve, since people—including those with a Congolese background—do resort to and mobilise state institutions in family conflicts. However, our interviews with and observations of people with a migratory background, perhaps more so than for other families, indicate that their expectations of state institutions are largely disappointed since these do not deliver the promises they were invested with. Moreover, migratory regulations fuel the normative plurality in which families navigate. But more importantly, migratory regulations also act upon the economy of relationships inside transnational families, granting some members special statutory roles on which others depend.

5.1. Human rights standards and family internormativity

Both for young people negotiating family normative models with their parents and state agents, and for spouses whose intimate lives are haunted by suspicions and dependencies, the plurality of norms in the family realm is not contained to specific and separate normative orders. On the contrary, in our case studies, plurality is dramatically reinforced by the inability of the state properly to acknowledge its own indeterminacy and cacophony when concrete practices are at play.

As explained above, we have observed that young people coming from a family with a history of migration might struggle to find their marks when navigating the private and the public spheres. The internormativity between hierarchical and egalitarian visions of family relationships and modes of handling the conflict can produce paradoxical effects at the subjective level, leading to great confusion for youths struggling to give meaning to the situation. This confusion is a key feature of the family life of transnational families and should be taken into account, as it contributes to the intensification of the conflicts and constitutes a major source of social rupture between youths and their families. Accordingly, the conception of the protection of family life used by public agents should take into account the diversity of norms that fuels the conflicts in order to have a better understanding of the cases and a greater impact on their resolution. Training programmes for state agents acting in and upon this internormativity seem therefore necessary in order to give a better application to the right to the respect of family life.

By attributing an egalitarian vision of family to the public sphere and a traditional one to the private sphere of the 'Congolese community', public agents feed cultural stereotypes stemming from an essentialist approach. This approach is fundamentally what diverts the adolescents from state institutions concerning family matters. Moreover, the essentialist approach blinds state agents in that they cannot grasp the tensions between egalitarian and hierarchical norms both in the private and public spheres. If state agents want to tackle family conflicts, they have to make room for the lived experience of tensions and confusions experienced by the youths. And this is valid for both families with and without migration histories. In our view, such training in internormativity stakes pertains to a general obligation to balance the necessity of state interferences according to human rights standards.

5.2. Human rights standards and state legal pluralism

Ultimately, the plurality of sources of state law expands the normative plurality in which families navigate. First, it strongly limits the relationships upon which children and parents might rely when going through conflicts. But more importantly, migratory regulations also act upon the economy of relationships inside transnational families, granting some members special statutory roles on which others depend. The role played by the issues of papers in matrimonial disputes as empirically illustrated through this research represents too high a cost to social and familial cohesion, but also to an accessible and working family justice, in comparison with the necessity of controlling family reunification rights. Therefore, a better equilibrium between state control and the right to family life should be urgently sought. Acknowledging these specific disparities inside state law affecting family relationships, the right to family life should integrate into the decision-making process a systematic evaluation of the consequences of the decision in regard to the administrative and economic status of the families.

References

Adedeji JL (2001) 'The Legacy of JJ Rawlings in Ghanaian Politics, 1979–2000' 5(2) *African Studies Quarterly* 1–27.

Adler D, Porter D and Woolcock M (2009) 'Legal Pluralism and Equity: Some Reflections on Land Reform in Cambodia' 2(2) *Justice for the Poor*.

Agyei-Mensah S and Owusu G (2012) 'Ethnic Residential Clusters in Nima, Ghana' 23 *Urban Forum* 133–49.

Ahearn LM (2001) 'Language and Agency' 30 *Annual Review of Anthropology* 109–37.

Ahmad N (2009) 'A Critical Appraisal of "Triple Divorce" in Islamic law' 23(1) *International Journal of Law, Policy and the Family* 53–61.

Ahmed F (2013) 'Religious Norms in Family Law: Implications for Group and Personal Autonomy' in M Maclean and J Eekelaar (eds), *Managing Family Justice in Diverse Societies* (Oxford, Hart Publishing).

Ainuson KG (2009) 'Adequate Water Supply to Disadvantaged Urban Communities in Ghana', PhD Dissertation, Clemson University.

Akosa-Sarpong K (2006) 'Ghana: Dawn of a Culture of Rights' *The Patriotic Vanguard*.

Albertyn, C (2007) "Equality" in E Bonthuys, and C Albertyn (eds) *Gender, Law and Justice* (Johannesburg, Juta).

Albo X (2012) 'Justicia Indigena en la Bolivia Plurinacional' in B de Sousa Santos and JL Exeni Rodriguez (eds), *Justicia Indigena, Plurinacionalidad e Interculturalidad en Bolivia* (Quito, Fundacion Rosa Luxemburg/Abya-Yala).

Ali Sardar S (2000) *Gender and Human Rights in Islam and International Law: Equal before Allah, Unequal before Man?* (The Hague, Kluwer Law International).

—— (2007) 'Religious Pluralism, Human Rights and Muslim Citizenship in Europe: Some Preliminary Reflections on an Evolving Methodology for Consensus, in LP Loenen and JE Goldschmidt (eds), *Religious Pluralism and Human Rights in Europe: Where to Draw the Line?* (Antwerp, Intersentia).

Alidou O (2005) *Engaging Modernity: Muslim Women and the Politics of Agency in Postcolonial Niger* (Madison, University of Wisconsin Press).

—— (2011) 'Rethinking Marginality and Agency in Postcolonial Niger: A social Biography of a Sufi Woman Scholar' in M Badran (ed), *Gender and Islam in Africa: Rights, Sexuality, and Law* (Stanford, CA, Stanford University Press).

Alidou O and Alidou H (2008) 'Women, Religion, and the Discourses of Legal Ideology in Niger Republic' 54(3) *Africa Today* 21–36.

Alistar Nicaragua (2003) *Diagnóstico de Tenencia y Uso de la Tierra de la Comunidad Mayangna de Awas Tingni (RAAN)* (Managua, Cidca UCA).

Allen S and Xanthaki A (eds) (2011) *Reflections on the UN Declaration on the Rights of Indigenous Peoples* (Oxford, Hart Publishing).

Allievi S (2011) 'Muslim Voices, European Ears: Exploring the Gap between the Production of Islamic Knowledge and its Perception' in M van Bruinessen and

S Allievi (eds), *Producing Islamic knowledge : transmission and dissemination in Western Europe* (London and New York, Routledge).

Allievi S and Dassetto F (1997) *Facettes de l'islam belge* (Louvain-la-Neuve, Academia Bruylant).

al-Qayrawani, Ibn Abi Zayd (c. 10th century) *La Risâla ou Epître sur les éléments du dogme et de la loi de l'Islam selon le rite Mâlikite.*

Alvarado LJ (2007) 'Prospects and Challenges in the Implementation of Indigenous Peoples' Human Rights in International Law: Lessons from the Case of Awas Tingni vs Nicaragua' 24(3) *Arizona Journal of International & Comparative Law* 609–43.

Álvarez Molinero N (2009), 'The International Convention on the Elimination of All Forms of Racial Discrimination and the evolution of the concept of racial discrimination' in F Gómez Isa and K de Feyter (eds), *International Human Rights Law in a Global Context* (Bilbao, Deusto University Press).

Amdouni H (2011) 'Le divorce—question 2: Une femme a t'elle le droit de demander le divorce et dans quelle condition ?', fatawas.be available at: http://www.fatawas. be/fatawas/Droit_familial_et_relations_sociales/Dissolution_du_mariage/divorce. html.

Ameh RK (2004) 'Reconciling Human Rights and Traditional Practices: The Anti-trokosi Campaign in Ghana' 19(2) *Canadian Journal of Law and Society* 51–72.

—— (2006) 'Doing Justice after Conflict: The Case for Ghana's National Reconciliation Commission' 21(1) *Canadian Journal of Law and Society* 85–109.

Amien W (2008) 'Muslim Personal Law (MPL) in Canada: A Case Study Considering the Conflict between Freedom of Religion and Muslim Women's Right to Equality' in E Brems (ed), *Conflicts between fundamental rights Conflicts between Fundamental Rights* (Antwerp, Intersentia).

Amien W (2010) 'A South African Case Study for the Recognition and Regulation of Muslim Family Law in a Minority Muslim Secular Context' 24(3) *International Journal of Law, Policy and the Family* 36196.

Anaya SJ (1996) *Indigenous Peoples in International Law* (Oxford, Oxford University Press).

—— (2004) *Indigenous Peoples in International Law*, 2nd edn (Oxford, Oxford University Press).

—— (2007) 'Indigenous Law and its Contribution to Global Pluralism' 6(1) *Indigenous Law Journal* 3–12.

Anaya SJ and Campbell M (2009) 'Gaining Legal Recognition of Indigenous Land Rights: The Story of the Awas Tingni Case in Nicaragua' in D Hurwitz and ML Satterthwaite (eds), *Human Rights Advocacy Stories* (New York, Foundation Press).

Anaya, SJ and Grossman, C (2002) 'The Case of Awas Tingni v. Nicaragua: A new step in the international law of indigenous peoples' 19 *Arizona Journal of International and Comparative Law* 1–15.

Anaya SJ and Macdonald T (1995) 'Demarcating Indigenous Territories in Nicaragua: The Case of Awas Tingni' 19 *Cultural Survival Quarterly* 69–73.

An-Na'im A (1995) 'Towards a Cross-Cultural Approach to Defining International Standards of Human Rights: the Meaning of Cruel, Inhuman, or Degrading Treatment or Punishment' in A An-Na'im (ed), *Human Rights in Cross-Cultural*

Perspective: A Quest for Consensus (Philadelphia, University of Pennsylvania Press).

An-Na'im A (ed) (2002) *Islamic Family Law in a Changing World: A Global Resource Book* (London, Zed Books).

Ansere JK (1977) 'Local Government and Chieftaincy' 11 *Ghana Journal of Sociology* 71–78.

Anyidoho NA (2011) 'Ghana: Review of Rights Discourse' Norwegian Centre for Human Rights RIPOCA Research Notes 5-2011.

Appiagyei-Atua K (2013) 'Alternative Dispute Resolution and its Implications for Women's Access to Justice in Africa—Case-Study of Ghana' 1(1) *Frontiers of Legal Research* 36–57.

Apter DE (1972) *Ghana in Transition*, 2nd rev edn (New York, Atheneum).

Ardito W (1997) 'The Right to Self-Regulation. Legal Pluralism and Human Rights in Peru' 39 *Journal of Legal Pluralism and Unofficial Law* 1–42.

Ariza LJ (2009) *Derecho, Saber e Identidad Indígena* (Bogotá, Ediciones Uniandes).

Arslan L (2014) 'Vous avez dit halal? Normativités islamiques, mondialisation, sécularisation' (138/139) *Journal des Anthropologues* 265–71.

Ashamu E (2011) 'Centre for Minority Rights Development (Kenya) and Minority Rights Group International on Behalf of Endorois Welfare Council v Kenya: A Landmark Decision from the African Commission' 55 *Journal of African Law* 300–13.

Assies W (2003) 'Indian Justice in the Andes: Re-rooting or Re-routing?' in T Salman and A Zoomers (eds), *Imagining the Andes, Shifting Margins of a Marginal World* (Amsterdam, Aksant Academic Publishers).

Aylwin J (2011) 'Struggling to Localise Human Rights: The Experience of Indigenous Peoples in Chile' in K De Feyter, S Parmentier, C Timmerman and G Ulrich (eds), *The Local Relevance of Human Rights* (Cambridge, Cambridge University Press).

Bakht N (2006) 'Were Muslim Barbarians Really Knocking on the Gates of Ontario: The Religious Arbitration Controversy—Another Perspective' 40 *University of Ottawa Law Review* 67–82.

Bakht N (2007) 'Religious Arbitration in Canada: Protecting Women by Protecting them from Religion' 19(1) *Canadian Journal of Women and the Law* 119–44.

Bakker LGH, Gehring AJ, van Mourik K, Claessen MM, Harmsen C and Harmsen E (2010) Sharia in Nederland: een studie naar islamitische advisering en geschilbeslechting bij moslims in Nederland (Nijmegen, Instituut voor Culturele Antropologie en Ontwikkelingsstudies, Instituut voor Rechtssociologie, Radboud Universiteit Nijmegen, WODC) available at: http://wodc.nl/onderzoeksdatabase/sharia.aspx?cp=44&cs=6837.

Banda F (2005) *Women, Law and Human Rights: An African Perspective* (Oxford, Hart Publishing).

Bano S (2007) 'Muslim Family Justice and Human Rights: The Experience of British Muslim Women' 2(2) *Journal of Comparative Law* 38–67.

—— (2012) *Muslim Women and Shariah Councils: Transcending the Boundaries of Community and Law* (Basingstoke, Palgrave Macmillan).

—— (2013) 'Muslim Dispute Resolution in Britain: Towards a New Framework of Family Law Governance' in M Maclean and J Eekelaar (eds), *Managing Family Justice in Diverse Societies* (Oxford, Hart Publishing).

Barrera A (2011) 'Turning Legal Pluralism into State-Sanctioned Law: Assessing the Implications of the New Constitutions and Laws in Bolivia and Ecuador', GIGA Working Papers 176.

Baxi U (2006) *The Future of Human Rights* (New Delhi, Oxford University Press).

Beck U and E Beck-Gernsheim (2010) 'Passage to Hope: Marriage, Migration and the Need for a Cosmopolitan Turn in Family Research' 2 *Journal of Family Theory & Review* 401–14.

Bell L, Nathan A and Peleg I (2001) *Negotiating Culture and Human Rights* (New York, Columbia University Press).

Bengoa J (2007) *La Emergencia Indígena en América Latina* (Santiago de Chile, Fondo de Cultura Económica).

Bentzon AW, Hellum A, Stewart J, Ncube W and Agersnap T (1998) *Pursuing Grounded Theory in Law. South–North Experiences in Developing Women's Law* (Oslo/Harare, TANO/Mond Books).

Berger M (2006) 'Sharia Law in Canada—Also Possible in the Netherlands?' in P van der Grinten and T Heukels (eds), *Crossing Borders: Essays in European and Private International Law, Nationality Law, and Islamic Law in Honour of Frans Van Der Velden* (Alphen aan den Rijn, Kluwer).

Beristain M (2009) *Diálogos sobre la Reparación. Qué reparar en los casos de violaciones de derechos humanos* (Quito, Ministerio de Justicia y Derechos Humanos).

Berman PS (2007) 'Global Legal Pluralism' 80 *Southern California Law Review* 1155–238.

Blocher J (2006). 'Building on Custom: Land Tenure Policy and Economic Development in Ghana' 9(1) *Yale Human Rights and Development Law Review* 166–202.

Boafo-Arthur K (2001) 'Chieftaincy and Politics in Ghana since 1982' 3(1) *West Africa Review* 1–16.

—— (2003) 'Chieftaincy in Ghana: Challenges and Prospects in the 21st Century' 2(2) *African and Asian Studies* 125–53.

Bousetta H and Bernes L-A (2007) *Muslims in the EU: Cities Report—Belgium. Preliminary Research Report and Literature Survey* (New York, London, Budapest, Open Society Institute).

Boye A, Hill K, Isaacs S and Gordis D (1991) 'Marriage Law and Practice in the Sahel' 22(6) *Studies in Family Planning* 343–349.

Brems E (2001) *Human Rights: Universality and Diversity* (The Hague, Martinus Nijhoff Publishers).

—— (2013) 'Inclusive Universality and the Child-Caretaker Dynamic' in K Hanson and O Nieuwenhuys (eds), *Reconceptualizing Children's Rights in International Development: Living Rights, Social Justice, Translations* (Cambridge, Cambridge University Press).

—— (2014) 'Should Pluriform Human Rights Become One? Exploring the Benefits of Human Rights Integration' 3 *European Journal of Human Rights* 447–70.

Brems E, Corradi G and Schotsmans M (2015) *International Actors and Traditional Justice in Sub-Saharan Africa. Policies and Interventions in Transitional Justice and Justice Sector Aid* (Antwerp, Intersentia).

Brinig MF and Allen DW (2000) '"These Boots Are Made for Walking": Why Most Divorce Filers Are Women' 2(1) *American Law and Economics Review* 126–69.

Bryan J (2005) 'Map or be Mapped: The Awas Tingni Case, Human Rights and the Tactics of Being Indigenous', paper presented at the 2005 Annual Meeting of the American Association of Geographers, University of Canterbury.

—— (2006) 'Dilemmas of Indigenous Lands in Awas Tingni v Nicaragua' 47(6) *Anthropology News* 22.

Burgorgue-Larsen L and Ubeda de Torres A (2011) *The Inter-American Court of Human Rights, Case Law and Commentary* (Oxford, Oxford University Press).

Burke KC (2012) 'Women's Agency in Gender-Traditional Religions: A Review of Four Approaches' 6(2) *Sociology Compass* 122–33.

Burke-White WW (2004) 'International Legal Pluralism' 25 *Michigan Journal of International Law* 963–79.

Buur L and Kyed HM (2006) 'Contested Sources of Authority: Re-claiming State Sovereignty by Formalising Traditional Authority in Mozambique' 37(4) *Development and Change* 847–69.

Cadoret A (2006) 'Le champ de la parenté aujourd'hui' 28 *Cités* 49–59.

Caeiro A (2011a) 'Fatwas for European Muslims: the Minority Fiqh Project and the Integration of Islam in Europe, PhD dissertation, Utrecht University.

—— (2011b) 'The Making of the Fatwa' (155) *Archives de sciences sociales des religions* 81–100.

—— (2003) 'Debating Fatwas in the Cyberspace: the Construction of Islamic Authority in Four Francophone Muslims Internet Forums' in SACRED MEDIA (Jyväskylä, Finland) available at: www.sacredmedia.jyu.fi/mainpage.php#caeiro.

Campese J, Borrini-Feyerabend G, Cordova M de, Guignier A and Oviedo G (2007) '"Just" Conservation? What Can Human Rights Do for Conservation… and Vice Versa?!' 15 *Policy Matters* 6–9.

Canessa A (2012) *Intimate Indigeneities, Race, Sex and History in the Small Spaces of Andean Life* (Durham, NC and London: Duke University Press).

Centre de Recherche en Démographie et Société (DEMO) (2013) 'Migrations et populations issues de l'immigration en Belgique'.

Cesari, J (2004) 'Quand la religion aide à l'intégration. Analyse comparée des élites musulmanes en Europe et aux Etats-Unis' in M Cohen, J Joncheray, PJ Luizard, and Association française de sciences sociales des religions (eds), *Les transformations de l'autorité religieuse* (Paris, L'Harmattan).

—— (2012) 'Foreword: Sharia and the Future of Western Secularism' in AC Korteweg and JA Selby (eds), *Debating Sharia: Islam, Gender Politics, and Family Law Arbitration* (Toronto, Buffalo, London, University of Toronto Press).

Chanock M (1985) *Law, Custom and Social Order: The Colonial Experience in Malawi and Zambia* (Cambridge, Cambridge University Press).

Charrad MM (2010) 'Women's Agency across Cultures: Conceptualizing Strengths and Boundaries' 33(6) *Women's Studies International Forum* 517–22.

Chaussebourg L, Carrasco V and Lermenier A (2009) 'Le divorce' (Paris, Ministère de la justice) available at: www.justice.gouv.fr/art_pix/1_1_1_stat_divorce_20090722.pdf.

Chinkin C, Wright S and Charlesworth H (2005) 'Feminist Approaches to International Law: Reflections from another Century' in D Buss and A Manji (eds), *International Law: Modern Feminist Approaches* (Oxford and Portland, OR, Hart Publishing).

Chirayath L, Sage C and Woolcock M (2005) 'Customary Law and Policy Reform: Engaging with the Plurality of Justice Systems', Background Paper for the World Development Report 2006: Equity and Development.

Clapham A (2006) *Human Rights Obligations of Non-State Actors* (Oxford, Oxford University Press).

Clarke KM (2009) *Fictions of Justice: The International Criminal Court and the Challenge of Legal Pluralism in Sub-Saharan Africa* (Cambridge, Cambridge University Press).

Classens A and Cousins B (eds) (2008) *Land, Power and Custom. Controversies generated by South Africa's Communal Land Rights Act.* (Athens: Ohio University Press).

Clavero B (1998) 'De los ecos a las voces, de las leyes indigenistas a los derechos indígenas' in *Derechos de los Pueblos Indígenas* (Vitoria-Gasteiz, Servicio Central de Publicaciones del Gobierno Vasco).

Colchester M (2011) 'Divers Paths to Justice: Legal Pluralism and the Rights of Indigenous Peoples in Southeast Asia—An Introduction' in M Colchester and S Chao (eds), *Divers Paths To Justice: Legal pluralism and the rights of indigenous peoples in Southeast Asia* (Chiang Mai, Thailand, Forest Peoples Programme (FPP) and Asia Indigenous Peoples Pact (AIPP)).

Commaille J (2006) 'La famille, l'Etat, le politique: une nouvelle économie des valeurs. Entre tensions et contradictions' 136 *Informations sociales* 100–11.

Comaille J and Martin C (1998) *Les enjeux politiques de la famille* (Paris, La découverte).

—— (2001) 'Les conditions d'une democratisation de la vie privée' in E Fassin and D Borillo (eds) *Au-delà du Pacs* (Paris, Presses universitaires de France).

Comaroff J and Comaroff J (1991) *Of Revelation and Revolution, Christianity, Colonialism, and Consciousness in South Africa* (Chicago and London, University of Chicago Press).

Commission on Legal Empowerment of the Poor (2008) *Making the Law Work for Everyone*, vol 1 (New York, United Nations Development Program).

Connolly B (2005) 'Non-State Justice Systems and the State: Proposals for a Recognition Typology' 38 *Connecticut Law Review* 239–94.

Coomaraswamy R (2005) 'Preface: Violence against Women and Crimes of Honor' in IL Welch and S Hossein (eds), *Honour Crimes, Paaradigms and Violence against Women* (London, Zed Books).

Cooper B (2009) 'Chronic Malnutrition and the Trope of the Bad Mother' in X Crombé and J Jézéquel (eds), *A Not-So Natural Disaster: Niger 05* (New York, Columbia University Press).

—— (2010) 'Secular States, Muslim Law and Islamic Religious Culture: Gender Implications of Legal Struggles in Hybrid Legal Systems in Contemporary West Africa' 59 *Droit et cultures* 97–120.

Coordinadora de la Mujer (2009) *Detrás del Cristal con que Se Mira: Mujeres Quechuas, Aymaras, Sirionó, Trinitarias, Chimane, Chiquitanas y Ayoreas, Órdenes Normativos e Interlegalidad* (La Paz, Nuevo Periodismo Editores).

Corradi G (2012a) 'An Emerging Challenge for Justice Sector Aid in Africa: Lessons from Mozambique on Legal Pluralism and Human Rights' 4(3) *Journal of Human rights Practice* 289–311.

—— (2012b) 'Advancing Human Rights in Legally Plural Africa: The Role of Development Actors in the Justice Sector', PhD dissertation, Faculty of Law, Ghent University.

—— (2014) 'Can Legal Pluralism Advance Human Rights? How Development Actors Can Contribute' 26(5) *European Journal of Development Research* 783–97.

—— (2015) 'Justice Sector Aid in Legally Plural Africa' in E Brems, G Corradi and M Schotsmans (eds) *International Actors and Traditional Justice in Sub-Saharan Africa* (Antwerp, Intersentia).

Cottyn H (2014) 'Renegotiating Communal Autonomy, Communal Land Rights and Liberal Land Reform on the Bolivian Altiplano. Carangas, 1860–1930', PhD dissertation, Ghent University.

Cowan JK, Dembour MB and Wilson RA (eds) (2001a) *Culture and Rights: Anthropological Perspectives* (Cambridge, Cambridge University Press).

—— (2001b) 'Introduction' in JK Cowan, MB Dembour and RA Wilson (eds.) *Culture and Rights: Anthropological Perspectives.* (Cambridge: Cambridge University Press).

Crawford G and Andreassen BA (2013) 'Human Rights, Power and Civic Action: Theoretical Considerations' in BA Andreassen and G Crawford (eds), *Human Rights, Power and Civic Action: Comparative Analyses of Struggles for Rights in Developing Societies.* (New York, Routledge).

Crook RC (2004) 'Access to Justice and Land Disputes in Ghana's State Courts: The Litigants' Perspective' *Journal of Legal Pluralism* 1–28.

Cutting C (2012) 'Faith-Based Arbitration or Religious Divorce: What Was the Issue?' in A C Korteweg and JA Selby (eds), *Debating Sharia: Islam, Gender Politics, and Family Law Arbitration* (Toronto, Buffalo, London, University of Toronto Press).

—— (2013) 'Sharia and Constraint: Practices, Policies, and Responses to Faith-Based Arbitration in Ontario', PhD dissertation, University of Waterloo.

D'Engelbronner-Kolff FM (2001) 'A Web of Legal Cultures: Dispute Processing amongst the Sambyu of Northern Namibia', PhD dissertation, Free University (VU) Amsterdam.

D'Hondt S (2009) 'Others on Trial: The Construction of Cultural Otherness in Belgian First Instance Criminal Hearings' 41(4) *Journal of Pragmatics* 806–28.

D'Ursel D (2010) *La Médiation entre Tradition et Modernité Familiale* (Bruxelles, Presses Universitaires de Louvain).

Danida (2010) *How to Note on Informal Justice Systems* (Copenhagen, Ministry of Foreign Affairs of Denmark).

Daniels E (1996) 'The Impact of the 1992 Constitution on Family Rights in Ghana' 40 *Journal of African Law* 183–93.

Danish Institute for Human Rights (2013) *Informal Justice Systems. Charting a Course for Human Rights Based Engagement* (New York, UN Women).

Dassetto F (2011) *L'Iris et le Croissant* (Louvain-la-Neuve, Presses Universitaires de Louvain).

Davies JA and Dagbanja DN (2009) 'The Role and Future of Customary Tort Law in Ghana: A Cross-Cultural Perspective' 26(2) *Arizona Journal of International and Comparative Law* 303–34.

De Feyter K and Gómez Isa F (eds) (2005) *Privatisation and Human Rights in the Age of Globalisation* (Antwerp, Intersentia).

De Feyter, K (2006) Localizing Human Rights (Antwerp, Institute of Development Policy and Management, Antwerp University) available at: http://www.ua.ac.be/objs/00152976.pdf.

De Feyter K, Parmentier S, Timmerman C and Ulrich G (eds) (2011) *The Local Relevance of Human Rights* (Cambridge, Cambridge University Press).

De Sousa Santos B (1987) 'Law: A Map of Misreading. Toward a Postmodern Conception of Law' 14 *Journal of Law and Society* 279–302.

—— (1995) *Toward a New Common Sense: Law, Science and Politics in the Paradigmatic Transition* (New York and London, Routledge).

—— (2002) *Toward a New Legal Common Sense. Law, Globalization and Emancipation*, 2nd edn (London, Edinburgh Dublin, Butterworths).

—— (2009) 'Toward a Multicultural Conception of Human Rights' in F Gómez Isa and K de Feyter (eds), *International Human Rights Law in a Global Context* (Bilbao, Deusto University Press).

De Sousa Santos B and Exeni Rodriguez JL (eds) *Justicia Indigena, Plurinacionalidad e Interculturalidad en Bolivia* (Quito, Fundacion Rosa Luxemburg/Abya-Yala).

Demart S (2008) 'Le "combat pour l'intégration" des églises issues du Réveil congolais (RDC)' 24(3) *Revue européenne des migrations internationals* 147–65.

Derman B, Hellum A and Bergtora Sandvik K (2013) *Worlds of Human Rights. The Ambiguities of Rights Claiming in Africa* (Leiden, Boston, Brill).

Derman B, Hellum A and Sandvik K (eds) (2013) 'Introduction' in *Worlds of Human Rights: Ambiguities of Rights Claiming in Africa* (Leiden, Brill).

Derman B, Lahiffe E and Sjaastad E (2010) 'Strategic Questions for Claimant Communities, Government and Strategic Partners: Challenges and Pitfalls in South Africa's New Model of Land Restitution' in C Walker, A Bohlin, R Hall and T Kepe (eds), *Land, Memory, Reconstruction and Justice: Perspectives on Land Claims in South Africa* (Athens, Ohio University Press).

Desmet E (2011) *Indigenous Rights Entwined with Nature Conservation* (Cambridge, Intersentia).

—— (2011) 'Interaction between Customary Legal Systems and the Formal Legal System of Peru' in J Ubink and T McInerney (eds), *Customary Justice: Perspectives on Legal Empowerment* (Rome, International Development Law Organization).

—— (2014) 'Analysing Users' Trajectories in Human Rights (law): A Conceptual Exploration and Research Agenda' 8(2) *Human Rights & International Legal Discourse* 121–41.

Dessing N (2002) 'An Islamic Wedding in a Dutch Living Room' 10 *ISIM Newsletter* 1.

DfID (2004) *Non-State Justice And Security Systems*, www.gsdrc.org/docs/open/SSAJ101.pdf.

Donelly J (1984) 'Cultural Relativism and Universal Human Rights' 6(4) *Human Rights Quarterly* 400–19.

—— (2007) 'The Relative Universality of Human Rights' 29(2) *Human Rights Quarterly* 281–306.

Drzewieniecki J (1995) '*Indigenous People, Law, and Politics in Peru*', paper presented at the Meeting of the Latin American Studies Association, Washington, DC, 28–30 September 1995.

Dunbar RA (1991) 'Islamic Values, the State, and "the Development of Women": The Case of Niger' in C Coles and B Mack (eds), *Hausa Women in the Twentieth Century* (Madison, University of Wisconsin Press).

—— (2000) 'Muslim Women in African History' in N Levtzion and RL Pouwels (eds), *The History of Islam in Africa* (Athens, Ohio University Press).

Dupret B (1999) 'Legal Pluralism, Normative Plurality, and the Arab World' in B Dupret, M Berger and L al-Zwaini (eds), *Legal Pluralism in the Arab World* (The Hague, Kluwer Law International).

—— (2007) 'Legal Pluralism, Plurality of Laws and Legal Practices: Theories, Critiques and Praxiological Re-specification' 1 *European Journal of Legal Studies*.

Eberhard C (2002) *Droit de l'Homme et Dialogue Interculturel* (Paris, Editions Des Ecrivains).

Eckert J, Donahoe B, Strumpell C and Ozlem Biner Z (eds) (2012) *Law Against the State. Ethnographic Forays into Law's Transformations* (Cambridge, Cambridge University Press).

Eilenberg M (2014) 'Frontier Constellations: Agrarian Expansion and Sovereignty on the Indonesian–Malaysian Border' 41(2) *Journal of Peasant Studies* 157–82.

El Fadl KA (1994) 'Islamic Law and Muslim Minorities: The Juristic Discourse on Muslim Minorities from the Second/Eighth to the Eleventh/Seventeenth Centuries' 1(2) *Islamic Law and Society* 141.

—— (1994) 'Legal Debates on Muslim Minorities' 22(1) *Journal of Religious Ethics* 127–62.

Engle Merry S (2006) *Human Rights and Gender Violence. Translating International Law into Local Justice* (Chicago, University of Chicago Press).

Engle K (2011) 'On Fragile Architecture: The UN Declaration on the Rights of Indigenous Peoples in the Context of Human Rights' 22 *European Journal of International Law* 141–63.

Englund H (2006) *Prisoners of Freedom: Human Rights and the African Poor* (Berkeley, University of California Press).

Enwright W (1985) 'Customary Law in Zimbabwe: Traditional Mechanisms and Colonial Control' 49(1) *Saskatchewan Law Review* 37–48.

Erlanger H, Garth B, Larson J, Mertz E, Nourse V and Wilkins D (2005) 'Foreword: Is it Time for a New Legal Realism?' 2 *Wisconsin Law Review* 335–63.

European Council for Fatwa and Research (2002) *First and Second Collections of Fatwas (Qararat wa-Fatawa li-l-Majlis al-Urubbi li-l-Ifta' wa-l-Buhuth)* (Cairo, Egypt, Islamic INC/Al-Falah Foundation).

—— (2009) 'mā ḥukm taṭlīq al-qāḍī ghair al-muslim bil-nisbat li-l-muslimīn al-muqīmīn fī balad ghair islāmiya? [What is the ruling on divorce by a non-Muslim judge for Muslims living in a non-Muslim country?]' European Council for Fatwa and Research (new website) available at: http://e-cfr.org/new/fatwa/ام-حكم-تطليق-القاضي-غير-المسلم-بالنسبة/3.

—— (2009) 'mā ḥukm taṭlīq al-mar'at nafsihā? [what is the ruling on divorce initiated by the woman?]' European Council for Fatwa and Research (new website) available at: http://e-cfr.org/new/fatwa/ام-حكم-تطليق-المرأة-نفسها؟/3.

Ewick P and Silbey SS (1998) *The Common Place of Law: Stories from Everyday Life* (Chicago, University of Chicago Press).

Fadil N (2011) 'Belgium' in JS Nielsen (ed), *Yearbook of Muslims in Europe*, vol 3 (Leiden, Boston, Brill).

Fallon K (2003) 'Transforming Women's Citizenship Rights within an Emerging Democratic State: The Case of Ghana' 17(4) *Gender and Society* 525–43.

Farran S (2006) 'Is Legal Pluralism an Obstacle to Human Rights? Considerations from the South Pacific' 52 *Journal of Legal Pluralism and Unofficial Law* 77–105.

Faundez J (2012) 'Legal Pluralism and International Development Agencies: State Building or Legal Reform' in B Tamanaha, C Sage and M Woolcock (eds), *Legal Pluralism and Development, Scholars and Practitioners in Dialogue* (Cambridge, Cambridge University Press).

Favell A and Martiniello M (1998) 'Convergence and Divergence between British and Belgian Multiculturalism' in M Martiniello (ed), *Multicultural Policies and the State: A Comparison of Two European Societies* (Utrecht, European Research Centre on Migration and Ethnic Relations, Utrecht University).

Feltoe (2003) 'The Role of Civil Society in Helping Overcome the Crisis in Zimbabwe. The Constitution, the Legal System and Political Violence', paper prepared for the Crisis in Zimbabwe Coalition, Harare.

Fenrich J and Higgins T (2001) 'Promise Unfulfilled: Law, Culture, and Women's Inheritance Rights in Ghana' 25 *Fordham International Law Journal* 259–41.

Fernandez Juarez G (2008) *Kharisiris en Accion, Cuerpo, Persona y Modelos Medicos en el Altiplano de Bolivia* (Quito, Abya-Yala).

Fernandez M (2000) *La Ley Del Ayllu, Practica de Jach'a Justicia y Jisk'a Justicia (Justicia Mayor y Justicia Menor) en Comunidades Aymaras* (La Paz, Fundacion PIEB).

Flores Condori P (2012) *Sistemas Juridicos Indigena Originario Campesinos en Bolivia, Tres Aproximaciones: Curahuara de Carangas (Oruro), Sacaca (Potosi) and Charagua Norte (Santa Cruz)* (La Paz, Projuride, GIZ).

Fluet E, Calaguas M and Drost C (2006) 'Legal Pluralism & Women's Rights: A Study in Post-Colonial Tanzania', Working Paper 1683 ExpressO Preprint Series (online: http://law.bepress.com/expresso/eps/1683).

Forsyth M (2007) 'A Typology of Relationships between State and Non-State Justice Systems' 56 *Journal of Legal Pluralism and Unofficial Law* 67–112.

Fournier P (2012) 'Calculating Claims: Jewish and Muslim Women Navigating Religion, Economics and Law in Canada' 8(1) *International Journal of Law in Context* 47–72.

Francis EK (1968) 'The Ethnic Factor in Nation Building' 46 *Social Forces* 338–46.

Gadea E (2010) 'La Loi chez les Aymaras: Justice Communautaire et Pluralisme Juridique à Curahuara de Carangas', unpublished Masters dissertation, Université de Lyon.

Gal S (1989) 'Between Speech and Silence: The Problematics of Research on Language and Gender' 3(1) *Papers in Pragmatics* 1–38.

Galanter M (1981) 'Justice in Many Rooms: Courts, Private Ordering and Indigenous Law' 19 *Journal of Legal Pluralism and Unofficial Law* 1–47.

—— (1981) 'Justice in Many Rooms: Courts, Private Ordering, and Indigenous Law' 19 *Journal of Legal Pluralism* 1–48.

Garcia Canclini N (2001) *Culturas Hibridas: Estrategias para Entrar y Salir de la Modernidad* (Grijalbo, Mexico).

Garth B (2006) 'Symposium: New Legal Realism. Introduction: Taking New Legal Realism to Transnational Issues and Institutions' 31(4) *Law and Social Inquiry* 939–44.

Gaventa J (2006) 'Reflections on the Uses of the "Power Cube"', 4 *CFP Evaluation Series* 2003–06, MFP Breed Netwerk, the Netherlands.

Gershon I (2011) 'Studying Cultural Pluralism in Court versus Legislative' 34(1) *Political and Legal Anthropology Review* 155–74.

Giddens A (1992) *The Transformation of Intimacy. Sexuality, Love and Eroticism in Modern Societies* (Cambridge, Polity Press).

Glendon M (2003) 'The Forgotten Crucible: The Latin American Influence on the Universal Human Rights Idea' 16 *Harvard Human Rights Journal* 27–40.

Glenn P (2004) *Legal Traditions of the World* (Oxford, Oxford University Press).

Goedde P (2010) 'Legal Mobilization for Human Rights Protection in North Korea: Furthering Discourse or Discord?' 32(3) *Human Rights Quarterly* 530–74.

Goldstein D (2007) 'Human rights as culprit, human rights as victim: rights and security in the state of exception' in M Goodale and S Engle Merry (eds), *The Practice of Human Rights. Tracking the Law Between the Global and the Local* (New York, Cambridge University Press).

Gómez Isa F (2011) 'Freedom from Want Revisited from a Local Perspective: Evolution and Challenges Ahead' in K De Feyter, S Parmentier, C Timmerman and G Ulrich (eds), *The Local Relevance of Human Rights* (Cambridge, Cambridge University Press).

Gómez Isa F (ed) (2013) *El Caso Awas Tingni. Derechos Humanos entre lo Local y lo Global* (Bilbao: Universidad de Deusto).

Gómez Isa F (2015) 'The Right to Development, Translating Indigenous Voice(s) into Development Theory and Practice' in J Wouters, A Ninio, T Doherty and H Cissé (eds), *The World Bank Legal Review*, vol 6: *Improving Delivery in Development: The Role of Voice, Social Contract, and Accountability* (Washington, DC, World Bank Publications).

Goodale M (2007) 'Locating Rights, Envisioning Law between the Global and the Local' in M Goodale and SE Merry (eds), *The Practice of Human Rights. Tracking the Law Between the Global and the Local* (New York, Cambridge University Press).

—— (2009a) *Surrendering to Utopia: An Anthropology of Human Rights* (Stanford, Stanford University Press).

—— (2009b) *Dilemmas of Modernity, Bolivian Encounters with Law and Liberalism* (Stanford, Stanford University Press).

—— (2006) 'Toward a Critical Anthropology of Human Rights' 47(3) *Current Anthropology* 485–511.

Goodale M and Merry SE (eds) (2007) *The Practice of Human Rights. Tracking Law between the Global and the Local* (Cambridge, Cambridge University Press).

Griffiths A (1996) 'Legal Pluralism in Africa: The Role of Gender and Women's Access to Law' 19(2) *Political and Legal Anthropology Review* 93–107.

—— (1997) *In the Shadow of Marriage: Gender and Justice in an African Community* (Chicago, University of Chicago Press).

—— (1998) 'Legal Pluralism. Women's Access to Law' 42 *Journal of Legal Pluralism* 123, 139.

—— (2002) 'Legal Pluralism' in R Banakar and M Travers (eds), *An Introduction to Law and Social Theory* (Oxford and Portland, OR, Hart Publishing).

Griffiths J (1986) 'What Is Legal Pluralism?' 24 *Journal of Legal Pluralism and Unofficial Law* 1–55.

Grillo R (2008) 'The Family in Dispute: Insiders and Outsiders' in R Grillo (ed), *The Family in Question: Immigrant and Ethnic Minorities in Multicultural Europe* (Amsterdam, Amsterdam University Press).

Grindal B (1973) 'Islamic Affiliations and Urban Adaptations: The Sisala Migrant in Accra, Ghana' 43(4) *Africa: Journal of the International African Institute* 333–46.

Hale C (2006) 'Activist Research v Cultural Critique: Indigenous Land Rights and the Contradictions of Politically Engaged Anthropology' 21 *Cultural Anthropology* 96–120.

Harper E (2011a) *Customary Justice: From Program Design to Impact Evaluation* (Rome, International Development Law Organization).

—— (2011b) *Working with Customary Justice Systems: Post-Conflict and Fragile States* (Rome, International Development Law Organization).

Harvey ME and Brand R (1974) 'The Spatial Allocation of Migrants in Accra, Ghana' 64(1) *Geographical Review* 1–30.

Haynes J (1991) 'Human Rights and Democracy in Ghana: The Record of the Rawlings' Regime' 90 *African Affairs* 407–25.

Hellum A (1995) 'Actor Perspectives on Gender and Legal Pluralism in Africa' in H Petersen and H Zahle (eds), *Legal Polycentricity: Consequences of Pluralism in Law* (Aldershot, Darthmouth).

—— (1999) *Women's Human Rights and Legal Pluralism in Africa: Mixed Norms and Identities in Infertility Management in Zimbabwe* (Oslo and Harare: TANO Aschehoug/ Mond Books).

—— (2000) 'Human Rights and Gender Relations in Postcolonial Africa: Options and Limits for the Subjects of Legal Pluralism' 25(2) *Law & Social Inquiry* 635–55.

—— (2013) "Gender, human rights and legal pluralities: experiences from Southern and Eastern Africa" in Sieder R and McNeish JA (eds) *Gender Justice and Legal Pluralities: Latin American and African Perspectives.* (New York: Routledge).

Hellum A and Derman B (2009) 'Government, Business and Chiefs: Ambiguities of Social Justice through Land Restitution in South Africa, in F von Benda Beckmann, K von Benda Beckmann and J Eckert (eds), *Rules of Law and Laws of Ruling: On the Governance of Law* (Farnham and Burlington, VT, Ashgate).

—— (2013) 'Between Common Community Interest and Gender Difference: Women in South Africa's Land Restitution Process' in B Derman, A Hellum and K Sandvik, Kristin (eds), *Worlds of Human Rights: Ambiguities of Rights Claiming in Africa* (Leiden, Brill).

Hellum A and Farhat T (2011) 'Taking What Law Where and To Whom? Legal Literacy as Transcultural "Law-Making" in Oslo' in A Hellum, S Sardar Ali and A Griffiths (eds), *From Transnational Relations to Transnational Laws: Northern European Laws at the Crossroads* (Burlington, VT, Ashgate).

Hellum A, Derman B, Feltoe G, Sithole E, Stewart J and Tsanga A (2013) 'Rights Claiming and Rights Making in Zimbabwe: A Study of Three Human Rights NGOs' in BA Andreassen and G Crawford (eds), *Human Rights, Power and Non-Governmental Action: Comparative Analyses of Rights-Based Approaches and Civic Struggles in Development Contexts* (London, Routledge).

Hellum A, Sardar Ali S and Griffiths A (eds) (2011) *From Transnational Relations to Transnational Laws, Northern European Laws at the Crossroads* (Farnham, Ashgate).

Hellum A, Stewart J, Sardar Ali S and Tsanga A (eds) (2007a) *Human Rights, Plural Legalities and Gendered Realities. Paths are Made by Walking* (Harare, Southern and Eastern African Regional Centre for Women's Law).

—— (2007b) 'Paths are Made by Walking: Introductory Thoughts' in A Hellum, J Stewart, S Sardar Ali and A Tsanga (eds), *Human Rights, Plural Legalities and Gendered Realities: Paths are made by walking* (Harare, Weaver Press).

Henquinet K (2007) 'The Rise of Wife Seclusion in Rural South-Central Niger' 46 *Ethnology* 57–80.

—— (2013) 'Translating Women's Rights in Niger: What Happened to the Radical Challenge to Patriarchy?' in B Derman, A Hellum, and K Bergtora Sandvik (eds), *Worlds of Human Rights: The Ambiguities of Rights Claiming in Africa* (Leiden, Brill).

—— (2014) 'Reformulating Participation in Nigerien Development Programs: An Examination of Conflicting Messages Concerning Gender and Class' in N Akua Amponsah (ed), *Beyond the Boundaries: Toyin Falola and the Art Of Genre-Bending* (Trenton, NJ, Africa World Press).

Herrera JI (2011) *Unveiling the Face of Diversity: Interlegality and Legal Pluralism in the Mayan Area of the Yucatan Peninsula* (Amsterdam, Universiteit van Amsterdam).

Hespel S, Put J and Rom M (2012) 'Navigating the Maze: The Interrelation of International Legal Norms, with Illustrations from International Juvenile Justice Standards' 6 *Human Rights & International Legal Discourse* 329–65.

Hessbruegge JA and Ochoa Gracia CF (2011) 'Mayan Law in Post-Conflict Guatemala' in D Isser (ed) *Customary Justice and the Rule of Law in War-Torn Societies* (Washington, DC, United States Institute of Peace).

Hilgers M (2012) 'The Historicity of the Neoliberal State' 20 *Social Anthropology* 80–94.

Hinz MO (2012) 'The Ascertainment of Customary Law: What Is *Ascertainment of Customary Law* and What Is it For? The Experience of the Customary Law Ascertainment Project in Namibia' 2(7) *Oñati Socio-Legal Series* 85–105, http://ssrn.com/abstract=2100337.

Hodzic S (2009) 'Unsettling Power: Domestic Violence, Gender Politics, and Struggles Over Sovereignty in Ghana' 74(3) *Ethnos* 331–60.

Hoekema A (1999) 'Hacia un pluralismo jurídico formal de tipo igualitario' in M Castro Lucic and MT Sierra (eds), *Pluralismo Jurídico y Derechos Indígenas en América Latina*, special issue of *América Indígena* 261–30.

—— (2008) 'Multicultural Conflicts and National Judges: A General Approach' 2 *Law, Social Justice & Global Development* 1–14.

Hoekema AJ (2003) 'A New Beginning of Law among Indigenous Peoples' in FJM Feldbrugge (ed), *The Law's Beginning* (Leiden and Boston, MA, Martinus Nijhoff).

—— (2012) 'If Not Private Property, Then What? Legalising Extra-Legal Rural Land Tenure via a Third Road' in JM Otto and AJ Hoekema (eds), *Fair Land Governance, How to Legalise Land Rights for Rural Development* (Leiden, Leiden University Press).

Holtmaat R (2013) 'CEDAW: A Holistic Approach to Women's Equality and Freedom' in A Hellum and H Sinding Aasen (eds), *Women's Human Rights: CEDAW in International, Regional and National Law* (New York, Cambridge University Press).

Holtmaat R and Naber JMM (2011) Women's Human Rights and Culture: From Deadlock to Dialogue (Cambridge and Antwerp, Intersentia).

Hussain J (2011) 'More than One Law for All: Legal Pluralism in Southeast Asia, 7 *Democracy & Security* 374–89.

IACHR (Inter-American Commission on Human Rights) (2007) Access to Justice and Social Inclusion: The Road Towards Strengthening Democracy in Bolivia, www.cidh.org (accessed 1 October 12).

Ibn'Uthaymeen (n.d.) 'Muslim Minorities/Divorce Procedures in Non-Muslim countries', available at: www.fatwa-online.com/fataawa/muslimminorities/0000920_2.htm.

Ibn Baz and Ibn Uthaymeen S (1998) *Muslim Minorities: Fatawa Regarding Muslims Living as Minorities* (Middlesex, Message of Islam).

ICHRP (2009) *When Legal Worlds Overlap: Human Rights, State and Non-State Law* (Versoix, International Council on Human Rights Policy).

IIDH (Instituto Interamericano de Derechos Humanos) (2006) *Ombudsman y Acceso a la Justicia de los Pueblos Indigenas: Estudio de Caso en Bolivia, Colombia, Guatemala y Nicaragua* (San Jose, Instituto Interamericano de Derechos Humanos).

Inksater K (2006) 'Resolving Tensions between Indigenous Law and Human Rights Norms through Transformative Juricultural Pluralism', Research Paper, Faculty of Law, University of Ottowa, Canada (DCL 7066T).

—— (2010) 'Transformative Juricultural Pluralism: Indigenous Justice Systems in Latin America and International Human Rights' 60 *Journal of Legal Pluralism* 105–42.

Institut national de statistique (Belgium) (2006) *Mariages et divorces en 2006* (Brussels, Institut national de statistique).

Islamopedia Online (2010a) 'The European Council for Fatwa and Research Upholds the Validity of a Divorce Issued by a Non-Muslim judge', www.islamopediaonline. org/fatwa/european-council-fatwa-and-research-upholds-validity-divorce-issued-non-muslim-judge.

—— (2010b) 'The European Council for Fatwa and Research Discusses the Permissibility of Divorce Initiated by the Wife', www.islamopediaonline.org/fatwa/european-council-fatwa-and-research-discusses-permissibility-divorce-initated-wife.

Issa O (2011) 'Le gouvernement abandonne le statut personnel devant la fronde des islamistes' *Inter Press Service News Agency*, 18 March, www.awid.org/fre/Library/NIGER-Le-gouvernement-abandonne-le-statut-personnel-devant-la-fronde-des-islamistes (accessed 6 May 2014).

Kagné B (2001) 'Immigration, stratégies identitaires et mobilisations politiques des Africains en Belgique' in G Gosselin and JP Lavaud (eds), *Ethnicité et Mobilisations Sociales* (Paris, L'Harmattan) 207–43.

Kamali MH (2010) *Shari'ah law: An Introduction* (Richmond, Oneworld).

Kang A (2013) 'The Effect of Gender Quota Laws on the Election of Women: Lessons from Niger' *Women's Studies International Forum* http://dx.doi.org/10.1016/j.wsif.2013.03.005 (accessed 18 March 2014).

Karman K-LJ (2011) 'Interpreting Islamic Law for European Muslims: The Role and the Work of the European Council for Fatwa and Research' in JS Nielsen (ed), *Yearbook of Muslims in Europe*, vol 3 (Leiden, Brill).

Katsande RK (2014) 'Interrogating Marriage as an Organizing Framework in Land Based Businesses: A Case Study of Women Horticulture Farmers in Mashonaland West Province of Zimbabwe', PhD dissertation, University of Zimbabwe.

Kaufmann JC (1992) *La Trame Conjugale: Analyse du Couple par son Linge* (Paris, Aramand Colin).

Kaya A, Kentel F and Zemni S (2008) *Belgische Turken: een brug of een breuk tussen Turkije en de Europese Unie?* (Brussels, Koning Boudewijn Stichting).

Keck ME and Sikkink K (1998) *Activists Beyond Borders. Advocacy Networks in International Politics* (Ithaca, NY, Cornell University Press).

Keshavjee M (2007) 'Alternative dispute resolution in a diasporic Muslim community in Britain' in P Shah (ed), *Law and Ethnic Plurality: Socio-Legal Perspectives* (Leiden and Boston, Martinus Nijhoff).

Keshavjee MM (2013) *Islam, Shari'a and Alternative Dispute Resolution: Mechanisms for Legal Redress in the Muslim Community* (London, IB Tauris).

Khir BM (2006) 'The Right of Women to No-Fault Divorce in Islam and its Application by British Muslims' 17(3) *Islam and Christian–Muslim Relations* 295–306.

Kinley D (2012) 'Bendable Rules: The Development Implications of Human Rights Pluralism' in B Tamanaha, C Sage and M Woolcock (eds), *Legal Pluralism and Development, Scholars and Practitioners in Dialogue* (Cambridge, Cambridge University Press).

Koning M de (2009) 'Sheikh Google, Sharia & Arbitrage', *Closer—Anthropology of Muslims in Europe*, available at: http://religionresearch.org/closer/2009/07/01/sheikh-google-sharia-arbitrage/.

Korteweg AC (2008) 'The Sharia Debate in Ontario: Gender, Islam, and Representations of Muslim Women's Agency' 22(4) *Gender & Society* 434–54.

—— (2012) 'Agency and Representations: Voices and Silences in the Ontario Sharia Debate' in AC Korteweg and JA Selby (eds), *Debating Sharia: Islam, Gender Politics, and Family Law Arbitration* (Toronto, Buffalo, London, University of Toronto Press).

Kymlicka W (2005) *Multicultural Citizenship* (Oxford, Oxford University Press).

Langford M, Derman B, Madlingozi T, Moyo K, Dugard J, Hellum A and Shirinda S (2012) 'South Africa: From Struggle to Idealism and Back Again' in BA Andreassen and G Crawford (eds), *Human Rights, Power and Non-Governmental Action: Comparative Analyses of Rights-based Approaches and Civic Struggles in Development Contexts* (London, Routledge).

Lecoyer K (2017) 'Belgian Muslim Women Navigating through Transnational Social Spaces with Regard to Marriage Conclusion' 14 *Migration Letters* 11.

Lecoyer K and Simon C (2015) 'The Multicultural Family in Conflict: Legal and Socio-Anthropological Perspectives on Child Residency' 47(2) *Journal of Legal Pluralism and Unofficial Law* 190–207.

Levitt P and Merry SE (2011) 'Making Women's Human Rights in the Vernacular: Navigating the Culture/Rights Divide' in DL Hodgson (ed), *Gender and Culture at the Limit of Rights* (Philadelphia, University of Pennsylvania Press).

Littlechild W (2009), 'When Indigenous Peoples Win, the Whole World Wins' in C Chartres and R Stavenhagen (eds), *Making the Declaration Work: The United Nations Declaration on the Rights of Indigenous Peoples* (Copenhagen, IWGIA).

Liversage A and Jensen TG (2011) *Parallelle retsopfattelser i Danmark: Et kvalitativt studie af privatretlige praksisser blandt etniske minoriteter* (Copenhagen, Denmark, SFI) available at: www.sfi.dk/rapportoplysninger-4681.aspx?Action=1 &NewsId=3144&PID=9267.

Lugard F (1918) 'Revisions of Instructions to Political Officers on Subjects Chiefly Political and Administrative' in AHM Kirk-Greene (ed), *The Principles of Native Administration in Nigeria: Selected Documents, 1900–1947*. (London, Oxford University Press).

Lukes S (1974) *Power: A Radical View* (Basingstoke, Macmillan).

Macdonald T (1996) *Awas Tingni, an Ethnographic Study of the Community and its Territory* (The Awas Tingni Territorial Demarcation Project).

Macfarlane J (2012a) *Islamic Divorce in North America : A Shari'a Path in a Secular Society* (Oxford and New York, Oxford University Press).

—— (2012b) 'Understanding Trends in American Muslim Divorce and Marriage' ISPU Report (Washington, DC, Institute for Social Policy and Understanding) www.ispu.org/GetReports/35/2399/Publications.aspx.

Mack P (2005) 'Religion, Feminism, and the Problem of Agency: Reflections on Eighteenth-Century Quakerism' in S Knott and B Taylor (eds), *Women, gender and enlightenment* (London, Palgrave Macmillan).

Magagi AM (2002) *Le mariage précoce en milieu rural haoussa de Maradi (Niger)* (Collège Coopératif Province-Alpes-Méditérranée Centre agrée par le Ministre de l'Emploi et de la Solidarité).

Mahmood S (2001) 'Feminist Theory, Embodiment, and the Docile Agent: Some Reflections on the Egyptian Islamic Revival' 16(2) *Cultural Anthropology* 202–36.

—— (2005) *Politics of Piety: Islamic Revival and the Feminist Subject* (Princeton, NJ, Princeton University Press).

Mamdani M (1996) *Citizen and Subject: Contemporary Africa and the Legacy of Late Colonialism* (Princeton, NJ, Princeton University Press).

Manço U (2004) 'Turcs d'Europe: une présence diasporique unique par son poids démographique et sa complexité sociale' in A Manço (ed), *Turquie: vers de nouveaux horizons migratoires?* (Paris, L'Harmattan).

Manço U and Kanmaz M (2004) 'Belgique. Intégration des musulmans et reconnaissance du culte islamique: un essai de bilan' in U Manço (ed), *Reconnaissance et discrimination: présence de l'islam en Europe occidentale et en Amérique du Nord* (Paris, L'Harmattan).

Mann K and Roberts R (eds) (1991) *Law in Colonial Africa* (Portsmouth, NH, Heinemann).

Maskens M (2013) 'L'amour et ses frontières: Régulations étatiques et migrations de mariage (Belgique, France, Suisse et Italie)' no 150 *Migrations et Société* 43–60.

Max Planck Encyclopedia of Public International Law, www.mpepil.com (accessed 5 October 2012).

Mazzocchetti J (2011) 'Fermeture des frontières et liens transnationaux: un terrain auprès de primo-migrants africains en Belgique' 1 *Autrepart* 263–79.

Mazzocchetti J and Jamoulle P (2011) *Adolescences en Exil* (Louvain-la-Neuve, L'Harmattan).

Mdidech J (2013) 'Divorce au Maroc: les demandes sont de plus en plus formulées par les épouses' *La Vie éco*, www.lavieeco.com/news/societe/divorce-au-maroc-les-demandes-sont-de-plus-en-plus-formulees-par-les-epouses-25671.html.

Medina C (2014) *The American Convention on Human Rights. Crucial Rights and their Theory and Practice* (Antwerp, Intersentia).

Meerschaut K and Gutwirth S (2008) 'Legal Pluralism and Islam in the Scales of the European Court of Human Rights: The Limits of Categorical Balancing', in E Brems (ed), *Conflicts Between Fundamental Rights* (Antwerp, Intersentia).

Megret F (2012) 'Is There Ever a 'Right to One' Own Law'? An Exploration of Possible Rights Foundations for Legal Pluralism' 45(1) *Israel Law Review* 3–34.

—— (2013) 'International Human Rights and Global Legal Pluralism: A Research Agenda' in R Provost and C Sheppard (eds), *Dialogues on Human Rights and Legal Pluralism* (Dordrecht, Heidelberg, New York, London, Springer Verlag) 69–95.

Meijknecht A (2001) *Towards International Personality: The Position of Minorities and Indigenous Peoples in International Law* (Antwerp, Intersentia).

Merry S (1988) 'Legal Pluralism' 22 *Law and Society Review* 869–96.

Merry SE (1988) 'Legal Pluralism' 22 *Law and Society Review* 869.

—— (1990) *Getting Justice and Getting Even: Legal Consciousness among Working-Class Americans* (Chicago, University of Chicago Press).

—— (1992) 'Culture, Power and the Discourse of Law' 37 *New York Law School Law Review* 209–25.

—— (1997) 'Global Human Rights and Local Social Movements in a Legally Plural World' 12(2) *Canadian Journal of Law and Society* 247–71.

—— (1998) 'Law, Culture and Cultural Appropriation' 10 *Yale Journal of Law and the Humanities* 575–603.

—— (2003a) 'Constructing a Global Law—Violence against Women and the Human Rights System' 28(4) *Law & Social Inquiry* 941–77.

—— (2003b) 'Human Rights Law and the Demonization of Culture (And Anthropology along the Way) 26(1) *Political and Legal Anthropology Review* 55–76.

—— (2006) *Human Rights and Gender Violence: Translating International Law into Local Justice.* (Chicago, University of Chicago Press).

—— (2006) 'New Legal Realism and the Ethnography of Transnational Law' 31(4) *Law and Social Inquiry* 975–95.

—— (2006) 'Transnational Human Rights and Local Activism: Mapping the Middle' 108(1) *American Anthropologist* 38–51.

—— (2010) 'What Is Legal Culture? An Anthropological Perspective' 5(2) *Journal of Comparative Law* 40–58.

Merry S (2011) 'Gender Justice and the CEDAW: The Convention on the Elimination of All Forms of Discrimination against Women' 9 *Hawwa* 49–55.

Merry SE, Levitt P, Rosen MŞ and Yoon DH (2010) 'Law from Below: Women's Human Rights and Social Movements in New York City' 44 *Law & Society Review* 101–28.

Mikell G (1992) 'Culture, Law, and Social Policy: Changing the Economic Status of Ghanaian Women. 17(1) *Yale Journal of International Law* 225–40.

Ministère Chargé des Marocains Résidant à l'Etranger (2012) 'MRE en chiffres', www.marocainsdumonde.gov.ma/minist%C3%A8re-des-mre/mre-en-chiffres. aspx.

Ministerio de Justicia y Derechos Humanos de Bolivia (1999) Justicia Comunitaria (La Paz, SIERPE).

Ministry of Housing (1958) *Accra: A Plan for the Town* (Accra, Town and Country Planning Division).

Mittlebeler EV (1976) *African Custom and Western Law. The Development of the Rohodesian Criminal Law for Africans* (New York and London, Africana).

Moore SF (1973) 'Law and Social Change: The Semi-Autonomous Social Field as an Appropriate Subject of Study' 7(4) *Law & Society Review* 719–46.

—— (1978) *Law as Process: An Anthropological Approach* (Oxford, Oxford University Press).

Morse B and Woodman G (1987) *Indigenous Law and the State* (Dordrecht, Foris).

Moustafa T (2013) 'Islamic Law, Women's Rights, and Popular Legal Consciousness in Malaysia' 38(1) *Law & Social Inquiry* 168–88.

Municipal Government and Council of Indigenous Authorities of Curahuara de Carangas (2007) *Plan de Desarrollo Municipal Originario. Quinquenio 2007–2011.* Oruro, Bolivia.

Municipal government of Curahuara de Carangas (2009) 'El Municipio de Curahuara de Carangas', *Revista de Promocion del Territorio Curahuara de Carangas*, Marzo de 2009.

Mutua M (2002) *Human Rights. A Political and Cultural Critique* (Philadelphia, University of Pennsylvania Press).

—— (2009) 'The Transformation of Africa. A Critique of the Rights Discourse' in F Gómez Isa and K de Feyter (eds), *International Human Rights Law in a Global Context* (Bilbao, Deusto University Press).

Nader L and Todd H (1978) *The Disputing Process—Law in Ten Societies* (New York, Columbia University Press).

Nkrumah K (1958) 'African Prospect' 37(1) *Foreign Affairs* 45–53.

—— (1962) 'Ghana' 6(2) *Journal of African Law* 103–12.

—— (1963) *Africa Must Unite* (Portsmouth, NH, Heinemann).

Noortmann M, Reinisch A and Ryngaert C (eds) (2015) *Non-State Actors in International Law* (Oxford, Hart Publishing).

Nourse V and Shaffer G (2009) 'Varieties of New Legal Realism: Can a New World Order Prompt a New Legal Theory?' 95 *Cornell Law Review* 61–137.

Nugent P (1996) 'An Abandoned Project? The Nuances of Chieftaincy, Development and History in Ghana's Volta Region' 37/38 *Journal of Legal Pluralism* 203–25.

Nyamu-Musembi C (2000) 'How Should Human Rights and Development Respond to Cultural Legitimization of Gender Hierarchy in Developing Countries?' 41(2) *Harvard International Law Journal* 381–418.

O'Connell R (2008) 'Let's Talk: Dealing with Difference in Human Rights Law' in K de Feyter and G Pavlakos (eds), *The Tension Between Group Rights and Human Rights. A Multidisciplinary Approach* (Oxford, Hart Publising).

Odinkalu CA (2006) 'Poor Justice or Justice for the Poor? A Policy Framework for Reform of Customary and Informal Justice Systems in Africa' in C Sage and M Woolcock (eds), *The World Bank Legal Review, Law, Equity and Development*, vol 2. (Washington, DC, Martinus Nijhoff).

OHCHR (Office of the High Commissioner for Human Rights) (1984) *CCPR General Comment No 13: Equality before the courts and the right to a fair and public hearing by an independent court established by law (Art 14).*

Onana EO (2012) 'The Confluence of Investments and Environmental Protection and the States Obligations under International law: Can we Really Prioritize

Parallel Standards in the Practice of International Law?' in V Sancin (ed), *International Environmental Law: Contemporary Concerns and Challenges* (Ljubljana, Zalozba).

Oomen B (2014) 'The Application of Socio-Legal Theories of Legal Pluralism to Understanding the Implementation and Integration of Human Rights Law' no 4 *European Journal of Human Rights* 471–95.

Oppermann B (2006) 'The Impact of Legal Pluralism on Women's Status: An Examination of Marriage Laws in Egypt, South Africa, and the United States' 17(1) *Hastings Women's Law Journal* 65–92.

Oquaye M (1995), 'Human Rights and the Transition to Democracy Under PNDC in Ghana' 17(3) *Human Rights Quarterly* 566–73.

—— (2000) 'The Process of Democratisation in Contemporary Ghana' 38(3) *Commonwealth and Comparative Politics* 53–78.

Otto JM (ed) (2011) *Sharia Incorporated. A Comparative Overview of the Legal Systems in Twelve Muslim Countries in Past and Present* (Leiden, Leiden University Press).

Ouali N (2004) *Trajectoires et dynamiques migratoires des Marocains de Belgique* (Louvain-la-Neuve, Academia Bruylant).

Oubrou T (2000) 'Introduction théorique à la charî'a de minorité', Oumma.com, http://oumma.com/Introduction-theorique-a-la-chari.

Padilla G. (2012) 'Aplicacion Practica del Principio de Legalidad y Debido Proceso en Contexto de Interculturalidad' in JC Martinez, C Steiner and P Uribe Granados (eds), *Elementos y Tecnicas de Pluralismo Juridico, Manual para Operadores de Justicia* (Berlin, Konraad Adenauer Stiftung).

—— (2008) 'La historia de Chico. Sucesos en torno al pluralismo jurídico en Guatemala, un país mayoritariamente indígena' in R Huber, JC Martínez, C Lachenal, R Ariza (eds) *Hacia Sistenas Jurídicos Plurales. Reflexiones y Experiencias de Coordinación entre el Derecho Estatal y el Derecho Indígena* (Mexico: Konrad Adenauer Stiftung).

PDHRE (2007) *Human Rights Learning and Human Rights Cities Achievement Report* (New York PDHRE International Office).

Pedziwiatr K (2008) 'The New Muslim Elites in European Cities: Religion and Active Social Citizenship Amongst Young Organized Muslims in Brussels and London', PhD thesis, KU Leuven.

Pellow D (2001) 'Cultural Difference and Urban Spatial Forms: Elements of Boundedness in an Accra Community' 103(1) *American Anthropologist* 59–75.

Peluso N and Lund C (2011) 'New Frontiers of Land Control: Introduction' 38(4) *Journal of Peasant Studies* 667–81.

Pentassuglia G (2014) 'Ethnocultural Diversity and Human Rights: Legal Categories, Claims, and the Hybridity of Group Protection' 6 *Yearbook of Polar Law*.

Perry R (2011) 'Balancing Rights or Building Rights? Reconciling the Right to Use Customary Systems of Law with Competing Human Rights in Pursuit of Indigenous Sovereignty' 24 *Harvard Human Rights Journal* 71–114.

Phillips A (2010) *Gender and Culture* (Cambridge, Polity Press).

Piccoli E (2009a) 'Las rondas campesinas y su reconocimiento estatal, dificultades y contradicciones de un encuentro: un enfoque antropologico sobre el caso de Cajamarca, Perú' 71 *Nueva Antropologia* 93–113.

—— (2009b) 'Pluralisme juridique: Defis de terrain et fonctionnements pratiques le cas de Cajamarca, Pérou' 1 *REU* 159–70.

—— (2010) 'Justicia mixta en Cajamarca (Perú): análisis etnológico de un pluralismo práctico', paper presented at the Meeting of the Latin American Network of Legal Anthropologists (RELAJU), Lima, 2010.

—— (2011) *Les Rondes Paysannes. Vigilance, Politique et Justice dans les Andes Péruviennes* (Louvain La Neuve, Académia-l'Harmattan, Université Catholique de Louvain).

Pimentel D (2010) 'Rule of Law Reform without Cultural Imperialism? Reinforcing Customary Justice through Collateral Review in Southern Sudan' 2(1) *Hague Journal on the Rule of Law* 1–28.

—— (2011) 'Legal Pluralism in post-colonial Africa: linking statutory and customary adjudication in Mozambique', htpp://ssrn.com/abstract=1668063.

Porqueres i Gené E (2014) 'Personne et parenté' 210 *L'Homme* 17–42.

Pospisil L (1971) *The Anthropology of Law: A Comparative Theory of Law* (New York, Harper and Row).

Preis B (1996) 'Human Rights as Cultural Practice: An Anthropological Critique' 18 *Human Rights Quarterly* 286–315.

Provost R and Sheppard C (2013) 'Introduction: Human Rights Through Legal Pluralism' in R Provost and C Sheppard (eds), *Dialogues on Human Rights and Legal Pluralism* (Dordrecht, Heidelberg, New York, London, Springer Verlag).

al-Qaradawi Y (2003) Fiqh of Muslim Minorities: Contentious Issues and Recommended Solutions (Cairo, al-Falah Foundation) http://islamfuture.files. wordpress.com/2009/12/fiqh-of-muslim-minorities.pdf.

Quane H (2013) 'Legal Pluralism and International Human Rights Law: Inherently Incompatible, Mutually Reinforcing or Something in Between?' 33 *Oxford Journal of Legal Studies* 675–702.

Raisz A (2008) 'Indigenous Communities before the Inter-American Court of Human Rights. New Century, New Era?' 5 *Miskolc Journal of International Law* 35–51.

Rajagopal B (2003) *International Law from Below. Development, Social Movements and Third World Resistance* (Cambridge, Cambridge University Press).

Rathbone R (2000) *Nkrumah and the Chiefs* (Oxford, James Currey).

Ray DI (1996) 'Divided Sovereignty: Traditional Authority and the State in Ghana' 37/38 *Journal of Legal Pluralism* 181–202.

Razack SH (2007) 'The "Sharia Law Debate" in Ontario: The Modernity/ Premodernity Distinction in Legal Efforts to Protect Women from Culture' 15(1) *Feminist Legal Studies* 3–32.

Red Participacion y Justicia (2010) Mapeo de la Administracion de Justicia en Bolivia, Documento Consolidado (on file with author).

Regino Montes A and Torres Cisneros G (2009) 'The United Nations Declaration on the Rights of Indigenous Peoples: The Foundation of a New Relationship between Indigenous Peoples, States and Societies' in C Chartres and R Stavenhagen (eds), *Making the Declaration Work, The United Nations Declaration on the Rights of Indigenous Peoples* (Copenhagen, IWGIA).

Report of the Special Rapporteur in the Field of Cultural Rights, Farida Shaheed. United Nations General Assembly, 10 August 2012, AA/67/287.

Report of the Working Group on the Issue of Discrimination against Women in Law and Practice. United Nations General Assembly, 5 April 2012, A/HRC/20/28.

République du Niger (1994) *Recueil des lois et réglements*, 2nd edn (Secretariat General du Gouvernement).

—— (2004) *Rapport de synthèse des élections municipales du 24 juillet 2004* (Commission Electorale Nationale Indépendante CENI).

République du Niger and Fonds des Nations Unies pour l'Enfance (2000) *Programme de cooperation entre le gouvernement de la République du Niger et le Fonds des Nations Unies pour l'Enfance (UNICEF), 2000–2004.*

Riviere G (1991) 'Lik'ichiri y Kharisiri … A Proposito de las Representaciones del "otro" en la Sociedad Aymara' 20(1) *Bulletin de l'Institution Française d'Etudes Andines* 23–40.

Roberts R and Mann K (1991) 'An Introduction: Law in Colonial Africa' in K Mann and R Roberts (eds), *Law in Colonial Africa* (Portsmouth, NH: Heinemann).

Robinson D (2000) 'Revolutions in Western Sudan' in N Levtzion and RL Pouwels (eds), *The History of Islam in Africa* (Athens, Ohio University Press).

Rodas Arano CV (2013) 'De la Llama Libre a la Llama Cercada: Cambios en la Construccion Territorial de Curahuara de Carangas (Prov Sajama, Dpto Oruro, Bolivia 2007–2013)', Masters dissertation, Facultad Latinoamericana de Ciencias Sociales, Sede Ecuador.

Rodríguez-Piñero L (2004) 'El caso Awas Tingni y el régimen de derechos territoriales indígenas en la Costa Atlántica de Nicaragua' in J Aylwin (ed), *Derechos Humanos y Pueblos Indígenas. Tendencias internacionales y contexto chileno* (Temuco, Instituto de Estudios Indígenas-Universidad de La Frontera).

Rosaldo R (1989) *Culture and Truth: The Remaking of Social Analysis* (Boston, MA, Beacon Press).

Ross R (2006) *Dancing With a Ghost. Exploring Aboriginal Reality* (Toronto, Penguin Canada).

Ruiz Vieytez EJ (2006) *Minorías, Inmigración y Democracia en Europa. Una Lectura Multicultural de los Derechos Humanos* (Valencia, Tirant lo Blanch).

Sánchez Botero E (2000) 'Reflexiones antropológicas en torno a la justica y la jurisdicción especial indígenas en une nación multicultural y multiétnica' in F Garcia (ed), *Las Sociedades Interculturales: Un Desafío para el Siglo XXI* (Quito, FLACSO).

—— (2004) *Justicia y Pueblos Indigenas de Colombia* (Bogota, Universidad Nacional de Colombia).

—— (2006) 'Entre el Juez Salomón y el Dios Sira, Decisiones Interculturales e Interés Superior del Niño', PhD dissertation, Faculty of Law, University of Amsterdam.

Sayo A (2003) *The Pursuit of Gender Equity in Niger* (CARE-Niger Document).

Schmid U (2001) 'Legal Pluralism as a Source of Conflict in Multi-Ethnic Societies: The Case of Ghana' 46 *Journal of Legal Pluralism and Unofficial Law* 1–47.

Selby JA (2012) 'Construing the Secular: Implications of the Ontario Sharia Debate' in AC Korteweg and JA Selby (eds), *Debating Sharia: Islam, Gender Politics, and Family Law Arbitration* (Toronto, Buffalo, London, University of Toronto Press).

Service Public Fédéral (SPF) (2013) 'Monitoring socio-économique'.

Shachar A (1998) 'Group Identity and Women's Rights in Family Law: The Perils of Multicultural Accommodation' 6(3) *Journal of Political Philosophy* 285–305.

—— (2006) *Multicultural Jurisdictions Cultural Differences and Women's Rights* (Cambridge, Cambridge University Press).

Shah S (2010) 'Administration of Justice' in D Moeckli, S Shah and S Sivakumaran (eds), *International Human Rights Law* (Oxford, Oxford University Press).

Sieder R and McNeish J-A (2013) 'Introduction' in R Sieder and J-A McNeish (eds), *Gender Justice and Legal Pluralities: Latin American and African Perspectives* (Abingdon and New York, Routledge).

Sieder R (2011) 'Building Mayan Authority and Autonomy: The 'Recovery' of Indigenous Law in Post-Peace Guatemala' 55 *Studies in Law, Politics and Society* 43–75.

—— (2013) 'Sexual Violence and Gendered Subjectivities: Indigenous Women's Search for Justice in Guatemala' in R Sieder and JA McNeish (eds), *Gender Justice and Legal Pluralities* (Abingdon and New York, Routledge).

—— (2002) *Multiculuralism in Latin America, Indigenous Rights, Diversity and Democracy* (New York, Palgrave MacMillan).

Sierra MT (1995). 'Indian Rights and Customary Law in Mexico: A Study of the Nahuas in the Sierra de Puebla' 29(2) *Law and Society Review* 227–54.

Smith R (2012) *Textbook on International Human Rights* (Oxford, Oxford University Press).

Soares BF (2011) 'Family Law Reform in Mali: Contentious Debates and Elusive Outcomes' in M Badran (ed), *Gender and Islam in Africa: Rights, Sexuality, and Law* (Stanford, CA, Stanford University Press).

Solanki G (2011) *Adjudication in Religious Family Laws; Cultural Accommodation, Legal Pluralism and Gender Equality in India*, Cambridge Studies in Law and Society (Cambridge, Cambridge University Press).

Stephen M (2006) *Local, not Traditional Justice: The Case for Change in Non-State Justice in Indonesia* (Jakarta, World Bank, Justice for the Poor Program, Social Development Unit).

Stewart J and Tsanga A (2007) 'The Widow's and the Child's Portion: The Twisted Path to Partial Equality for Widows and Daughters under Customary Law in Zimbabwe' in A Hellum, JE Stewart, SS Ali and A Tsange (eds), *Human Rights Plural Legalities and Gendered Realities: Paths are Made by Walking* (Harare, Weaver Press).

Stewart J and Damiso C (2013) 'Limping along the Journey of a Thousand Miles: Implementing CEDAW in Zimbabwe' in A Hellum and H Sinding Aasen (eds), *Women's Human Rights: CEDAW in International, Regional and National Law* (New York, Cambridge University Press).

Szablowski D (2007) *Transnational Law and Local Struggles: Mining Communities and the World Bank* (Oxford, Hart Publishing).

Tamanaha B (1993) 'The Folly of the "Social Scientific" Concept of Legal Pluralism' 20(2) *Journal of Law and Society* 263–323.

—— (2000) 'A Non-Essentialist Version of Legal Pluralism' 27(2) *Journal of Law and Society* 296–321.

—— (2008) 'Understanding Legal pluralism: Past to Present, Local to Global' 30 *Sydney Law Review* 375–411.

—— (2010) 'A Framework for Pluralistic Socio-Legal Arenas' in MC Foblets, JF Gaudreault-DesBiens and AD Renteln (eds), *Cultural Diversity and the Law. State Responses from Around the World* (Bruxelles, Bruylant) 381–401.

Tamanaha B, Sage C and Woolcock M (eds) (2012) *Legal Pluralism and Development, Scholars and Practitioners in Dialogue* (Cambridge and New York, Cambridge University Press).

Tapia Pinto IS (2008) *Curso de Derecho Internacional de los Derechos Humanos en Bolivia* (La Paz, Latinas Editores Ltdas).

Tarrow S (2006) *The New Transnational Activism* (New York, Cambridge University Press).

Thornberry P (2002) *Indigenous Peoples and Human Rights* (Manchester, Manchester University Press).

Tønnessen L (2013) 'Between Sharia and CEDAW in Sudan: Islamist Women Negotiating Gender Equity' in R Sieder and J McNeish (eds), *Gender Justice and Legal Pluralities: Latin American and African Perspectives* (New York, Routledge).

Torrekens C (2005) 'Le pluralisme religieux en Belgique' 4 *Diversité Canadienne* 3.

Truffin B and Laperche F (2011) '"Ils emportent leur secret": Regards ethnographiques sur le traitement judiciaire des conflits conjugaux en contexte multicultural' in J Ringelheim (ed), *Le droit et la diversité culturelle* (Bruxelles, Bruylant) 657–98.

Tsanga A (2007) 'Reconceptualizing the Role of Legal Information Dissemination in the Context of Legal Pluralism in African Settings' in A Hellum, J Stewart, S Sardar Ali, and A Tsanga (eds), *Human Rights, Plural Legalities, and Gendered Realities* (Harare, Weaver Press).

Twinning W (ed) (2009a) *Human Rights, Southern Voices* (Cambridge, Cambridge University Press).

—— (2009b) 'Some elusive -isms' in W Twining (ed), *General Jurisprudence: Understanding Law from a Global Perspective* (Cambridge, Cambridge University Press).

—— (2010) 'Normative and Legal Pluralism: A Global Perspective' 20 *Duke Journal of Comparative & International Law* 473–517.

US Department of State (2010) *International Religious Freedom Report 2010* (Bureau of Democracy, Human Rights, and Labour).

Ubink J (2008) 'Negotiated or Negated? The Rhetoric and Reality of Customary Tenure in an Ashanti Village in Ghana' 78(2) *Africa* 264–87.

—— (2011a) 'Gender Equality on the Horizon: The Case of Uukwambi Traditional Authority, Northern Namibia, in E Harper (ed), *Working with Customary Justice Systems: Post-Conflict and Fragile States* (Rome, International Development Law Organization).

—— (2011b) 'Stating the Customary: An Innovative Approach to the Locally Legitimate Recording of Customary Law in Namibia' in J Ubink (ed), *Customary Justice: Perspectives on Legal Empowerment* (Rome, International Development Law Organization).

UN Women (2011) *Progress of the World's Women* (New York, United Nations).

United Nations (2005) *Niger: Initial and Second Report of the Niger on the Convention on the Elimination of All Forms of Discrimination against Women.* (New York, United Nations Committee on the Elimination of Discrimination against Women).

—— (2007) *Committee on the Elimination of Discrimination against Women, 38th Session, Summary Record of the 790th Meeting* (New York, United Nations).

—— (2013) *Statistical Yearbook 2011, Fifty-sixth issue* (New York: United Nations Department of Economic and Social Affairs, Statistics Division).

United Nations Development Programme (2013) *Human Development Report 2013: The Rise of the South: Human Progress in a Diverse World* (New York, UNDP).

Van Cott DL (2002) *The Friendly Liquidation of the Past, The Politics of Diversity in Latin America* (Pittsburgh, University of Pittsburgh Press).

—— (2003) 'Legal Pluralism and Informal Community Justice Administration in Latin America', paper prepared for the conference Informal Institutions and Latin American Politics, Notre Dame, IN, April 2003.

Van Rouveroy van Nieuwaal, E (1987) 'Chiefs and African States: Some Introductory Notes and an Extensive Bibliography on African Chieftaincy' 25–26 *Journal of Legal Pluralism* 1–41.

Van Waesberghe ES, Sportel I, Drost L, van Eijk E and Diepenbrock E (2014) 'Zo zijn we niet getrouwd. Een onderzoek naar omvang en aard van huwelijksdwang, achterlating en huwelijkse gevangenschap', Research Report (Maastricht, Verwey-Jonker Instituut; Universiteit Maastricht) www.stichtingwende.nl/wp-content/uploads/2014/05/Zo_zijn_we_niet_getrouwd_Stichting_Wende_20141003.pdf.

Vandenhole W (2015) *Challenging Territoriality in Human Rights Law: Building Blocks for a Plural and Diverse Duty-Bearer Regime* (London, Routledge).

Villalón R (2010) 'Passage to Citizenship and the Nuances of Agency: Latina Battered Immigrants' 33 *Women's Studies International Forum* 552–60.

Von Benda-Beckmann K (1981) 'Forum Shopping and Shopping Forums: Dispute Processing in a Minangkabau Village in West Sumatra' 19 *Journal of Legal Pluralism* 117–59.

Von Benda-Beckmann F (1997) 'Citizens, Strangers and Indigenous Peoples: Conceptual Politics and Legal Pluralism' in R Kuppe and R Potz (eds), *Law & Anthropology: International Yearbook for Legal Anthropology*, vol 9 (The Hague, Martinus Nijhoff).

—— (2002) 'Who's Afraid of Legal Pluralism?' 34 *Journal of Legal Pluralism and Unofficial Law* 37–82.

—— (2006) 'The Multiple Edges of Law: Dealing with Legal Pluralism in Development Practice' *The World Bank Legal Review: Law, Equity and Development* (Washington, DC, World Bank Publications).

—— (2009) 'Human Rights, Cultural Relativism and Legal Pluralism. Towards a Two-dimensional Debate' in K von Benda-Beckmann, F von Benda-Beckmann and A Griffiths (eds), *The Power of Law in a Transnational World: Anthropological Enquiries* (New York, Oxford, Berghahn Books).

Von Benda-Beckmann F and Von Benda-Beckmann K (2005) *Mobile People, Mobile Law. Expanding Legal Relations in a Contracting World* (London, Routledge).

Von Benda-Beckmann F, Von Benda-Beckmann K and Eckert J (eds) (2009) *Rules of Law and Laws of Ruling: On the Governance of Law* (Farnham, Ashgate).

Wainright J and Bryan J (2009) 'Cartography, Territory, Property: Postcolonial Reflections on Indigenous Counter-Mapping in Nicaragua and Belize' 16 *Cultural Geographies* 153–78.

Weilenmann M (2009) 'Project Law—A Legal Intermediary between Local and Global Communities: A Case Study from Senegal' 51 *Anthropologica* 1–13.

—— (2009) 'Project Law—A Power Instrument of Development Agencies: A Case Study from Burundi' in F Von Benda-Beckmann, K Von Benda-Beckmann and A Griffiths (eds), *The Power of Law in a Transnational World. Anthropological Enquiries* (New York, Oxford, Berghahn Books).

Wiggings A (2002) 'El Caso Awas Tingni o el futuro de los derechos territoriales de los pueblos indígenas del Caribe Nicaragüense' 30 *WANI: Revista del Caribe Nicaragüense* 6–31.

Wilson R (1997) 'Human Rights, Culture and Context: An Introduction' in R Wilson (ed), *Human Rights, Culture and Context: Anthropological Perspectives* (London, Pluto Press).

—— (2001) *The Politics of Truth and Reconciliation in South Africa: Legitimizing the Post-Apartheid State.* (Cambridge, Cambridge University Press).

Wilson, R and Mitchel, J (2003) Human Rights in Global Perspective. Anthropological Studies of Rights, Claims and Entitlements (London and New York, Routledge).

WLSA (1994) *Inheritance Law in Zimbabwe: Law, Customs and Practice* (Harare, WLSA).

Wojkowska E (2006) *Doing Justice: How Informal Systems Can Contribute* (Oslo, United Nations Development Programme).

Wojkowska E and Cunningham J (2009) 'Justice Reform's New frontier: Engaging with Customary Systems to Legally Empower the Poor', in …

Woodman G (1988) 'How State Courts Created Customary law in Ghana and Nigeria' in B Morse and G Woodman (eds), *Indigenous Law and the State* (Dordrecht, Foris).

—— (1998) 'Ideological Combat and Social Observation: Recent Debate about Legal Pluralism' 42 *Journal of Legal Pluralism* 21–54.

—— (2012) 'The Development "Problem" of Legal Pluralism: An Analysis and Steps Towards Solutions' in B Tamanaha, C Sage and M Woolcock (eds), *Legal Pluralism and Development, Scholars and Practitioners in Dialogue* (Cambridge and New York, Cambridge University Press).

World Bank (2003) *Legal and Judicial Reform: Strategic Directions* (Washington, DC, The World Bank).

—— (2009) 'Customary Justice and Legal Pluralism in Post-Conflict and Fragile Societies', proceedings of conference hosted by United States Institute of Peace, George Washington University, Washington, 17–18 November 2009.

Wyvekens A (2012) *Justice et diversité culturelle* (Paris, Mission Justice et Droit).

Xanthaki A (2007), *Indigenous Rights and United Nations Standards. Self-Determination, Culture and Land* (Cambridge, Cambridge University Press).

Yrigoyen R (1999) *Pautas de Coordinacion entre el Derecho Indigena y el Derecho Estatal* (Guatemala, Fundacion Myrna Mack).

—— (2002) 'Peru: Pluralist Constitution, Monist Judiciary—A Post-Reform Assessment' in R Sieder (ed), *Multiculuralism in Latin America, Indigenous Rights, Diversity and Democracy* (New York, Palgrave MacMillan).

Zine J (2012) 'Sharia in Canada? Mapping Discourses of Race, Gender, and Religious Difference' in AC Korteweg and JA Selby (eds), *Debating Sharia: Islam, Gender Politics, and Family Law Arbitration* (Toronto, Buffalo, London, University of Toronto Press).

Index

www.ingramcontent.com/pod-product-compliance
Lightning Source LLC
Chambersburg PA
CBHW050414280326
41932CB00013BA/1856